ASIAN AMERICANS

RECONCEPTUALIZING CULTURE, HISTORY, POLITICS

edited by
FRANKLIN NG
CALIFORNIA STATE UNIVERSITY
FRESNO

A GARLAND SERIES

DOING THE DESI THING

PERFORMING INDIANNESS IN NEW YORK CITY

SUNITA S. MUKHI

GARLAND PUBLISHING, Inc.
A MEMBER OF THE TAYLOR & FRANCIS GROUP
NEW YORK & LONDON / 2000

Published in 2000 by
Garland Publishing Inc.
A member of the Taylor & Francis Group
29 West 35th Street
New York, NY 10001

10 9 8 7 6 5 4 3 2 1

Library of Congress Cataloging-in-Publication Data is available from the
Library of Congress.

Mukhi, Sunita S.
        Doing the desi thing : performing Indianness in New York City /
    Sunita S. Mukhi
p. cm. — (Asian Americans) Includes bibliographical and references and index.
ISBN: 0-8153-3372-2 (alk. paper)

Printed on acid-free, 250-year-life paper
Manufactured in the United States of America

For
Papa, Mama,
Sujata, Suresh, Lin, and Anjali

though they may be in Manila,
they live here in my heart

Contents

Preface

This book is part of a life work in which I have grappled with, been bemused by, and have been intensely engaged with, that part of my identity and belongingness to *Indianness*. I have approached the question of what does it mean to be Indian outside India by looking at how this is conceptualized, understood and manifested in staged cultural productions by non-artists of the Indian community.

From a personal historical standpoint, I myself was an active practitioner of these cultural productions in the Sindhi Hindu community in Manila, Philippines. In my search for an authentic and true Indianness, I was solemnly involved in doing Indian culture through popular entertainments as part of my nationalist zeal for India and civic duty to the community I grew up in. Much pleasure and accolade, and affection I did derive during these productions and because of it. I was pleasantly amused and stimulated to discover that the impulse to perform and display are present and almost patterned amongst Indians in other diasporic sites, and particularly in New York. I begun to mull over the importance of these forms in stark contrast to the classical or more traditional forms of Indian artistic forms.

Whereas the traditional forms are treated with awe and some distance, these other forms are robust, egalitarian, participatory and of course popular. They are considered as "cheap" entertainment by cultural elites but are nevertheless practiced by them in private, and are very visible in the lifestyle of the community.

I came upon the term *desi* in conversations with others like me who trace their ancestry to the South Asian subcontinent. Desi has been appropriated to describe phenomena, people who practice a relationship or represent shared aspects of the South Asian subcontinent. Thus, to "do the desi thing" would mean to adopt, or enact gestures and behaviors that could trace its origins, or refers to one's relationship—imagined, imaginative or actual—to the South Asian Subcontinent.

Though the South Asian subcontinent includes nation-states of India, Pakistan, Sri Lanka, Nepal, Bangladesh, Bhutan and the Maldives, this study, however, is limited to the performance of an Indian desiness, but yet within it are performative genres that speak to the affiliations to other South Asians.

There is ample research being done on the life of the dispersed Indian but not much has been written on the substance and interpretation of particular performance events that take up much of the psychic energies and material resources of the community. There is acknowledgment that Indian immigrant life is saturated with popular expressive cultural forms, and even begrudging, embarrassed gesture to say that they are important, but I have just begun to come across any work that looks at these forms as a way for a group of people to build community, to express identity, and negotiate power within the community's hierarchies as well as with the host society. Much bubbles forth in these productions, if one casts asides biases against these popular forms.

What then do these forms say about Indianness in this diasporic site of NYC? Why the impulse to do the desi thing? I have attempted to answer this question by using the framework of urban folklore, i.e. at how people in the city make their lives more humane amidst alienation, competition, the servitude of work, racism and otherness. The racial politics of the U.S. play a major role in defining the contours of these inscriptions. Defining oneself as neither white nor black, though there may be aspirations to the former in lifestyle, a new category of "brown" Indian is conjured both to differentiate and include. The burgeoning influence of globalization of musics, media entertainments, cinema, audio and video cassettes have helped link communities in far-flung sites—a rhythm nation rather than a geopolitical one is created. The earnest urge to authenticate a pure heritage is constantly being challenged by the impulse and pleasure to adopt, adapt and appropriate the rhythms and sensualities/sensibilities that individuals confront from other sources specifically from the urban youth culture which is influenced by African-American as well as Latino ghetto aesthetics. Thus, hip-hop is Indianized or desified by breakdancing to an upbeat Hindi film song, a black bustier dress is accentuated with a scarf of Indian silk, bhangra disco parties are organized to raise funds for progressive social service groups such as Sakhi for South Asian Women and SALGA (South Asian Lesbian and Gay Association). Though Indians may not see themselves as black, or wish to be identified as Latino, the way the body is reconfigured—made vital and in movement allows for a visible, alive, energized presence to be achieved as a resistance to erasure.

The war goes on between the official rhetoric of pure Indianness and the convulsions of these hybrid forms. The events themselves, by virtue of their public nature, allows for the official rhetoric to be repudiated. The changing demographics of immigrants, the economic clout of community members—money and numbers place pressure on the official harbingers of culture to adapt, or at least acknowledge the existence of other classes and types of Indians, and even other Desis. Understand that the community leaders cannot reject them wholesale because we are a minority community and must cohere to gain power within a westernized host country. A too divided community does not "look good"—so it is best to let the new vernacular be. Disco bhangra, Hindi film dance reinterpretations, and fashion shows are begrudgingly considered by community elders as better than sexual diseases, drugs, gang wars, and exogamy.

Where do I go from here? Already I am being criticized by educated elites for overinterpreting these events, but participants, on the other hand, are grateful for the attention to this socio-cultural aspect of their lives. A number of performances are to come out of this. I have already outlined one in the concluding chapter. The subject matter begs for it.

Much more work can be done, and maybe even taken over by other interested scholars. The Sindhi diwali section in Chapter 3 can be expanded into a chapter. The Sindhis are a true migrant community with fidelity to a syncretic Sindhiness and pronounced link to a Hindu Indianness. The *Naya Andaaz* dance competition should be expanded as an example of institutionalizing the aesthetics of the reinterpreted film dance, as well as Dheeraj's School of Dance to acknowledge the involvement of the Indo-Caribbean community in changing the aesthetic of Indian popular dance to include broad soca and chutney gestures. The study of the performance of Desiness can be made more full by the analysis of other expressive forms of other South Asians. Perhaps the valences of religion, language, politics may nuance the performances, bringing to the fore other tense negotiations within and without the communities.

An epilogue on the necessity to Perform Indianness in so flamboyant a manner—the drag elements, the reconfigurations of space and time wrought out of dispersal—must be worked out as the substance of the text expands to include new forms, new phenomena. My life's work is cut out for me in my search for an always and already impure Indianness. While you will witness in the next few hours, in the forthcoming descriptions, Indianness performed in New York City.

But before you proceed, let me express my gratitude to people who have brought me this far in my scholarly pursuits, for the fruition of this book. First, I extend my gratitude to the Performance Studies Department, New York University—the dynamic faculty, my brilliant colleagues, the concerned administration, the exciting courses, books, articles, and performances that I struggled through but nevertheless enjoyed thoroughly—for opening my mind to the bold, brave, new world of performance theory, embodied knowledge, philosophy of the senses, emotion, rhythm & rhyme, movement and music, and the critical issues of representation, imaging, being & becoming. Specifically, I am indebted to my mentor Richard Schechner for encouraging my mad forays into Indianness, and for casting an incisive eye, together with my other professors Barbara Kirshenblatt Gimblett, May Joseph, Brooks McNamara, and Una Chaudhuri, and my dear colleague and dearest friend Radhika Subramaniam, for the detail and expression of my ideas, especially in its dissertation form.

I am indebted to Garland Publishing, specifically editor Franklin Ng and to editorial assistant Rebecca Wipfler and Richard Koss and the staff of Garland Publishing, for considering this project vital and engaging enough to find for it a niche in the vibrant landscape of multicultural/Asian American studies. The project reaches its completion when it can be shared with the public, otherwise this work would have festered in a musty corner of my room.

There are many others who have helped shape this opus. Even as I write this, it is being refined by the intellectual, economic, as well as psychic investments and, at times, huge sacrifices of **my friends, loved ones near and far, those I loved once, and love now**, and **my family**. I owe them all too much that this lifetime will not suffice to reciprocate their kindness, optimism, laughter and love.

And of course, I am indebted to the vibrant, at times perplexing and frustrating, but always fascinating **Asian Indian community in the New York tri-state area** who have provided me with much cultural fodder to chew, mull, (sometimes spit out!), digest, and be nourished by.

DOING THE DESI THING

CHAPTER 1

Introduction

> *What does it mean to be "Indian" outside*
> *India? How can culture be preserved without*
> *being ossified? How should we discuss the need*
> *for change within ourselves and our community*
> *without seeming to play into the hands of our*
> *racial enemies? What are the consequences of*
> *embracing those ideas and practices and turn-*
> *ing away from the ones that came here with*
> *us? . . . How to build a new, "modern" world*
> *out of an old, legend-haunted civilization, an*
> *old culture which we have brought in the heart*
> *of a newer one? . . . These questions are all a*
> *single, existential question: How are we to live*
> *in the world? (Rushdie, 1991: 17, 18, 19)*

Permit me to refine this question into a more phenomenological one—
How, indeed, do we Indians outside India live in the world?

Let me add more specific questions to Rushdie's simmering caul-
dron of concerns: What does it mean to perform an *Indian* cultural show
in New York City, United States of America? Is the Indianness expressed
a celebration of ethnic difference in a community of differences; an assertion of nationalistic allegiance to the Indian nation-state; a display of
cultural heritage and familiarity within and without the Indian community; an opportunity to reconstruct, enjoy and be admired for this complex and problematic concept of Indianness? The concept of Indianness
springs from a *self-acknowledgement* of having origins in India or what
is believed to be an Indian homeland and a *recognition* by others as having a relationship with that homeland even despite living for generations
outside it. Indianness is more fully explained in the next chapter. This
dissertation describes its manifestations in the performance events that
Asian Indians in New York City use to express Indianness. In this modest
project, I hazard to answer that existential query of how Indians live outside India. I am concerned with how one plays out or performs this dual
valence of self-acknowledgement and recognition of being Indian.
Through an interpretative analysis of three cultural variety shows that are

mounted in Manhattan, New York City, I analyze how Asian Indians residing in the United States perform their Indianness: What does it mean
to present one's self as "Indian" outside India, what does it mean to be
Indian in multi-cultural and cosmopolitan New York in this last decade of
the 20th century? Why does one do the Desi thing?

CULTURAL PERFORMANCES

Cultural performances in New York city present some expressive elements of Indian culture to both Indians and non-Indians primarily
through the genres of the variety show, parades, and arts, crafts, and food
fairs. An array of Indian performing arts and popular entertainments,
marking national and religious holidays, is presented from classical, to
folk to mass media traditions. Produced by Indian non-profit voluntary
associations, large and small, some of which are partially funded by arts
councils and the New York State Council of the Arts and the National Endowment for the Arts, these productions may include guest appearances
by professional performers though the bulk of the participants are non-
professional.

In his anthropological study of Southern Indian cultural forms in
India, specifically in Madras, Milton Singer also used the term 'cultural
performance' to describe the elementary constituents of culture which he
ultimately used as units of observation:

> [Cultural performances] include what we in the West usually call by
> that name - for example, plays, concerts and lectures. But [to Indians,
> cultural performances also] include prayers, ritual readings and recita-
> tions, rites and ceremonies, festivals, and all those things we usually
> classify under religion and ritual rather than with the cultural and artis-
> tic. [Indians] thought of their culture as encapsulated in these discrete
> performances, which they could exhibit to visitors and to themselves.
> (1980:71)

Using Singer's definition, the expressive behaviors that are enacted
in public life are presentations of Indian culture. They are part of an exhibition of Indianness to both Indians and non-Indians to be watched, enjoyed, understood, theatrically put on as in a production. This reflexivity
is the paramount manifest intent of these performances. These performances are "epistemological, a way of knowing self, culture, and others
more completely" (Fine & Speer, 1992:17).

More than the intent to be reflexive, what occurs in these productions is a dynamic confluence of multiple narratives regarding what it means to be Indian outside India, specifically in the United States. These narratives are the result of the changing demographics and policies of immigration, the current American multi-cultural climate, race relations, and the interactions amongst Indians who have come to settle here, or are born here, and those in India. These cultural productions are the sites upon which contested value systems—aesthetic and moral—are negotiated between audience and participants, among participants, between producers of the events, and those who perform. These productions are used to reveal the aspirations and anxieties of having a migrant sensibility, of *being* in America with Indian heritage, and of *becoming* American of Asian Indian heritage, and of creating a way of being that is both Indian and American or is neither Indian nor American.

These cultural artifacts are part of the "webs of significance that we have spun and are suspended from" as Max Weber has put forth, elaborated by Clifford Geertz's contention that these genres are texts which contain 'tales a culture tells itself', or texts that can display ourselves to ourselves:

> They [art, performance, theater] are [not only] elaborate mechanisms for defining social relationships, sustaining social rules, and strengthening social values . . . [but they] materialize a way of experiencing, bring a cast of mind out into the world of objects, where men can look at it. (Geertz, 1983:99).

The cultural productions that are analyzed in this book are the performance events produced annually for the Indian Independence Day (August 15) by the Federation of Indian Associations (FIA), the Deepavali Festival at the South Street Seaport mounted by the Association of Indians in America (AIA) usually around the first Sunday in October, and the productions of the New York University's (NYU) South Asian Organization—Shruti (throughout the school year). I witnessed and observed these productions very closely from 1989 to 1995. From 1996 to the present I have participated in these events as a casual observer, as a celebrant, if you will. The ostensible agenda of these cultural performances is to celebrate occasions of nationalistic pride such as Indian Independence Day, or a religious obligation and devotion during Deepavali, the Hindu festival of lights, or an exhibition of cultural/ethnic identity in the semestral projects of college-going youth of Indian origin. These expressions underscore that we are Indians, that these are our songs, dances, food, crafts for the non-Indian to see, learn from and consume, and for the Indian to reminisce, enjoy, and be validated by. These are prime opportunities to be amongst other Desis, and to participate in Desiness.

OFFICIAL/VERNACULAR: MARGA/DESI

These performances are where the "dialectic between continuity of tradition . . . and [where] the inventions of tradition find expression" (Fine & Speer, 1992:16). These productions display a tense negotiation between the preservation of and assimilation of Indianness. The tension is rooted in the definitions of what is considered 'high' art or culture, and what is 'low' art or culture.

In Hindu aesthetics, art forms that are derived from Sanskritic, brahmanic texts are called *marga*. They are codified in texts or *shastras* like the dramaturgical treatise, *Natyasastra*. These art forms should evoke in the initiated aficionado a *rasa*, a mood or sentiment that is of refined and subtle emotion, and of deep spiritual essence. The practitioner of these forms needs the guidance of a seasoned *guru*, a teacher, and is bound to him or her in service and respect for his lifetime (Goswami, 1986). According to Milton Singer, forms derived from such texts are considered today as part of the Pan-Indian Sanskritized "Great tradition". Classical art forms like *Bharatanatyam*, Kalidasa's *Shakuntala*, and Carnatic music are some examples of marga.

Please note that the marga traditional forms are based on the tenets of Hindu *upper caste* aesthetics. Besides caste elitism, a Pan-Indian "Great Tradition" is derived from a *Hindu* idiom, philosophy and iconography. Islamic influenced classical forms such as court miniature paintings, Hindustani music, Kathak dance, and Urdu poetry are somehow subsumed as Indian marga forms or are assumed to become Hinduized by virtue of syncretizing and thriving within the Pan-Sanskritic culture though patronized in Moghul courts. These courtly Islamic forms are allowed in the Marga coterie, precisely because they were encouraged, practiced and appreciated by both a Hindu and Islamic elite.

Within the Hindu aesthetic code, *desi* is the term applied to folk, or popular forms which run the gamut of theater, songs, music, dance and poetry in the various regional languages of the South Asian subcontinent. These are practiced by the 'folk', the country dweller, the uninitiated, the common person, by non-Brahmins, or the non-sanskritized. From the perspective of the marga aficionado, desi forms are:

> Not bound by strict rules and principles and [are] characterized by features likely to appeal to popular tastes: simple rendering; accentuated and obvious rhythm; group singing; stereotyped, monotonous form; emphasis on words; basis in a festival, a season, or an event; emotional and dramatic tone. (Singer, 1980:183)

They are described as part of the Little Traditions, as *prakrit*, as vernacular. With the influence of modernity, urbanization, and the rise of Indian nationalism, this hierarchy has spawned other categories. Mass mediated forms like cinema, TV, radio, video, and audio-cassettes allowed for the proliferation and interpenetration of Great and Little traditions, the invention of a host of other expressive forms. Intellectual and political elites—marga aficionados, began to be more concerned about preserving Indian forms from what they considered the corrupting influence of modernity, westernization and debauchery. Classical and folk, marga and desi forms were, therefore, recodified, frozen and preserved as artifacts of an official traditional Indianness, as expression of Indian nationality.

Official Indianness displayed and exhibited in international diplomatic circles, in National Holiday parades and celebrations, in Festival(s) of India, in Museum(s) of Natural History and Asia Society(ies), included forms of the great and little traditions as long as they did not have overt Western influence. Sanskrit/prakrit; marga/desi forms are displayed with nationalistic pride, shown off as a national treasures, as pure Indianness (with Sanskrit-marga forms being the pinnacle of Indianness in this official hierarchy). Official Indianness is imbued with brahmanic, and therefore casteist influences, as well as an atavistic return to what is believed to be a pre-modern lifestyle. Thus, the productions here in Manhattan are sometimes prompted by a manufactured nostalgia for a mythologized homeland, the "original," pre-colonial India, before the onslaught of modern urbanization. This imagined India is conceptualized as if it came into existence at the historic moment of India's independence (Prakash, 1992).

In presenting an official Indianness, there is an insistence on presenting our 'original' non-American, non-Western selves; an insistence on presenting ourselves as Indian *nationals* , as *traditional* Indians with a unified, homogenized, glorious, *pure* and ancient heritage. The type and nature of these performances are determined by the purpose of the producers and the response of the performers. If the intent is to show Americans, i.e., non-Indians, a reified "Indian culture," the performances are usually more classical, touristic, folkloric; Indianness portrayed is monolithic, traditional, and *defensively* non-Western. There is an ardent insistence that the forms presented are impervious to western influences, and have maintained the essence of Indianness. Such **official** Indianness employs a certain kind of technicolored Pan-Indian aesthetic portraying India as a "great civilization" or "great tradition" with a "great classical past" (Singer, 1980; Naipaul, 1989). This India is an exotic place, an image derived from Western orientalist constructions (Said, 1979), and adopted in a nationalistic fervor (Nehru, 1946; Anderson, 1991). Such performances are more likely to be produced with institutional support from various non-profit arts organizations run by Asian-loving individuals or "educated" professional Indians. The support may come from the New York State Council on the Arts' divisions on Folk Arts and on Special Arts, the National Endowment for the Humanities and other public and private foundations such as Indian merchant and cultural associations. The Association of Indians in America (AIA)'s Deepavali Festival of Lights at South Street Seaport provides one such instance of official Indianness.

DESI DIASPORA: A NEW VERNACULAR

Yet within these productions there is also an earnestness to represent our new "modernized," "westernized" or "contemporary" selves to ourselves. The other Indianness draws from the contact and interaction of what are perceived to be disparate socio-cultural milieus. The emerging demands and pleasures of Indian immigrants that have come in the 1980's expressed a new kind of **vernacular** Indianness, unlike the desi type described earlier by Milton Singer. The current immigrant demographics run the gamut of social classes, with a hefty number of lower-class, non-English speaking Indians, as well as an emerging second generation. There is an increased number of immigrants of Indian heritage coming from the West Indies, Africa, and Asia, even Europe and Canada—what Parminder Bhachu describes as 'twice or thrice migrant' who bring with them the traces of the domiciles they left, as well as their skills and savvy for the "game of migration" (1995: 224). There are enough Indians living in New York to form a self-sufficient community which I discuss in the forthcoming chapter entitled "The Migrant Sensibility". A person of Indian origin need not go far or out of his neighborhood to eat Indian food, watch an Indian movie, have Indian friends, find a job, or avail of health, legal, or merchant services owned and practiced by a compatriot, i.e., practice Desiness.

This emerging vernacular Indianness or Desiness includes song and dance sequences taken from Hindi popular films re-choreographed for the stage, folk dances specific to the particular regions in India, repertoires of songs from Hindi films and the provincial folk and religious traditions, fashion shows, Indian and contemporary disco music played by bands, and comedy skits. The variety shows organized for Indian Independence Day in August by the Federation of Indian Associations (FIA), and annual productions by the New York University (NYU) South Asian Student Association Shruti are examples of this kind of vernacular Indianness.

BECOMING INDIAN AMERICAN: EMERGING IDENTITIES

This project illustrates to what extent or in what ways we immigrant Indians adjust to the host country, how and why we are insistent on maintaining and constructing an "authentic" Indianness along with expressing our emergent hybrid Indian or Desi identity: The shift from being Indian in America to becoming Americans with Indian heritage, adjusting to life here in the U.S.A. and reaping the benefits of citizenship. The performances depict the dynamic processes and varieties of this pragmatic identity formation.

Aspects of the Indianness we perform here are a transcultural phenomenon (Appadurai, 1991, 1993; Taylor, May, 1991) shared by Indians all over the world (even in Indian cities) who find themselves in a cosmopolitan, heterogeneous, urban environment, whose Indianness is transmitted by mass media, international fashion, travel & tourism, and migration. (Chaudhuri, 1991; Steinberg, 1981; Kirshenblatt-Gimblett, 1983). Paul Gilroy elucidates that the special premium placed on expressive culture has helped dispersed peoples to organize a shared diasporic consciousness:

> Artistic forms [music, song, dance] have produced and sustained an interpretative community outside the orbit of formal politics in a long sequence of struggles which has been irreducibly and simultaneously both cultural and political. The internationalization of the leisure industries and the growth of important markets for cultural commodities

outside the overdeveloped world has provided new opportunities for
the consolidation of diaspora awareness. (Gilroy, 1993:33)

Through the availability of global electronic networks, and the relative
ease of travel, those of Indian heritage can experience and enjoy various
types of popular entertainments, the arts, and the scholarly dialog facilitated by diasporic artists. So for example, a New York Indian young adult
can be familiar with and understand the same type of music to some extent as a British Asian as well as with a Bombay Indian, having this commonality to discuss in a conversation or being able to participate in its
enactment. Though there may be specific circumstantial and geopolitical
differences amongst Indians in the diaspora, there are moments when
these boundaries dissolve, and an interpretative community is created
based on these commonalties of pleasure and sentiment. This commonality I call a type of Desiness.

Thus the Indianness or Desiness expressed is multi-faceted and
problematic, but always dynamic and nuanced. This book illustrates how
Indianness oozes from the fissure of tradition and innovation, authenticity and authentication, pastness and contemporaneity, purity and hybridity, erasure and visibility.

In all these performances, Indian immigrants are nourished and fortified in their adaptation to life in the United States. The official performance of Indianness is informed by an assertion of a distinct, though
archaic and revivalist ethnic identity (Graburn, 1975) that is spurred on
by a nationalistic fidelity to independent India (Anderson, 1991), enhanced by an impulse to use Indian exoticism as a commodity for socio-
political exchange (Appadurai, 1981, 1986; Kirshenblatt-Gimblett,
1990, 1991). Indian heritage is asserted against white American hegemony, generally against westernization, and metaphorically against non-
Indianness—a resistance to erasure or of dissolving into a pot of cultural
mush. The vernacular rendition of Indianness or Desiness usually depicts
a more fluid dialog, integration, fusion, and coalescing of value systems
(Wagner, 1975; Drewal, 1988). These events become sites upon which
hitherto unheard narratives, histories, and identities are expressed, are
exposed.

There is a confrontation between official rhetoric and community
vernacular needs. The identity that is expressed in the vernacular sphere
is a more natural, informal, spontaneous, and dare I say, "authentic" Indianness *in the diaspora*. The authenticity arises from the anti-orientalist
(Said, 1979), and anti-colonialist nature (Hall, 1988; Minh-ha, 1989;

Spivak, 1990) of these populist expressions (Bauman, 1992 a; McNamara, 1983), which are primarily produced and enjoyed by co-ethnics or those of Indian origin. These cultural productions manifest levels of resistance to westernization even as they appropriate modern technology, and official culture. These productions shatter the myth, yet again, that the U.S.A. is a melting pot; rather it is a multicultural mosaic or even a fluid kaleidoscope. Another American identity glimmers here: An identity spiced with curry, a kaleidoscope reflecting bright saffron, green, red, turquoise, and shades of rich brown.

SUMMARY OF SLIPPERY TERMS: INDIAN, DESI, SOUTH ASIAN, OTHERS

The terms *Indian* and *Desi* need to be clarified in this discussion of the performance of Indianness in New York City. As the discussion unfolds, the terms will slither and slip into each other, true to the attributes these terms possess. I present these terms now as distinct phenomena, if only to illustrate how those of South Asian origin have reconstructed their understanding of who they are as influenced by the places they find themselves living.

1. **Indian** - is officially a citizen of the nation-state known today as India. As a descriptive term as in "Indian culture", it refers to the lifeways, customs, values, traditions, history of those who claim descent, or citizenship or residence to the nation-state of India. To perform Indianness, or practice Indian culture is to enact behaviors that are acknowledged to reflect the lifeways, customs, values and traditions, and history of India. This discussion is concerned with what is defined as, how Indianness is defined, enacted, promoted in the cultural productions of the South Street Seaport Deepavali Festival, the Indian Independence Day Parade and Cultural Program, and the cultural programs produced by Shruti, the South Asian Student Organization at New York University.
2. **Indian American** is the term used to describe Americans of Indian descent, or offspring of Indian immigrants who are born American citizens. With this descriptive term is the acknowledgement that there is a negotiation of the differences between dominant White American value systems and lifestyles, and Indian value systems and lifestyles. From this negotiation emerges

another way of being. Some of the college going young adults who participate in the New York University cultural programs identify themselves as Indian American.

3. **Asian Indian** is the term used by the U.S. Census Bureau to describe persons who identify themselves as having Indian descent, specifically describing themselves as: Indian, Bengalese, Dravidian, Bharat, Goanese, East Indian (sic). The term 'Asian' added onto 'Indian' distinguishes these Indians from West Indians from the Caribbean, as well as American Indian or from Native Americans.

4. **South Asian** is the term used to describe any person who claims descent from any of the countries in the South Asian subcontinent such as India, Pakistan, Bangladesh, Sri Lanka, Bhutan, Nepal, and the Maldives Islands. In an attempt to acknowledge the overwhelming similarities that these distinct nation states share as far as colonial histories, lifeways, and values are concerned, and since people of South Asian descent confront the same issues of class, race, and gender in United States, the term South Asian is the preferred progressive term used to represent ourselves in the current climate of US multicultural politics. Progressive service organizations such as Sakhi for South Asian Women, or South Asian Lesbian and Gay Association(SALGA) or South Asian Women's Creative Collective (SAWCC), or South Asian Youth Action (SAYA!) strive to cater to all South Asians as a matter of mandate and canon. Their mission is to provide a venue, services and advocacy for particular issues that of concern to all South Asians such as domestic violence (Sakhi), sexual politics (SALGA), creative expression (SAWCC) and youth development (SAYA!) rather than celebrate and emphasize ethnic, regional, linguistic, or religious distinctions.

   In this book, I must confess that I have described primarily Indian cultural productions with an understanding derived from my familiarity and practice of Indian culture. I am keenly aware and have acknowledged the inclusionary appropriateness of the term South Asian.

5. **Desi** is a colloquial descriptive term that has been appropriated by young South Asians in the Diaspora, especially in the last 10 years to acknowledge, appreciate, and overcome the differences that divide South Asians such as religion, language, class. It is a term used by diasporic South Asians to describe the lifeways,

values, and socio-cultural negotiations that are being experienced by those of South Asian descent born and bred in countries that are not South Asian. A party that plays, reggae, hip-hop, bhangra, and Hindi film music, attended by primarily Pakistanis, Indians, and other South Asians is a Desi party. If someone says he or she is dating a Desi, one is actually saying that he or she is not dating a non-South Asian. Whether the person in question is of Indian, Pakistani descent, practices Hinduism or Islam, or is Punjabi or Gujurati speaking is only of secondary or tertiary importance. The Desi shares an understanding with other like-minded Desis that these differences are diluted in the diaspora. In this book, all the forms that emerge in response to the official definition of Indianness seem to be Desi forms, i.e., forms that are enacted by or have appeal to most South Asians, despite marked regional, linguistic, and religious differences. In this book, I use the terms Desi and Indian interchangeably because included in the performance of Indianness in the United States is Desiness, a realization that to perform Indianness outside India, is to acknowledge, at least some of the time, one's relationship and kinship to other South Asians—differences, notwithstanding.

METHODOLOGICAL ISSUES

How have I unearthed answers to my speculations? First, let me locate myself in this project, clarify whereof I speak. I am inspired by anthropologist Kirin Narayan's analysis of her own 'multiplex identity' as a native doing ethnography of story-telling and other performative genres of women in the Nasik and Kangra, in the state of Gujarat, Northwest of India. Her father is Gujarat, mother German. She was brought up in Bombay, did graduate work in California, and research in rural Gujarat, and is now teaching in Wisconsin. Despite her mixed and mixed up heritage, she identifies herself as Indian:

> Mixed ancestry is itself a cultural fact: the gender of the particular parents, the power dynamic between the groups that have mixed, and the prejudices of the time, all contribute to the mark that mixed blood leaves on a person's identity . . . Growing up in Bombay with strongly stressed patrilineage, a Hindu Indian identity has weighted more than half in my self-definition, pushing into the background Pilgrim fathers

and Bavarian burghers who are also available in my genealogical
repertoire. This would seem to mark me as Indian and, therefore, when
I study India, a 'native' anthropologist. After all, researching aspects of
India, *I often share an unspoken emotional understanding with people
with whom I work.* [italics mine] (1993:674)

Unlike Narayan, I am not of mixed blood, nor have I been brought
up in India but, like her, I have always had to define my cultural identity
in reference to Indianness. I have had to wrestle with that specter of India
that I have inherited, have had to live with it, and still continue to, outside
India, here in New York City. In terms of this project, I have the distinct
advantage of being myself a product of the Indian diaspora: Twice migrant—from the Philippines to the US—thrice migrant if I include my
parents' migration out of Hyderabad Sind, now Pakistan. Having grown
up in the Sindhi Hindu community in the Roman Catholic capital of that
Malayo-Polynesian archipelago of the Philippines, Manila, and finding
myself in the Western cosmopolitan milieu of New York City, I have always been dazzled by the perplexing and fascinating concept of "Indian
culture". The longest I have sojourned in India, in the cosmopolitan metropolis of Bombay is seven months at a stretch. India as my homeland
was also an imaginative construct besides it being an actual site to visit.
My parents of Sindhi Hindu heritage made us keenly aware of our being
Indian Hindus rather than Pakistani Muslims, and even Filipino
Catholics. This awareness of a particular ethnic identification evolved
first, because they left their bag, baggage, hearth and home, in their ancestral homeland Sind, during the India/Pakistan partition, and second
because their mercantile ambitions brought us not to another Indian city,
but to a city "across the black waters" in a Southeast Asian archipelago.

Though India and the Philippines do share similarities of colonial
and post-colonial history, oppression and ambivalence, and both belong
to Asia, and are subject to the whims of international economic foreign
policies, my not being perceived as having the looks, heritage, and sensibility of the Filipinos, who themselves are hybrid but differently so,
marked me, as foreign. To my classmates, I was a 'bumbay', a local,
sometimes derogatory term for Indian coined from 'Bombay' or "bhum
bhai"—'brother from the same soil' (Dusenbery, 1995: 22), a term that
the Punjabi Sikhs, who are the oldest and most assimilated Indian community in the Philippines, use to describe each other. To us bumbays, Filipinos were 'pakora', originally a term for a deep-fried flat appetizer
made from split pea flour. The flatness was in reference to their low-

bridged noses in comparison to our high-bridged ones. Among other differences, we were Hindus, unbaptized, our men were uncircumcised, we are pagan idol-worshippers, sometimes we showed our midriffs in a saree and wore a dot on our foreheads, ate very spicy, and odd-looking food. Filipinos on the other hand, were Roman Catholic, baptized, hygienically circumcised (a vestige of American medical and cleanliness myth), ate sour-bitter, fishy, and bland food, and were inheritors of heaven. We, 'bumbays', would come back, sometimes even as cockroaches—big, fat flying ones, mind you!

Not to say that my whole upbringing was fraught with hostility. On the contrary, despite this racist, and xenophobic 'official' backdrop in my community as well as within Filipino society, much love, warmth, and delight did and do percolate amongst Indians and Filipinos, through intermarriage, and life-long friendships, intellectual and artistic exchange, philanthropic organizations, business ventures, and voluntary conversions to Catholicism, or the worship of Jesus as yet another avatar of the Divine, and naturalization into Filipino citizenship (for business and patriotic purposes), and involvement in local and state politics.

Living with difference and an "impure" identity all my life has made me keenly aware of the constant necessity to define, negotiate, resist the definitions of a reified Indianness and yet use it to describe myself. I have acquired a great reverence for hybridity that emerges from living in a dynamically intercultural environment. In New York, I am recognized as Indian by fellow Indians, mistaken as Hispanic by other Hispanics. In a recent visit to Mexico, I was complimented for passing off as a "beautiful middle-class Mexican woman." The middle-class adjective as opposed to upper class was thrown in to underscore that I had *indio* blood—adding even more to my "authentic" passing off as an indigenous *mujer mexicana*. I am totally ignored by Filipinos, dismissed as another 'bumbay' (but whom I recognize by skin color, facial features and intonation) because I just do not look Filipina. In my Banyan tree imagination, India's history and its civilization grow roots beside Philippine history, and my lived reality. The Philippines, though, was not even part of the British Commonwealth, and therefore does not figure in the official Indian colonial, and post-colonial imagination. Since my looks and family background, intellectual inquiry, and sensibility, is "strategically" Indian (Spivak, 1987), and because I share an "unspoken emotional understanding" to some extent, and some of the time, with other Indians, I am Indian-identified due to my background, and my foreground. Yet, not purely so, because I bring with me a Filipinoness which changes my kind of Indianness. Call me an *Indipina¹ (Indian-Filipino)*, if you will. The matter of my Indianness is further complicated by living in multicultural New York City as if my future belonged here. I am a not-not Indian.

I have forged relationships with New Yorkers - Desis and non-desis alike, through my research, through my school work, and through my professional, personal, familial, and scholarly contacts and efforts. I participated in a video project as a talent for the activist group SAKHI and some others, have been involved in a cable TV commercial, many play readings and theatrical/performance productions. I have published, and presented papers on this problematic concept of Indianness. I compose performance pieces and poetry exploring and expressing the agonies and ecstasies of hybridity. I work as an arts and cultural programmer at the Asia Society with ample opportunities to mount, amongst others, Desi cultural productions, and engage sections of the Desi community in the animation of these productions. Through my personality, intellect, and talent, I have actively engaged in dialogues with people of Indian descent, with South Asianists, as well as with artists on what it means to have some part of our selves defined as Indian, and what happens with that part of the self outside India. This is the personal cultural arsenal that I deploy in this project. In my study of the diasporic community here, I have used this experience as an entry point, and then applied my scholarship to it. I concur with Narayan who asserts that:

> Those of us who study societies in which we have pre-existing experience absorb analytic categories that rename and reframe what is already known. The reframing essentially involves locating vivid particulars within larger cultural patterns, sociological relations, and historical shift. These categories also rephrase these particulars as evidence of theoretical issues that cross cultures and are the special province of trained academics. (1993:678)

I am, thus, an informed native—native, that is, to Indianness, not a native of India—a participant observer, and can systematize this knowledge as a scholar equipped with an interdisciplinary social science/ performance studies framework. This has given me access to a "diversity within this cultural domain" and "has lead me to the discovery of many strange and unfamiliar aspects of [this] society". After all, "one knows about a society [only] from particular locations within it" (Narayan, 1993:678–679). Indeed, I am merely an informed native cultural critic, not an omniscient one.

The methods I used to gather information are **personal observations** on how a performance is constructed, produced, and what choices are made to express Indian culture. Important too, is how the performance is evaluated as to its aesthetic appeal by the audience, and my own value judgements. My Geertzian interpretative analysis is guided by aspects of Joann Kealiinohomoku's dance guide which I use as spring board for my impressionistic study. Though her guide is to be used for dance, I have expanded its use for performance. Some of these aspects are hereby summarized:

1. **Identification**—name and type of dance; locality and environment; occasion; participants
2. **[Performance] Background**—function and purpose; meaning or story; owner of dance; transmission, learning and rehearsal; ethnoevaluation of performance
3. **Participants' Background**—number, age and sex; status of performer; training; role of audience
4. **Other Considerations**—texts; communication and projection of the performers; dance gestures and movements.

I began preliminary observations of NYC Asian Indian immigrant life in 1989 when I attended the Deepavali Festival, and the attendant celebrations, and participated in a moderately active social life. Serious research on the South Street Seaport Festival began in 1990 which resulted in a slide-lecture, and a short research paper for Brooks McNamara's New York University's Popular Entertainments' class. From 1990 until 1995, I have attended, participated and video-taped aspects of the South Street Deepavali festival, the India Day Parade, as well as attended four Shruti (NYU) shows. It was impossible to record and witness every aspect of these performance events every year, since I have not mastered the yoga of multiple simultaneous presences as yet. Each year I looked closely at different areas, and events within the festivals, and noted my observations. I do not feel that I have absorbed, or even observed everything of these productions, much less of the productions that occur in the NYC tri-state area (and there are so much of them that you can attend, at least two every month, if you are conservative!). These productions add events every year to lure audiences, and satisfy their need for novelty and variety. Since these particular occasions come once a year, or twice at the most in the case of Shruti, time constraints dictated when and how much I could record. I attended 14 shows: 6 Deepavali Festivals, 3 Rego Park

Sindhi Diwali shows, 4 India Day Parades, 4 Shruti events in a six year span 1989 to 1995. The list does not even include the gatherings and meetings, social occasions, religious ceremonies, and other performance events. But these other cultural events have left vivid impressions in my mind and have influenced and enhanced my understanding of the expanse, variety and dynamism of Indian cultural life in New York. This project analyzes only the most salient characteristics of Asian Indian expressive life in Manhattan as expressed in these three cultural productions.

I **analyze the contents** and formats of performances that I saw and videotaped personally. I look for thematic patterns, sources of innovations, and interpret the underlying socio-political ideational thrust of the various production numbers. I sought to understand how even as these performances operate within dominant cultural discourses they are always already transforming them, always already deconstructing its rhetoric of authenticity and purity. I am influenced by Stuart Hall's assertion that popular or vernacular forms are constantly being reorganized and or redefined by the aficionados of dominant or official culture:

> Culture is polarized around a cultural dialectic . . . this sense of tension and opposition between what belongs to the central domain of elite or dominant culture and the culture of the periphery(1981: 234).

I look at how these popular forms articulate these relations of dominance and subordination, the relation between vernacular culture and hegemony, how these cultural expressions are "organized around the contradiction of popular forces versus the power bloc" (1982: 238). These performances seem to me negotiations of what it means to be Indian in America, of being American with Indian heritage, of having a hyphenated identity, of being an Indian of the diaspora, of being neither wholly Indian nor wholly American.

I **interviewed** performers and the program producers using an informal open-ended question guide. Some of the questions were about their intent in composing their numbers, what influenced their aesthetic choices as to venue, music, choreography, theme, performers, production values. I also asked why it is important to perform this kind of show in the United States of America, on this particular occasion, why the need to represent themselves, their Indianness in this manner. I focus on the performers and program producers because I consider them the prime culture brokers who, through the process of participating in the productions, consume their socio-cultural milieu's ideas about Indian identity and, in turn, reconstitute this identity in their performances (Schechner, 1985; Geertz, 1973 & 1983). Examples of questions I asked are:

1. How did your organization decide on what items to include in this celebration? Why did you decide to perform this particular number? Who helped you with this number? How are your performances composed? How did you decide on this material?

2. For whom is this occasion? Why are we celebrating it? When you perform this number what are you saying about this occasion? About yourself? About being Indian? About being American? In your opinion, what do Indians experience or feel about this way of celebrating this occasion? What does it mean to non-Indians?

3. How did you feel about performing? What does performing mean to you? What do you feel while you are performing? When do you feel you are performing well?

4. What are some of the problems you (and your organization) experienced in preparing for this show? How did you solve these problems?

5. How long does it take to plan and organize this project? How much does it cost? Where do you get your funding?

6. What did you personally wish to achieve in your involvement with the project?

7. What prompted the choice of this site for this performance?

8. What is the primary appeal of this particular number? Do you think that this particular item is a good expression of Indian culture? How does it compare to other forms? Who understands this performance?

I was able to speak informally with many Asian Indians about their life and adjustments to the US. Many of my insights have been culled from these conversations and banterings. I have not quoted or identified these sources as I want to protect the privacy of those who cooperated with me. However, I have cited a number of community leaders and community artists by name since their position places them in the public eye already. I also have had the fortune of discussing my observations with academic colleagues in the various conferences and presentations that I have attended or in which I participated. In my current professional undertaking at the Asia Society, I have also been able to practice, research and administrate as a cultural worker. This has provided me much insight and access.

Significance and Limits of the Inquiry

I hope this study contributes to the storehouse of knowledge in intercultural communication, the problems of cultural identity and adaptation, global migrations and the problematics of diaspora, urban hybrid subcultures and the socio-cultural processes of performances. Moreover, this project illustrates how a "pluralistic ambience [is created] in which people are able to discover positive pleasure in their inescapable diversity" (Gilroy, 1993: 33). Inspired by Raymond Williams (1958) and Stuart Hall (1981), my project focuses on the community productions of Indian immigrants performed by non-professionals—i.e., ordinary people rather than professional artists. In the Indian context it would mean dealing with non-Sanskritized or non-Brahmanized art forms, these forms which are looked down on with disdain by the upper castes and classes, the intellectual and artistic elites. Not that the producers of these festivals and variety shows are disenfranchised, or that those who participate in them are from the disadvantaged classes only. The forms of cultural expression that emerge, that insist upon appearing due to 'popular demand' include quite prominently non-marga, non-elitist forms, i.e., Desi forms. It is in this way that they are 'ordinary'. This study tries to shed light on why they are employed, giving credibility and validation as to their cultural meaningfulness. While these performances provide much pleasure to the spectators (as well as to myself) they speak against "dominant" white hegemony, and also against mainstream "official" Indian hegemony.

Studies on 'official', marga performances, festivals, traditional art forms of India have already been done by Richard Bauman (1992 a, 1992 b) and Richard Kurin (1985, 1991). Academic departments all over the United States, which have some Indian Studies components, already heavily emphasize India's classical and/or folkloric traditions. Their analysis emphasize India as their original source. When you witness these performances, you experience India or Indian culture as untouched, never-changing. The otherness, the purity, the ancientness attributed to these type of forms are the poignant ingredients of their appeal.

Asian-American studies, diaspora studies, cultural and performance studies are exciting fields requiring shifts in paradigms brought about by

the disillusioning realities of the artificiality of the nation-state, the ubiquity of orientalist thought and other post-colonial theories, vast global
migrations, the phenomenon of being once–twice migrant, and the dismantling of the essentialist notions of a reified cultural identity that has
brought about the crises of representation. Rather than looking at cultures and their forms as pure entities, as whole and unchanging, these
contemporary disciplines demand that culture be viewed as hybrid and
emerging, straddling multiple definitions, histories, and being represented by forms that are intercultural, popular, wrought out of the experience of dislocation, relocation, multiplicity, difference (be it gender,
class, culture, etc.)

Influenced by certain performance-oriented folklorists' penchant for
investigating "native systems of aesthetics in their own terms, as these
condition the making, consumption, and interpretation of aesthetic productions" and studying "the functional role of artfulness in the conduct
of social life: to enhance rhetorical efficacy, to elicit the participative energies of an audience, as a medium of reflexivity or self-aggrandizement,
as entertainment and so on" (Baumann, 1992: 39) and as representation,
and political exchange, I look at performance events that have participants who are not necessarily professional artists, or who are practitioners only of the Great Traditions. They may have artistic talent, they may
like to sing and dance, but their life is not necessarily that of the artist.
They participate in these performances as a way to express in an 'artful'
way their sense of community, belonging and political savvy. Taking
time out of their daily workaday routines, they appropriate, reject, innovate, invent forms that best express their life and that can entertain and
delight themselves. The voluntary associations that they participate in
provide opportunities for creative expression, leadership, philanthropy,
political representation, and a social life.

Singer (1980) discusses the impact of urbanization on the Sanskritic
expressive and artistic behaviors in Madras, India. He posits that this
learned, literate, highly specialized and systematized Great Tradition
prevailed all over India through the efforts of a self-perpetuating intellectual group who mediated alien cultural influences to the non-elites and
interpreted these forms to the foreigners. In his anthropological research
on the social imbeddedness of this tradition in Madras City life, Singer
looked toward the literati, scriptural texts, and leading practitioners of
the cultural performances of the Great Traditions to understand how
these forms were transformed and elevated from the parochiality of the
Little traditions. This dominant tradition has strong elements of sacred

Hindu scriptural tenets, and therefore, has a deep spiritual essence, specifically a spirituality espoused by Sanskritic, brahmanic upper caste and Aryan traditions. In the field of folklore studies, Singer's theory is based on the framework of social evolution which posits that vernacular forms are the unpolished, raw, and more primitive versions of the Great Tradition. This view is at best conservative, and presumptuous of the lack of structure and vitality of folk forms or non-Great Tradition forms in and of themselves. The Little traditions are not taken as serious art forms because they are not learned, not evolved yet, not mediated by an elite—they are Neanderthal to the *Homo sapiens*. The sardonic and self-evident question is, then, which is the more human, the more civilized of the practices, as well as of the practitioners?

As Singer looks at the transformations of the Great Tradition in the urban metropolitan city of Madras, I look at cultural performances that take place in the city of New York, specifically Manhattan. Similar to Herman Bausinger's analysis of folklife in cities (1990), I look for urban folk forms that emerge from their relationship to the urban megalopolis, either as a place of work, or a place to be entertained by, or a place to go to school in, or as a place to live. Folklife is not only to be found in the perceived natural and simple life of the peasants who are fantasized, especially by city dwellers, to be living a life of goodness, peace, harmony, and innocence. Bausinger asserts that there is a vibrant folklife in urban and technologized cities. These forms have redefined the social, temporal, and spatial limits of the city. The overmechanized city life has, in fact, expanded human social relations and created new cultural forms:

> Technology [has not] invaded and dissolved all forms of community that support folk culture . . . Without doubt the increased mobility due to technology has made relationships more wide ranging and has dissolved traditional groups. Old neighborhood relations, for example, are often replaced by circles of acquaintances and social contacts which also characterize the structure of societies and clubs. Overall, however, group life is no less intensive than it used to be . . . Popular songs are not only heard but also sung. Membership in choral societies has not decreased; on the contrary, it has vastly increased since the introduction of the radio. . . . the traditional pilgrimage prayers are still said, led over the microphone. (1990: 23, 24)

The folklorist Dan Ben Amos elaborates on Bausinger's assertions regarding the place of tradition in city life in his introductory remarks:

Tradition is not passed on from generation to generation in language, art, and music as a time-honored body of knowledge and values. Rather, it is in a constant stage of disarray, about to disintegrate under the pressures of change; and members of the society strive to restore and maintain it in new rituals, displays, and diverse forms of entertainment—constructed and if necessary invented—or the revival of old ones . . . Tradition is not only made self-conscious but often [it is] up for sale . . . an object of multiple perspectives and different systems of evaluation. (1990: vii–viii, ix)

In Bausinger's understanding of folk life in a world of technology—"the city, with its congested streets, polluted air, and multi-ethnic population, becomes . . . as much a 'natural environment' for folklore as open fields, clear sky and tradition-steeped peasantry of the countryside" (Ben Amos, 1990: vii).

Thus South Street Seaport becomes ever more colorful on one of the Sundays of October or November with dances, food, crafts, and fireworks produced and enacted by Asian Indians. Madison Avenue on one Sunday in mid-August is overwhelmed by the dramatics of people of South Asian descent, and Greenwich Village comes all the more alive with a fashion show, jokes, and young couples dancing in an extravaganza produced by young Indian NYU students. Asian Indian worlds are created, marked off, valorized, and celebrated in these urban frontiers with expressive forms that have been innovated or invented by these Desi folks. The island of Manhattan becomes pronouncedly Asian Indian on these days, during these performances. This visibility is especially significant amidst the carnival of difference and cosmopolitanism that New York purports to espouse but whitewashes (pun intended) with ruthless competition, a high crime rate, homelessness, and hostile racism.

In this study, I am guided by these questions that Kirshenblatt-Gimblett has outlined for the urban folklorist. I have restructured these questions in list form:

1. What is the relationship between peculiar features of urban settings and the expressive forms found [here]?
2. How do people use expressive behavior to personalize and humanize the urban environment?
3. How do they insert themselves into the larger power structures, or find ways in which to exercise choice and control?

4. How do they appropriate and rework mass-produced commodities?
5. How can expressive behavior reveal complex interplay of formal controls, tacit understandings and custom?
6. What forms does the traditionalizing process take in a heterogeneous and competitive urban setting?
7. How do the inhabitants of a city form images of the larger whole and their place in it? (1983: 185)

Succinctly put: How does the Asian Indian leave a vivid imprint of his or her humanity and dynamism in NYC? I discuss these human and dynamic processes, these "indigenous solutions [and] arrangements that inhabitants themselves evolve, often independently of the authorities, if not in defiance of [them]" (Kirshenblatt-Gimblett, 1983: 183). The "authorities" who are defied are "white" America, as well as the propagators of official Indianness by the cultural elites of the Asian Indian American community.

This project destabilizes India's place as referent and looks, albeit Janus-faced, at Indianness outside India. Ample research has been done already on Indians in Britain (Agnihotri, 1987; Watson, 1977; Bhachu, 1985; Davison, 1966; Burghart, 1987; and so forth) and in the Caribbean (Birbalsingh, 1989; Brereton, 1982; Morton, 1991; La Guerre, 1974; Vertovec, 1988; Korom, 1994 a&b). Indianness in North America is a growing field of interest. For this study, I have used information thoroughly researched in the work of Madhulika Khandelwal (1992) wherein she updates the general histories of Indian immigration formulated by Saran et al. (1980, 1985). Whereas Saran et al, base their understanding of immigrant life on interviews with highly professional and affluent immigrants who arrived in the U.S. in the 1960s as graduate students or highly qualified professionals, Khandelwal, in her dissertation, narrates the stories of the more diverse immigrants who came after the 1970s until 1993 as a result of the liberal Immigration Reform Act of 1965. This reform allowed the legal immigration of family members of settled and successful model minority. The 1960s batch of immigrants are by now sending their children to college, or maybe even having grandchildren. Maxine Fisher (1980a, 1980b) and the Helwegs (1990) focused on the life, lifestyles, and adjustments of the 1960s elites. Fisher primarily focuses on the roles of voluntary associations in the life of Indian immigrants with special emphasis on the Association of Indians in America. On the other hand, Khandelwal deals with later immigrants who are not always model minorities, who take on semiskilled and unskilled labor, are not necessarily highly educated, and may not speak English. Khandelwal discusses an immigrant profile that is diversifying. My project adds a new perspective on the socio-cultural life of these Indian immigrants. Specifically, I look at how Indian diasporic identity is expressed in performance.

Since this Indianness is "invented" (Wagner, 1975; Anderson, 1991; Sollors, 1988, since it occupies the imagination of people who define some part of their selfhood as Indian (Rushdie, 1992; Naipaul, 1990), this project continues to contribute to the understanding of the culture/identity-making processes of migrating peoples, of which Indians are the most active. The cultural productions or the performances are seen as a special, heightened, and vivid instance of human adaptive behavior. It is behavior in which humans make sense of their circumstances and adjust themselves to their perceived reality and their own aspirations. These cultural productions are the entry point to understanding the adaptive behavior of a cultural minority whose sense of self is continually in a state of anxiety, in flux, processual, and performed.

Lastly, since I myself am a product of the Indian diaspora enmeshed in pleasures and pains of performing Indianness as a New York resident, I contribute an informed and enriched native's perspective to this complex problematic of hybrid identity. I could not be, nor do I wish to be, a passive observer in the production of this book. Indeed, I intervene, have my say, and at times seem to disappear as this project unfolds. The project is as much about my understanding of my Indianness, corroborated and contradicted, in parallel to the Indianness of all others I am studying. The text is thus, interrupted by anecdotes of memories as a participant in Indian diasporic culture in the Philippines and my ambivalent reactions to the material that I have gathered. My ethnographic research was a venue for the performance of my Indianness, allowed me to practice my Desiness. It is, as Kirin Narayan describes it, my own "enactment of hybridity" (1993: 681). It is a hybridity wrought out of the split of my professional and personal life, and a cultural hybridity that has emerged from my engagement with difference.

PROFILE OF THE BOOK

This book has been organized around three performances of Pan-Indianness that are produced annually in Manhattan, New York by voluntary associations. Before discussing these, in chapter 2 I sketch Asian Indian immigration in the US, specifically of NYC Indians. I discuss briefly the importance of cultural productions in the life of the Indian in America. Specific questions asked are: What is the role of staged performances in the life style of Indian immigrants? What are their attitudes to the partic-ipation in, enjoyment of, exhibition of these performances? Where can I locate this study in the history of the Asian Indian diaspora? The core of this inquiry concentrates on specific performances, each of which illumi-nates a vital aspect of Indianness.

The third chapter entitled "Currying the Big Apple: Creating Pan-In-dian Authentic Ethnic Aesthetic" describes the performance events sur-rounding the Deepavali festival at the South Street Seaport as asserting an exotic, folkloric, and, yes, pastoral Indian identity. These cultural per-formances assert a nationalistic allegiance to a secular India problema-tizing the Hindu base of the festival. Issues of creating an authentic identity, orientalism and tourism are threshed out.

In the fourth chapter entitled "Underneath My Blouse Beats My In-dian Heart: Hindi Film Dance, Indian Womanhood & Nationalism at the India Day Parade" speaks about how through the genre of popular Hindi cinema and its systemics, Indian womanhood and varieties of sexualities are redefined. This chapter also illustrates how regional and religious dif-ferences are homogenized by the processes of the transculturalization via the electronic media.

In chapters 3 and 4, I first describe the assertion of official Indian-ness as prescribed by the community leaders or officers of these organi-zations. I then proceed to discuss how this official Indianness is rebuffed by other more popular and vernacular forms which spring up. The per-formance organizers are thus forced to acknowledge these forms, and therefore the assertions of the populace that enact these genres.

The fifth chapter whimsically entitled "The GlamoroU.S. Bride Snow White Dances Disco Bhangra with Desi Groom: Performing Hy-bridity at NYU" is about how young college-going first- and second-gen-eration Asian Indian immigrants are nurtured by the cultural memory of India and the impact of their social reality of the United States. India–America, as represented by Shruti, the South Asian Student Orga-nization at New York University, is comprised of the ersatz elements of the popular, commercial cultures of both countries. This chapter de-scribes how these cultural forms are used to represent their hybridity, and their interactions with disparate intergenerational value systems.

The book's sixth and concluding chapter, entitled "It's a Drag Grow-ing Rutabagas in the Shrinking Himalayas: A Performance (Ambi)Va-

lence to Indianness," deals with the twofold question of identity politics:
(1) How does a minority group express and preserve the particularities
and varieties of its identity despite the pull, impulse, and necessity to assimilate, and (2) what does it mean to perform this multifaceted and
problematic identity within the U.S. of the late 1990s? I am very aware,
at this point, of the tragic drama of Indian communalism in the resur-
gence and dominance of Hindu fundamentalism in India and its spill
over here. A specific and quasi-monotheistic version of Hinduism is
being conjured and advocated to justify the fascism and exclusivity of a
Hindu state. In the performances that I discuss, Hindu fascism rears its
ugly head, only to be chopped off by the syncretic vernacular forms. The
current rhetoric of "multiculturalism" in the United States allows the cel-
ebratory expression of difference. Concurrent with this celebration of
difference, is the spate of racial crimes against South Asian Americans. I
am more concerned with how does the performance of Indianness empower Indians in the diaspora. Does it arm them against racism, the homogenizing forces of capitalism, and Western cultural hegemony?
Included in this final chapter is a performative response to the enactment
of Indianness, my personal ambivalences as an Indian woman in diaspora.

Before you are taken up into the kaleidoscopic whirlwind of Indianness in NYC, allow me to locate this book in the continuing history of the
motility of Indian peoples. The next chapter guides us in the journeys of
the diasporic Desi, landing us rather squarely on the ever shifting terrain
of the New York cultural landscape.

NOTES

[1] I performed a monologue which unravels what it means to be a woman of Indian descent, born and brought up in Manila, Philippines entitled: *From Manila
to Manhattan: On Being a Filipino-Indian-American* at the American Museum
of Natural History's People Center in May of 1997.

CHAPTER 2

The Migrant Sensibility

> *One of the effects of mass migration has been*
> *the creation of radically new types of human*
> *being: of people who root themselves in ideas*
> *rather than places, in memories as much as in*
> *material things: people who have been obliged*
> *to define themselves—because they are so de-*
> *fined by others—by their otherness: People in*
> *whose deepest selves strange fusions occur,*
> *unprecedented unions between what they were*
> *and where they find themselves. The migrant*
> *suspects reality. Having several ways of being,*
> *he understands their illusory nature. To see*
> *things plainly, you have to cross a frontier.*
> *(Rushdie, 1992:124)*

In the history of the Indian diaspora, this book is located in a desire to understand the sensibility of migrating peoples, to understand how home,
the *hereland,*[1] place, displacement and dislocation have created a new
type of human being. In this case the new type of being is the Indian in
the diaspora, or the diasporic Desi, for whom the concept of 'being Indian' is continually called into question. This movement out of the geographic boundaries of the subcontinent creates, thus, an Indianness, a
self-acknowledgement of having origins in a particular elsewhere, and
being recognized as coming from that particular elsewhere despite living
for generations in a hereland. Whether or not, persons of Indian heritage
do travel back to the subcontinent, speak any or none of the Indian languages, or practice any of the religions, or enact any of the ethnic markers, there seems to be an affiliation to the cultural landscape of
Indianness, there is a designation of self as Desi. This affinity may be expressed in the form of culinary preferences, the affection for Desi popular entertainments and to a limited extent, a reverence for the classical or
traditional arts, or the formal study of "Indian culture" or the practice of
Hindu religions[2], and startlingly, in wedding ceremonies which may be
described as generically Indian. The Indianness that emerges in a hereland insists upon the amalgam of pleasurable components of the "native"

culture, reaping the benefits of a local economy, making a home in the hereland that contains sometimes inchoate notions of Indianness, and most importantly, in creating a community in relation to the homeland they have left or that their forefathers came from. (Karamcheti, 1992)

Indianness wrought out of the migrant sensibility has also a definite global sweep rather than only a connection to that particular geographic land mass or even to the hereland. This new *diasporic* Indianness is characterized by the emergence of a global community that is unified by their common experience of dispersal—the problems of identity, racism, intergenerational conflicts, the building of community in relation to the South Asian subcontinent- and a claim to an essential identity that is Indian or Desi, even though its manifestations vary. This diasporic Indian community may be maintained by travel to India as well as to other Indian diasporic sites, telecommunications, electronic media, and the widespread distribution and saturation of Indian popular entertainments. Diasporic Indians need not have the shared memory of having actually lived as Indians in India to be Indian. (Nelson in Karamcheti, 1992:268 Karamcheti; 1992). Indianness is claiming a cultural and/or ancestral link to India while not necessarily ever having lived or gone there. Indianness is transnational, i.e., it transcends the limits of nationalist geography. Participating in "Indian Culture" makes one Indian.

More books than one would be required to do justice to the narratives of Indians in the diaspora, and by extension to all peoples who move by force of economic circumstance, colonial oppression, or personal ambition. Indeed, this history has contributed to the diasporic imagination of Indianness—an invention of an identity that bespeaks an attachment and belonging to a particular ancestral homeland, and a difference from the peoples and cultures encountered in the hereland(s). Though I begin by describing the dispersal of Indian peoples globally due to the economic mechanisms of indentured labor, the forthcoming sketch brings to the fore only the most relevant, and salient details of the history of Indians in the U.S. Though I have not relied on a strict chronological framework, the history of dispersal is arranged in two time periods: colonial and post-colonial because this divide marks the emergence of the independent Indian nation-states of India and Pakistan, and the attendant sense of nationalism instilled in Indians (as well as Pakistanis) everywhere. Within these broad time periods I have developed themes in which the varying attitudes towards Indianness are marked—focusing primarily on the depreciatory attitudes towards Indian immigrants while Indian culture and philosophy are exalted in the United States. The issues of race, class and orientalism complicate this ambivalent attitude towards peoples of Indian descent in the U.S.

The chapter concludes with the description of categories of expressive behaviors which Indians in the U.S. use to manifest aspects of their Indianness. These expressive behaviors are vital features of their lives in this country For historical details, I am indebted here to historian Dr. Madhulika Khandelwal's up-to-date and exhaustive description and research of NYC Asian Indian immigration history from 1965 to 1990. I have included a brief chronology, and a table of the number of Asian Indian immigrants to the U.S., in the appendix to summarize the discussion. Interwoven with this discussion are my personal encounters with dispersal, as what I perceived to be a shard of color in this kaleidoscope of Indianness.

COLONIAL DISPERSALS: LABOR, MERCHANTS, AND GODMEN

Indians have been pulled from the subcontinent during the last two centuries for structural as well as for personal/economic reasons. In 1833, slavery was abolished in the British empire (subsequently in other European empires as well). This created a labor shortage on the plantations and the factories in the colonies. Indentured laborers were exported from India to the Empire. Losing lands in India to the British, to the wealthy indigenous landlords who were given lands in exchange for their loyalties towards the British, high taxes, natural disasters and extremely poor living conditions, prompted huge numbers of Gujuratis, Punjabis, Malayalees, Tamils and Uttar Pradeshis of either Christian, Islamic, Sikh or Hindu faiths to work as indentured laborers in the colonies of the vast British Empire in east (Kenya, Nigeria), west (Ghana), and in South Africa (inc. Mauritius and Reunion Islands), Southeast Asia (Malaysia, Singapore, Hongkong, Fiji), and the Caribbean Islands (Guyana, Trinidad).

Five to six year contracts bound them to the colonial and economic masters. After which they could either return to India, or renew their contracts. From the laborer's point of view, the near-slavery conditions of indenture was a step up from the terrible poverty and the religious and caste discrimination which they experienced in the subcontinent. Although some Indians returned to India when their term of indenture was over, many others elected to stay abroad. These Indians saw opportunity for economic advancement and relief from the social rigidity of their homeland. Depending on the miscegenation laws, and the economic viability of returning to India to find a wife, male indentured workers brought wives and brides from their ethnic group in the subcontinent, or intermarried with local women, or other Indian women who came as indentured workers. These indentured workers were for the most part from the lower castes or totally disenfranchised classes. Indeed, a few upper caste Indians—brahmins and others—indentured themselves, but they were a small and negligible number. From 1833 to as late as 1924, this indentured labor force involved the migration of about 1.4 million people, taking Indians to 11 British colonies, 3 French, and 1 Dutch (Parekh, 1993).

V. S. Naipaul, the distinguished author, who comes from this West Indian indentured laborer ancestry, describes how the idea of Indianness was formed in Trinidad:

> These overseas Indian groups [in Trinidad] were mixed. They were miniature Indias, with Hindus and Muslims, and people of different castes. They were disadvantaged, without representation, and without a political tradition. They were isolated by language and culture from the people they found themselves among; they were isolated, too, from India itself. In these special circumstances they developed something they would never have known in India: a sense of belonging to an *Indian community*. This feeling of community could override religion and caste. [my italics] (1990:7)

As these indentured laborers left a poverty-stricken homeland, they created a new sense of self and community with others who came along with them from the same subcontinent. They began to define themselves as generically "Indian," whereas in the subcontinent they may have defined themselves according to their ethnic linguistic group Gujarati, Malayalee, or according to their religious affiliation—Hindu, Muslim, Christian, or even according to caste and other subdivisions.

Besides being contracted laborers, Indians were prompted to migrate from the subcontinent due to their mercantile ambition. There has been a history of seafaring tradesmen amongst the Gujuratis, Parsees, Sindhis, and even Punjabis. Business opportunities mushroomed as the need arose to rebuild and rejuvenate cities after the world wars, as well as when various colonies gained independence as nation states. The rise of American economic power in the 20th century due to the force of colonial/imperialist ambitions, allowed for more doors to be opened for Indians wanting to earn a living outside India. As early as 1784, there was trade between India and the U.S. As early as the 19th century, successful Indian merchants and traders were already living in the U.S., especially on the East coast. From the middle of the 19th century to the 1930's, New York City was the U.S.'s leading seaport, "headquarters of the most important Atlantic shipping lines, an entrepot for goods from the South, North, and West, and the terminus for most of the ships that brought immigrants from Europe" (Berrol in Saran & Eames, 1980:90). By jumping English and other Western European trading ships in the Eastern Seaboard, some Indians arrived in New York and were absorbed in the garment and diamond trades. Even in the imagination of poets and thinkers like Emerson, Thoreau, and Whitman, India was conceived as a land of ancient wisdom, great wealth, glory, despite its despotism (Sharma, 1995:15–16).

One of the first contacts that the average American citizen had with "Indianness" was at the 1893 First World Parliament of Religions held in Chicago. Swami Vivekananda, disciple of the ecstatic mystic Ramakrishna, in flawless English, expounded on Vedantic Philosophy. After this successful stint, Vedanta Society centers were established throughout the U.S.—San Francisco and New York City being the strongholds.

Via the Philippines and Hawaii, many Indian tradesmen also penetrated the West Coast market in the earlier half of this century. Between 1907 and 1914, California and Vancouver experienced the surging "tide of turbans." About three thousand Punjabi Sikhs arrived in the West coast via Canada or the Philippines. Sikhs are distinctive, even in the subcontinent, because of their robust, tall physiques, their full beards, and long hair wrapped in cotton turbans. Other Indians made a distinct impression also, because of their skin color, clothing, cuisine, religious practices, and other cultural ways. Despite these differences, all peoples from the subcontinent were generalized as "Hindoos" at the turn of the century, here in the U.S.

Like the Chinese and the Japanese, these Sikhs—"Hindoos"—tilled farms, built railways, and worked in the steel, iron, and lumber mills. And like these East Asians, these "Hindoos" experienced discrimination. The local white population blamed these newcomers for the depletion of the job market, because they felt they were losing their jobs to these over eager foreigners. Asians were denied citizenship and the right to own land. In 1908, they were even driven out of their homes and jobs by local white residents of Live Oak, Sacramento Valley in California and rioted against in Bellingham, Washington. According to the Commissioner of the California State Bureau of Labor Statistics in 1920:

The Hindu is the most undesirable immigrant in the state. His lack of
personal cleanliness, his low morals and his blind adherence to theories and teachings, so entirely repugnant to American principles
make him unfit for association for American people. (Melendy,
1977:195)

However, the commissioner went on to explain that this criticism
was primarily against lower caste and low-class Hindus. His tone of disdain cannot be missed in this description of the "workingmen or peasant-
laborer specimens of the Hindoo genus homo":

The man with the Western cap wears clothes of pseudo-Occidental
style, which he fondly believes to be up-to-date, measured by Western
standards; but the sleeves invariably are too short and end nearer the
elbow than the wrist, while the coat and nether garments are tight
where they should be loose, and baggy where they should be tight. As a
rule, the clothes are dilapidated in appearance and frequently second-
hand, and the whole combination is grotesque except in the eyes of the
newcomer himself. (Melendy, 1977:189)

In contrast, listen to the tone of grudging admiration for the upper-
class, upper-caste "Hindoo immigrant":

Some there are in the group straggling across the gang-plank with
whose dress even the most fastidious American could find no fault.
Their clothes are of the latest approved style in cut, color, and material.
The well-dressed East Indians are merchants, students, or men of
means . . . (Melendy, 1977:189)

Already, as early as the first part of the 20th century, Indians were
discriminated against for their appearance and their class affiliations.
Education was another reason for the early 20th century migration
to England or to the United States. Sons of the privileged classes were
sent to advance themselves by becoming "westernized oriental gentle-
men" and learned Western political philosophy. Many of these returned
to India as the educated elite, who helped forge the independent nation
states of India and Pakistan. M. K. Gandhi, J. Nehru, and M. Jinnah, the
most decisive leaders of the independence movement against British imperialism, had an Indo-Anglian education.
While these highly politicized Anglo-educated elite in the Indian

subcontinent was forging independence from British rule, here in the U.S. between 1910 to 1920 an Indian independence movement was also taking root. Through the efforts of Har Dayal, a lecturer in Stanford University, and Tarakanath Das, an activist student in University of Seattle, the San Francisco-based Gadar Party was formed. But the U.S. government, allied with the British government, squelched this movement. Har Dayal was deported in 1914, Das and other leaders were imprisoned in 1918 (Melendy:209–212).

On the East Coast however, there was much sympathy for the plight of colonial India. In New England, motivated by principles of democracy, freedom, and peace the "Boston Brahmins," aficionados of the Theosophy Society and the Vivekananda Society supported the Independence Movement. However, officially, the U.S.–U.K. alliance prevailed, and the U.S. adopted a neutral stand regarding India's independence. But it was clear, with the cases of the Gadar party and with Das, Dayal and companions, that active and vocal participation in the independence movement against the British, a U.S ally, could cost the Indian his sojourn in the U.S.

After World War II, Gandhi's method of non-violent resistance attracted many American supporters, especially on college campuses in the East that by the time India attained independence in 1947, the U.S. was an important military ally of India.

Through these highly romantic words of Thoreau we can see that what stimulated affection for Indianness, especially in the East Coast, were the perceived spiritual niceties, that brand of other-worldly Hinduism, as well as class and caste hierarchy:

> In the morning I bathe my intellect in the stupendous and cosmogonal philosophy of the Bhagavat-Geeta . . . I meet the servant of the Brahmin, priest of Brahma and Vishnu and Indra, who still sits in his temple on the Ganges reading the Vedas, or dwells at the root of a tree with his crust and water jug . . . Furthest India is nearer to me than Concord and Lexington. (in Singer, 1990:22)

This pro-Indian, specifically, pro-Hindu sentiment was wrought out of the racist supremacist myth and the orientalist fantasy that Sanskritized traditions had pure, good and solid Aryan origins. Specifically focusing on the glory of the Sanskrit language and its being part of the Indo-Euro-Aryan linguistic group, in 1786, Sir William Jones, a scholar of the "oriental renaissance" observed that:

The Sanskrit language, whatever be its antiquity, is a wonderful structure; more perfect than the Greek, more copious than the Latin, and
more exquisitely refined than either. Yet bearing to both of them a
stronger affinity, both in the roots of the verbs and the forms of the
grammar, than could possibly have been produced by accident; so
strong, indeed, that no philosopher could examine them all without believing them to have sprung from some common source, which perhaps no longer exists. (Singer, 1990:25)

This observation was the springboard for comparative Indo-European studies in Europe as well as in America. Sanskrit language and literature became a worthy study because it was surmised to have origins in
the more advanced civilization of Europe.

On the West Coast, the "tide of turbans" was considered a scourge,
much like the "yellow peril" of the Chinese laborer. Though Thoreau,
Emerson, and their ilk may have waxed eloquent the glory of Hindu spirituality, workaday laboring Indians were considered barbarian, uncouth,
untrustworthy, stingy, and ever too willing to work for too little money,
with a very low standard of living:

The Hindoo invasion is yet in its infancy; only the head of the long pro-
cession has entered the Golden Gate but for miles their turbaned figures may be seen wielding crow-bar or shovel along the tracks . . .
their usual expenses amount to little more than three dollars a month—
a sum that would scarcely support a white man for three days . . . they
must always be reckoned with as a factor strongly affecting the pros-
perity of the white inhabitants. They [will] cease to become the ser-
vants of Americans [and will become] dangerous rivals. (Scheffauer,
June 1910 in *Little India*, Jan. 1993: 23–24)

In 1923, it was decided by Justice Sutherland in the classic case of
Bhagat Singh Thind, that though Hindus of the upper caste may be of
Aryan origin, they were not to be considered white precisely because:

The physical group characteristics of the Hindus render them readily
distinguishable from the various groups of persons in this country
commonly recognized as white. The children of English, French, German, Italian, Scandinavian, and other European parentage, quickly
merge into the mass of our population and lose the distinctive hall-

marks of their European origin. On the other hand, it cannot be doubted that the children born in this country of Hindu parents would retain indefinitely the clear evidence of their ancestry. (in Hing: 231)

All "Hindus," upper caste or not, were not allowed U.S. citizenship or the right to own land in 1923, because they were not considered of the 'white' race. As I will show in the forthcoming section, very little has changed in the attitudes today towards Indians. This seems to be the sentiment expressed by U.S. Americans in the early part of this century towards Indians: "We love the idea of the exotic, peaceful, and passive you, but not the scruffy reality of your hairy, hardworking, robust and non-white presence."

POST-COLONIAL DIASPORA: TRANSCONTINENTAL FAMILIES AND HYPHENATED IDENTITIES

With Indian independence in August of 1947, came the partition of the subcontinent, and soon after, the dismantling of the British empire. Vast populations were forced to move within the South Asian land mass based on their religious as well as nationalistic allegiance. A person from the subcontinent may have grown up thinking that her homeland was "India", only to discover that she would be considered "Pakistani" today. Pakistan was further divided into the Bengali-speaking but yet Islamic East Pakistan (subsequently, the independent state of Bangla Desh in 1972) and the officially Urdu speaking Pakistan.

In the divided Punjab, Sikhs were forced to relocate to India but still retained memories of their homes across the border in what became "Muslim" Pakistan. Yet, in India, too, many Sikhs, feeling unjustly treated by the predominantly Hindu polity in India, crave for a portion of the Indian land mass in the Indian state of Punjab to be carved out as a separate Sikh nation of Khalistan. Though Pakistan was created based on the tenets Islamic politics, and as a resistance to Hindu political hegemony, India's largest minority group consists of Muslims (10%) whose nationalist allegiance is to secular India, not Islamic Pakistan.

The complexity of Indianness wrought out of partition is manifested in Rashmi Sharma's description of this composite family:

The father was born in Mandalay in 1917, while it is still part of British India, but later became Burma and is now Myanmar; one child was

born to this man in 1938 in Bombay, before India's independence in
1947, and the other child was born in Karachi in 1948, after Karachi
became part of the new nation of Pakistan in 1947. In the United States
these three persons, from the same family, would be classified in three
separate categories by nationality based on place of birth—the father
would be classified as Burmese, the older child as Indian, and the
younger as Pakistani. (in Rustomji-Kerns, 1995:12–13)

My own family history lies at these crossroads: My Sindhi Hindu
parents and others members of the Sindhi community have currently
very limited access to, or no family in Hyderabad, Sind Province, Pakistan. They have brought with them blurred memories of a carefree child-
hood, some culinary delicacies, songs and music, cultural and religious
practices, and language as remnants of their Sindhi homeland to their
new herelands.

After partition, the homeland for my parents was the amorphous
India where some of my kinfolk still live, specifically Mumbai and Pune
with connections that fade as my maternal grandparents have passed
away. Business opportunities bring them to various parts of the globe.
For me now in New York, the Philippines is where I go "home" to because Mama and Papa are there and because I grew up there. I go home
to Manila for a respite, from the daily grind of New York. Or I can go
"home" to San Francisco where my aunt is, or to Los Angeles (where
other Manila-born Sindhis have migrated), or to Toronto where another
aunt and my Iranian Shi'ite Uncle live, or to Singapore or Malaysia or to
Hongkong, or to Indonesia, or to London, or to Spain, or to Surinam, or
to New York where my network of aunts, uncles, grand-aunts, cousins,
second-cousins, and almost-like-blood friends live and will welcome
me, even if they have never met me: they know my family. Scattered all
over the globe these people are my "transcontinental family" with ties
that we maintain through travel, telecommunications (phone, fax, electronic mail), occasional letters and newsletters, and yes, even through
gossip. (Kelly, 1990: 251). Home is not, therefore, one set place. My
roots are not set down—I take them with me. However, I still recognize
myself and am recognized by compatriots as 'Indian' by other South
Asians as Desi, as still having "Indianness" or still *being* Indian.

My passport is Indian, but I was born in the Philippines, even though
I was once a permanent resident there (due to my too long sojourn here
have 'lost' it (more ways than one!)). Despite living there until the age of
25, I have to return to the Philippines as a tourist. Still a much better fate

than my parents who will not be allowed to visit the home of their child-hood—Hyderabad Sind because of the hostile Indo-Pakistani relation-ship! I was surprised but pragmatic when I entered my Mama and Papa in an immigration lottery as "Pakistan-born," though they would be hor-rified to be considered such, and have no intention to migrate to the U.S., least of all as Pakistanis!

My parents practice a type of syncretic and popular Hinduism based on the teachings of the founding father of Sikhism, Guru Nanak, the folklore of the Islamic Sufi saint Shabaz Kalander, the mythology of Sindhi deity Jhoolelal, the whole gamut of Vaishnavite and Shaivite Hin-duism, with Jesus and Mary placed alongside Nehru and Gandhi—also Indira Gandhi and the Mahatma (never ever Jinnah, though) and some other dead relatives of mine. Brahmanic Hinduism, Sanskrit texts or Marga type Indianness do not figure as the only exalted medium of a way of living. This hybrid Indianness is very different than what was pro-pounded by "official" brahmanic culture, and the homogeneity of a Rama-centered nationalist Hinduism currently propagated by the Bharati Janata Party in India today.

The creation in 1947 of the modern independent state of India also underscored the creation of Indianness based on a secular nationality ideally above sectarian and communal fissiparousness. In the imagina-tion of the dispersed people of the subcontinent, this Indianness was and still is a precious and proud identity. Again, I turn to Naipaul:

> India was the India of the independence movement, the India of great
> names. It was also the India of great civilization and the great classical
> past. It was the India by which, in all the difficulties of our circum-
> stances, we felt supported. It was an aspect of our identity, the commu-
> nity identity we had developed, which in multi-racial Trinidad, had
> become more like a *racial identity*. (1990:8)

Naipaul eloquently describes the attachment that dispersed peoples of Indian origin have to a mythologized Indianness, especially made salient when the Indian nation-stare was formed. Faced with difference in their new herelands, their identity is marked as Indian, anchored to a newly formed nation-state of India. The community coalesces on the basis of this shared myth. Creating distinctions between the native popu-lation which may be of African or Asian (or what have you) descent, and the imperial/colonial elites which are European allowed for the invention of a not-black, and not-white racial category of "brown" Indian *race* in the imagination of those of Indian descent. To be Desi is to be "brown." Besides being a cultural category, Indianness becomes a racial designation. In the Asian Indian immigrant history in the US, too, Asian Indianness is defined by the community leaders to be distinct from whites (Europeans) and blacks (African Americans). The result is the invention of a new racial category of "brown" within the Indian cultural imagination.[3]

Against this backdrop of global dispersal wrought out of the vagaries of colonial history and circumstance, this study focuses particularly on the Indian dispersal into the U.S.. Indian immigration to the U.S. has been colored, even tainted, by U.S. immigration policy and policing. Indians in the U.S. have experienced, like their other Asian counterparts, racial discrimination and an ambivalence towards their presence in the U.S. Only since 1946 has citizenship been granted to those of Asiatic descent. There was much debate around whether those of Indian ancestry are of Caucasian descent due to their Aryan (Indo-Germanic) and therefore European background, and were therefore qualified to be U.S. citizens, since citizenship at that time in the early 1900's was awarded only to those of the Caucasian race. However, Aryans or not, it was argued that Indians are shades of brown—not pure white, not from the European continent, were again disqualified (Melendy, 1977; Hing, 1993). This obsession with racial definitions is based on the black and white racial binarism that is constructed to justify slavery. In the imagination of the Europeans, blacks were rationalized as inferior, simian-like and are therefore useable inhumanly as slave labor. The black-white binarism is, however, complicated with the shades of brown of other "races." Even within "black" complexions here in the United States, there are varieties of shades, complicating and subverting notions of "race," citizenship, and Americanness. Differences multiply. The worlds of "brown" and "yellow" especially from Asia decenter the superiority of whiteness, as well as dismantling the too easy binarisms of black (of African descent) and white (of European descent) in the U.S.

The "brown" "race" Indian is complicated by the notions of class elitism created by the immigration of highly qualified Indians into the U.S. between 1965 to 1975. In the first decades of independence, India saw an over-production of university graduates who were unwilling to relocate to rural or poorer centers to practice their medical, engineering, business, or other much needed professional skills and expertise. The newly formed Indian nation state was yet unable to absorb these graduates, coupled with the lag in adjustments to a post-colonial governmental system, and the lack of fit of their modern, industrial, and westernized skills with the demands and needs of the largely agricultural, rural India. This prompted many of these new educated elite to seek work elsewhere. The urban metropolises of the U.S. and U.K. being some of the prime choices for employment opportunities. This brain drain is a story shared by many of the newly formed nation states in Asia.

The late 1950's through the 1960's were very important years for U.S. immigration. Several developments in the U.S. provided powerful magnets opening up prospects to pull Asians, and specifically Indians into the country. The Cold War sponsored a hefty increase in research especially after the USSR's launching of Sputnik in 1957. Expenditure for research increased from $7 billion to $14 billion, allowing for the increase of scientists and engineers in the U.S. from 243,800 to 358,900. In 1965, government health payment programs—Medicare for the aged and disabled workers and Medicaid for low-income persons went into effect, opening new demands for medical personnel at every level. Since the U.S. was producing few physicians—only 7,000 in 1963, for example, the shortage of medical professionals created yawning vacancies in hospital staff. Physicians, nurses, technicians, and technologists were desperately needed. (Khandelwal, 1991:57–60).

This dire need for highly skilled professionals in the medical, scientific, and academic fields was taking place amidst the charged atmosphere of the Civil Rights' Movement, which sought to establish equal rights and freedoms for African Americans and consequently for other minority groups. The idealistic and ideological anti-racist shift was intertwined with the dire needs of a burgeoning super power for employable professionals and entrepreneurs, and the desperate need of an over-educated post-colonial foreign elite for employment. This co-dependency allowed Lyndon B. Johnson in 1965 to sign into law the Immigration Reform Act which removed the European bias in immigration laws. The doors of the U.S. opened, and a flood of Asian immigrants poured in. Many Indian immigrants also took advantage of the investor category, purchasing small motels, stores or food establishments in order to emigrate to the U.S. (Hing, 1990:102). Spouses and children rejoined their families already in the U.S. Thus, the profile of Indian immigration changed to not only include professionals, but also startlingly enterprising people. Whereas previously Indian immigrants were scattered and dispersed all over the U.S., the new wave concentrated in the major metropolitan centers where they could avail themselves of the employment opportunities in the sciences, engineering, medicine, business and acade-

mia. The 1965 immigration reform allowed for the creation of pronounced communities, especially in the urban metropolises of New York
City and its environs, Los Angeles and Northern California, Chicago,
and Houston, among others.

In contrast to the largely agricultural and blue-collar occupations of
the earlier wave of Indian immigrants in the West Coast in the early part
of the 20th century, the East Coast migration profile consisted of typically middle class, well educated, and professionally trained Indians.
Present NY tri-state Indians owe their visibility to the 1960 to 1970 immigrants who established a sense of community by forming organizations, producing performance events, circulation of ethnic newspapers,
and by lobbying for a distinct category of "Asian Indian" in the Census
Bureau.

In Khandelwal's research of New York Indians of the 1970's most
lived in Manhattan, and were university students, scientists, engineers or
doctors, members of the Indian government and diplomatic community,
Air India airlines' personnel, and the Indian delegation to the United Nations. Due to the small size of the Indian population, these groups inter-
mingled; their education, high social status, and shared Indianness being
primary features of cohesion. This cohesion was expressed in the organizing of artistic, secular, and religious events. Indian groups began
showing Hindi films at Columbia University. The first Indian newspaper
India Abroad was published and circulated in 1970. In 1976, the first Indian television program "Vision of Asia" started weekend transmission
on channel 47 in New York. Artists of classical music and dance were imported via the Indian Consulate in cooperation with student clubs and associations on university campuses. Also, a handful of artists and
academics of the Arts and Humanities migrated to the States and introduced Indian classical arts to non-Indian as well as Indian audiences
through classes and performances. In fact, many of the cultural activities
in the 1970's were animated by these student organizations.

Concurrent with the growing population of more elite Indians who
were made aware of their civil rights, was the organization of Pan-Indian
organizations. In 1967, The Association of Indians in America or the
AIA was founded by former students, now turned professionals. In 1977,
the AIA succeeded in lobbying with the U.S. Census Bureau to add a
new and distinct category of "Asian Indian" in the 1980 census, and to
designate it as a minority category. This category grows specifically out
of U.S. culture and history; it is "made in the U.S.A. [. . .] the shape of
which is determined by members of the host society and the new immi-

grants themselves" (Williams, 1988:9). Thus immigrants of Indian descent are transformed into Asian Indians in the U.S[4]. The term distinguishing them from "red Indian" or the Native American, and from the Caribbean of African descent, i.e., the West Indian. Currently, the Asian Indian designation is subsumed under the Asia Pacific Islander category, a political identity formation I discuss more fully in Chapter 3. In 1987, the AIA organized the first annual Deepavali festival at South Street Seaport, and began forming chapters throughout the United States. Its members continue to be drawn from the pool of professional, affluent, and highly educated Indian immigrants.

An extremely important part of 1965 Immigration reform was the family reunification program which allowed immigration based on relationship rather than occupation. Less skilled family members, or differently skilled family members came into the country, diversifying the profile of the Indian community. With the filling of the job market, and the severe cutting back of positions in the medical professionals open to immigrants due to the 1976 Health Professions Educational Assistance Act, many new immigrants could not find jobs in their professions. These immigrants then opened up small businesses primarily to cater to the food, clothing, and other service needs of the ever-increasing Indian population. To accommodate their families, many Manhattan residents moved to the less costly, and bigger apartments in Queens. Many small businesses were established in Jackson Heights, Flushing, and Elmhurst as the first Hindu temples, and Sikh gurduwaras were established. According to Khandelwal:

> By 1981, some 71 % of Indians arriving that year were sponsored relatives of resident aliens, 15% were sponsored relatives of Indian naturalized U.S. citizens, and only 13% immigrated under occupational preference categories. The professional predominance of the 1960's and early 1970's migration was now at an end. (1991:94)

An important result of this increase in family immigration was the formation of voluntary organizations based on linguistic, religious, and regional affiliations (Khandelwal, 1990), rather than based on a generic and secular Indianness. For example, The Cultural Association of Bengal, Inc. (founded in 1971), the Gujarati Samaj (f. 1973), and the Tamil Sangam (f. 1970) are some organizations based on linguistic/regional affiliations (Fisher, 1980:150-51). Concurrent with the completion of a Hindu temple Society of North America in Flushing in 1976, and the

Sikh *gurduwara* in Richmond Hill in 1972 was the formal inauguration
of the Hindu Temple Society of North America and the Sikh Cultural Society respectively (Khandelwal, 1993:69)

This was in studied contrast to the earlier 1960's immigration based
on profession, when pan-Indian organizations such as the AIA were organized despite regional, linguistic and religious differences. However,
membership in these new parochial organizations did not restrict participation or attendance in the pan-Indian events that were organized. The
immigrants' social life expanded to include both parochial and pan-Indian participation. The immigrants' Indianness included both the
parochial and pan-Indian assertions. To coordinate the celebrations of
major secular and nationalistic Indian holidays like Independence Day
(August 15), Republic Day (January 26), and Gandhi's Birthday (October 2), the Federation of Indian Associations (FIA) was formed in 1971.
It is the umbrella organization for the many parochial organizations in
the tri-state area (Fisher, 1980:187).

In 1987, the U.S. government declared an amnesty for illegal West
Coast farmworkers who wanted to apply for permanent and legal resi-
dency which again reconfigured the landscape of immigration. Clearly,
America was (is, and continues) browning, much to the dismay of the
Anglo/Arya-philic nativist. The Indian community was diversifying
rapidly, with many new immigrants opening up kiosks, driving cabs and
limousines, going into construction, managing restaurants, and performing. By 1990, there were 815,447 legal Asian Indian immigrants. According to recent 1995 statistics, there are 1.08 million Asian Indians. By
year 2000, Asian India immigrants may reach the 1.33 million mark!
This does not include undocumented aliens, Asian Indian foreign students, and semi-permanent business residents (Little India, 1998:39). In
1990, 35% of the legal immigrants of Indian descent lived in the Northeast Coast, of which 17.3% live in New York alone (Hing, 1990:103).
Asian Indians in the metropolitan areas of New York and New Jersey
boasts of being 1% and 1.6% of the total population, respectively. (Little
India, 1998:42) This high percentage of Asian Indian presence, makes
New York tri-state area one of the prime bastions for Indianness in the
United States.

The influx of "brown" and ethnically distinct Asian Indians has of
course created discontent amongst some other white immigrants. In
1987 many Indians were attacked by "dotbusters" in Jersey city, who
were able to recognize Asian Indians by the bindi or dot that some of
Hindu Indian women wear at the center of their foreheads. In the same

year an Asian Indian doctor, Navrose Mody, was beaten to death by a group of 11 white Hispanic youths in Hoboken, New Jersey. Mody's attackers got only a minimal five year sentence for assault. In 1988, worshippers leaving a mosque in Woodside, Queens were attacked by white Hispanics with baseball bats and iron rods. In 1989, the Indian business district on 74th Street, Jackson Heights, became the target of vocal opposition by the white residents of Irish, Italian, and Polish ethnicity of the area. They objected to garbage, clutter, parking and traffic congestion caused by the "bazaar-like" influx of Indians especially on the weekends. In late 1990, a rally was organized by the Jackson Heights Beautification Group to stop the increase of Indian businesses. In 1992, there was a petition to rename Jackson Heights "Little India." In fact, Mayor David Dinkins called Jackson Heights this name but protests were conducted on the basis that Jackson Heights was not only occupied by Indians.

Needless to say, Indian merchants and clients in Jackson Heights have frequently complained of incessant attacks and muggings (Khandelwal, 1991:1995). In 1992, the case of Dr. Kaushal Sharan who was beaten into a coma by a gang of youth in Jersey City finally went to trial as a civil rights crime through the persistent efforts of the civil rights organization Indian Youth Against Racism or YAR. Earlier Dr. Sharan's assailants were acquitted of all criminal charges in the state court. Again in 1994, Saleem Osman, a member of the Committee Against Anti-Asian Violence and coordinator of its Lease Driver's Coalition was dragged from his car by the hair and brutalized by plainclothes police officers who taunted him, "There's no black mayor any more...You better go back to your country!", while Osman was assisting another South Asian cab driver in an altercation with a passenger. (Tallapragada, 1994:31, 32, 34, 35).

The most recent hate crime has mobilized the NYC Desi community into a cohesive force. On September 20-1998, a 20 year-old Indo-Caribbean man, Rishi Maharaj, was beaten with baseball bats by three white men while hurling anti-Indian epithets at him in South Ozone Park, Queens. Peace vigils, rallies, and press conferences were conducted to protest the crime and advocate for a more stringent anti-hate crime law in NYC. Electronic mail, the South Asian ethnic press, and South Asian cable TV were saturated with discussions and calls to action to coalesce against the increase of hate crimes *as a Desi community*. The West Indian Indian Rishi Maharaj was adopted as a Desi by members of the South Asian community, blurring the differences and setting aside discriminations that abound between the Indo-Caribbean and South Asian communities. After all, Rishi Maharaj was attacked because he *looked Indian* in the eyes of his white attackers, even if he claims cultural citizenship to Caribbean culture rather than to South Asian, even if there is a simmering animosity between Indo-Caribbeans and other South Asians. The fight against racism necessitates a coalition. (Bahadur, 1998:20; Sengupta & Toy, 1998: NY Times Internet)

These are atavistic echoes of an earlier discrimination experienced in the West Coast by blue-collar Indian laborers. Only now, discrimination is hurled at any kind of Indian immigrant, whether they are doctors (Mody), activists (Osman), retail store owners (merchants of Jackson Heights), worshippers (Woodside mosque), ordinary citizens (Maharaj). More importantly, these racial hate crimes and incidents reveal that the Asian India community is inclusive of all South Asians in the diaspora. Non-South Asians can not discern one South Asian from another. We all *look* Desi to them or to use a more contentious phrase— "All Desis look Alike." As we recognize each other as Desi, we do have the capacity to discern the specifics of Desi particularities. These incidents reveal that Asian Indians thus share a history of discrimination with other South Asians, with others who are of South Asian descent, and non-white Americans, and must consider their belongingness to a community not only based on the relationship to the South Asian subcontinent, but a community which is part of U.S. American (racial) history.

The recognition of being part of a larger community was made palpable especially in the Rishi Maharaj case where organizations from the South Asian communities, Indo-Caribbean communities and Asian American communities have formed a coalition. These organizations are: The Asian American Legal Defense and Education Fund, Agenda 21, Asian Americans for Equality, Asian/Pacific Islander Coalition on HIV and AIDS, Associations for All Trinidadians and Tobagonians Inc., Catholic Charities, Committee Against Anti-Asian Violence, Cricket International, Federation of Indian Associations, Forum of Indian Leftists, KALI, New York Taxi Workers' Alliance, Queens Coalition Against Racism, Sakhi for South Asian Women, South Asian American Law Students Alliance, South Asian Lesbian and Gay Alliance, South Asian Women's Creative Collective, South Asian Youth Action, South Asian Youth Solidarity Summer, Worker's Awaaz, Youth Force–South Bronx Community Justice Center, Victim Services, and others.

THE ASIAN INDIAN PERFORMS INDIANNESS
IN NEW YORK CITY

The formation of organizations like the AIA, the FIA, the array of parochial associations, and student groups, and the participation of these immigrants in the activities of these organizations are a vital part of their socio-cultural life in the U.S. Involvement in these organizations facilitate a sense of being part of an Indian community. This dissertation focuses on these Pan-Indian expressions in Manhattan. Pan-Indian organizations like the AIA, and the FIA invariably organize their events in Manhattan. It is considered "the city" vis-a-vis Queens, New Jersey and Connecticut—the tri-state area. Manhattan is the public arena for the display of Indianness to both Indians and non-Indians. Queens, etc., is home, while Manhattan is the world, the outside. Queens and New Jersey are where one can *live* ethnically, while in Manhattan, one can *display* ethnicity with pride and pomp to an ethnically mixed audience. There are huge cultural events held in New Jersey but their audiences are primarily of Indian origin. Manhattan, too, has distinct areas of Asian Indian life such as "Indian" (Bangladeshi) restaurants on East 6th Street, and the variety of restaurants and Indian specialty stores from 23rd to 29th Street at Lexington Ave. which may be run by Pakistanis, Bangladeshis, Indo-Caribbeans or Indians. However, a majority of Indians live outside Manhattan, in Queens, Long Island, New Jersey. Moreover, Indianness becomes very present in Manhattan during the cultural performances I discuss in the forthcoming chapters.

A very important aspect of Indian immigrant life in New York city is the participation in behaviors that express, display and promote Indianness. This performance of Indianness has acquired a pronounced importance as the number of Indian immigrants have burgeoned. Besides having to make Indianness visible to non-South Asians, there is now an ample audience to participate in the production of these performances, to witness them, and finance them, too. Because the profile has diversified, and is continuously transforming due to the emerging second and third generation of "hyphenated" Americans, the gamut of cultural performances has also expanded. In her research on immigrant life and history on New York, Madhulika Khandelwal observes a dramatic increase in new Indian pop expressive culture. Both classical or marga and vernacular forms are participated in by NYC Asian Indians also (Khandelwal, 1991). This book specifies what these new popular expressive forms are. One woman declared to me, as we were dancing to a famous Hindi Film

song at one of the association parties that these activities were so important to her that:

> During the week, in those five days, I am just living [surviving], but in
> the weekends, I become alive in my community, in my association—I
> need my community, I need to attend a [an Indian] show, watch a [an In-
> dian] movie, or meet my [Indian] friends or else I die. (Interview: 1995)

Distinctively Indian leisure activities "becomes the right time and
space allocated for recovery and recuperation" from the joyless servitude
of work (Gilroy, 1993:36) in a world that is not Desi. Corporate life requires professional distance, cool demeanor and emotional sobriety. An
ethnic or cultural neutrality is required in dealing with fellow employees
or with one's superiors unless one is working for a Desi company. Frol-
icking with like-minded co-ethnic friends allows for relaxation and a
more casual stance for some. In a less melodramatic tone, a young NYU
student decided to participate in the South Asian organization on campus
because:

> I needed to learn more about my culture. In fact, since I became a
> member, my mother thinks I have become more Indian than she is! I
> have more Indian friends now, but this time, I chose friends who have
> the same interests as me, have the same crazy ideas that I have. [They
> are my friends] not just because they are the sons and daughters of my
> parents' friends—[yet] they are still Indian. (Conversation;1995)

These declarations stem from the dearth of Indianness in the work-
place:

> I do not hang out with anyone from work. It is so lonely there. I am so
> sick of these [white] people bragging about how they have this scarf
> from India, or how they can pronounce *mirchi masala* (chili spice) or
> how they love to meditate for hours to impress me about how much
> they like or know of India or whether I speak "Hindu." I need to be
> with people who can laugh at jokes in Hindi, who can sing Hindi film
> songs—just understand the meaning, and the humor, and the culture.
> (Conversation; 1996)

Another Indian American male confesses the erotic appeal of Indianness:

> You cannot imagine how exciting it is to walk into a party full of Desi
> women—with their brown complexion, dark eyes and black hair. And
> that they know the (Indian) music playing, and the same movies and
> food that I know. To think I only dated white girls when I was 18, 19,
> twenty years old. And could never imagine being with Indians even!
> But now (at 28) I feel I can be with my own, and still have romance,
> and so much fun!—it is such a thrill! (Conversation; 1997)

Much has been written by Saran, Helweg, and Khandelwal, on how
these voluntary organizations help in the identity formation and preservation of ethnicity. Research has been done on the performative behaviors of Asian Indian immigrants and I am indebted to the following
specific authors.

In her study of the Asian Indian voluntary associations that have
formed in the U.S., Maxine Fisher (1980) focuses her discussion on the
activities of the AIA, its history, and especially the political and bureaucratic processes involved in their petitioning for the addition of the
"Asian Indian" category in the U.S. Census. Her study illustrates the necessity of mastering the skills and savvy of dealing with bureaucracies in
national and urban politics. She also describes the ways in which Asian
Indians enjoy and participate in the parochial organizations that have
sprung parallel to the Pan-Indian AIA. However, neither Fisher's, nor
any of the other researches done by Saran (1985), or Helweg (1990), detail the contents or analyze the texts and structures of the performances
within these organizations. They spend much time describing the lifeways and strategies of adjustments of the immigrants especially from the
post-1960's who are successful, affluent, and educated.

Dance ethnologist Kiren Ghei's study (1988a, 1988b) on the reinterpretation of Hindi film dance sequences by Los Angeles Asian Indian
teenagers is groundbreaking. Until recently, much writing on the Hindi
Films is pejorative, lamenting over the crassness of the production values
and its formulaic approach catering to the degraded tastes of the masses;
Ghei's work, on the other hand, is concerned with how film dance is innovated, judged and reformulated for the stage using the resources of
theatrical films on video, folk aesthetics and individual intuition and talent. In her interviews with Los Angeles Asian Indian teenage choreogra-
phers and community dancers, she discusses how values of beauty,
grace, morality, ethnic pride, and community belongingness are enacted.
Dance transformations are labanotated.

My discussion of the dances and the performances are not of such a technical bent, but I am concerned with the themes of ethnic pride and community belongingness that are embodied in the dance, and in the other performance numbers that I have studied closely for this project. Much of Ghei's data is corroborated by the experiences of the performers I interviewed as well as by my own experience as a choreographer, director and producer in Manila, Philippines. I argue that transforming the film dance on video into live performance seems to be a humanizing intervention in a potentially homogenizing and aesthetically bankrupt mass mediated genre.

Contentious definitions of "authentic" Indianness are discussed forcefully in Annanya Bhattacharjee's (1992) analysis of how Roland Barthes' concept of the bourgeois habit of "ex-nomination" (1988) is practiced through the exclusionary policies of pan-Indian organizations like the AIA and the FIA. Class bias prompts members of these Pan-Indian organizations to disallow service oriented groups that deal with deviant, shameful, lower class concerns and issues to participate, be vocal or represent the ills and abuses afflicting the Asian Indian community in the U.S., NYC in particular. In her acerbic critique, Bhatacharjee lambasts these Pan-Indian organizations' denial of community ills and problems because they are perceived as marring the image of the Asian Indian community as a model minority.

My work directs attention toward how these organizations define what kind of Indianness is a proper and authentic representation. Further, I observe how those who are excluded assert their presence and visibility within the community, especially during these performative events. Consequently, in the forthcoming chapters, I begin my discussion by describing the manifestations of an official Indianness and then proceed to show how even in the same performance events, this kind of Indianness is being defiled, redefined, rebuffed by a more contemporary, hybrid Indianness.

My fieldwork indicates that there seems to be quite a number of productions that Indian immigrants participate in and witness. These events are rich and untapped sources of cultural information for further research. I have loosely categorized these performances[5] as aesthetic, cultural, religious, popular entertainments, and media performances, though these categories share elements that inevitably blur these distinctions.

Aesthetic performances include all productions that depict the classical arts of the South Asian subcontinent. These include song and dance recitals by professionals in and out of the United States, classical song and dance recitals by aspiring artists, traditional dramas staged by local South Asian troupes, or by troupes imported from the homelands, and other productions which depict what is considered as South Asia's older, traditional and purer art forms whether performed by Desis or non-Desis. These performances are produced and funded in part by arts councils or art organizations such as the World Music Institute, The Asia Society, and other governmental and endowment agencies. Audience's are expected to be cognizant of the forms' aesthetic framework in order to have a more refined enjoyment of the arts. And if not, efforts are made by the artists to annotate their performances with descriptions of the narratives, explanations of the syntax and semantics of the dance gestures or the music. These performances are based on the belief that these forms are untouched by westernization (Chatterjee, 1993), and that these forms require years of rigorous training from their practitioners. Important, too, is that these art forms are believed to be untainted by the vulgarity and loudness of popular art forms. Thus aesthetic performances depict a *class* art. Practitioners of aesthetic forms believe they are performing ART, uplifting the SPIRIT, and depicting what is true, good and beautifully DESI.

In this context, **cultural performances**, which I have discussed in the introductory chapter, are those productions which present Indian culture to both Indians and non-Indians primarily through the genres of the variety show, parades, and arts, crafts and food fairs. They are produced by Indian voluntary associations though they may be partially funded by arts councils and endowment foundations or they may be mounted by smaller community organizations. An array of Indian arts from classical, to folk to mass media traditions is presented. These productions mark national secular and religious holidays. The agenda of these cultural performances is to celebrate an occasion which is believed to be shared by all Indians such as Indian Independence Day, or the Deepavali Festival (festival of lights). The display is to underscore that we are Indians, that these are our songs, dances, food, crafts which the non-Indian can see and appreciate, occasions for Indians to reminisce, enjoy and be validated (Sollors, 1988). Indians participate in these productions to see themselves hyperbolized (Geertz, 1973). Reflexivity is the paramount intent of these performances rather than some intellectual delight derived from the purity of form that one ideally acquires from aesthetic performances.

If aesthetic performances depict Indian ART, and cultural performances depict Indian CULTURE, **religious performances** depict FAITH, particularly the Indian Hindu's faith[6]. The worship services in

the homes and the temples performed individually or in groups, the celebration of religious holidays, the devotional songs and dances performed
to mark the religious calendars, lectures/sermons/talks given by religious
leaders or luminaries are some examples of religious performances. For
example, *Navratri* [7]or Nine Nights festival of Goddess Durga and her sister Ambha are celebrated with an extravagant Garba—a round dance in
New Jersey during the Autumn months. A parade of the elephant-headed
God Ganesh during September occurs in the Flushing Hindu Temple.
Through these performances, the Indian immigrants express the religious aspect of their ethnicity.

Cultural performances and aesthetic performances emphasize the
secular aspects of Indian ethnicity even if they are steeped in religious
idiom and iconography. In the venues and genres of these non-religious
performances, songs, and dances, originally intended for religious efficacy are secularized. Hindu becomes Indian in aesthetic and cultural performances while in religious performances the Indian becomes Hindu.

Productions primarily intended for "escapist" fun and light enjoyment are **entertainments**. These include mega-productions that star popular Hindi film actors and actresses who perform songs and dances from
their films on stage. Songs and dances performed in parties, receptions,
and weddings fall under this category. Beauty pageants for Miss India-
U.S. A, Miss New York (California, Florida, etc.), Miss Diwali, Mother-
Daughter pageant, variety programs for New Year or Valentine functions,
talent contests like *Naya Andaaz* in New Jersey are also entertainments.
In these productions as in the variety programs of the cultural performances, may include songs and dances from Hindi films, and from the
folk and classical traditions.

Another emerging and powerful kind of performance I designate as
activist performances in which issues of sexual, race, class identity, and
bi-culturalism are the central themes exploited through the genres of poetry, spoken word, dance, and performance art. The annual showcases of
the South Asian Women's Creative Collective, South Asian Youth Action, Inc., and the Diasporadics—festival of activist arts and performance
are some examples of activist performances. They are mounted in hip alternative performance spaces in Manhattan.

Thus far, I have mentioned only live performances but **media performances** have the most far-reaching influence on the Indian immigrant
community here (Pfleiderer & Lutger, 1985) as well as for communities
globally. The song and dance sequences that pervade Hindi films have
determined the choreographies and aesthetics of live cultural and reli-

gious performances. U.S. Indian television broadcast shows excerpts from Hindi film song and dance sequences, talented amateur performers, coverages of performance events such as parades, celebrations, festivals, TV serials of Hindu epics, dramas, talk shows, advertisements, news, etc. produced both in India and locally. Included with these media performances are the songs, news and talk shows aired on the radio. Hundreds of Indian film on video tapes, and audio cassettes are available in shops and are distributed worldwide. Indians in different diasporic sites can experience the pleasures of similar musics, films, and dances, thus having much to share, and talk about—creating a community that is transnational. Media performances are experienced in the privacy of the Indian immigrant's home. These media performances feed back into the live public performances. Public shows are covered on TV, thus being doubly represented.

To limit the scope of this discussion on Indianness in New York City, I focus on the rich field of cultural performances in Manhattan, i.e., the productions in which Indian immigrants publicly announce, show and play with and enjoy "Indianness," where they can do their Desi thing. Examining the parades, the festivals, the variety programs, and the fairs that celebrate Indian ethnicity forms the bulk of this book.

The Asian Indian community is growing. Today there are many subcommunities divided by class, profession, regional and religious, and language differences. Opposing the centrifugal force of these divisions is the desire to come together, "to be Indian," as fellow Desis. The pushing and pulling, the vernacular and the official, the Pan-Indianness and the parochiality, the authentic Indianness versus the hybridizing identity find expression in these performance events. A fine example of what I am talking about is the subject of the next chapter, the colorful and expansive Deepavali Festival at the South Street Seaport.

NOTES

[1] I have appropriated Peter Van der Veer's term in *Nation & Migration*, 1995. The term 'hereland' suggests the sojourn in a place for now, having come from another place, and maybe even actually leaving it, or believing that one can, may or should leave it, in the future.

[2] I am aware that Hinduism is only one of the religions practiced amongst Indians in the diaspora. From my observations, I gleaned that Hindu iconography, idioms and practices are some of the hegemonic ethnic markers of Indianness.

[3] From my many conversations with members of the Indian community here, there is always an emphasis on being considered neither like a *white* European American nor a *black* African-American. Also there is a repudiation for being considered Latino or even 'oriental' such as East Asian or Southeast Asian. Indians here consider themselves as better aesthetically as well as socioculturally than Latinos or African Americans, and not as '"cultureless" or colorless as Americans of European descent. Those of Indian descent are therefore "brown".

[4] In the United Kingdom, immigrants of South Asian descent are described officially as "Asian", and as "Pakis" from Pakistani in somewhat derogatory terms. In this study, I refer to Indians in Britain, or British of South Asian descent as British Asians.

[5] I have limited the definition of performance to include only staged, purposive theatric events. Much performance happens during parties, informal gatherings, temple worships, weddings, and such that I have not even begun to discuss. My understanding of Desiness, has, nevertheless, been influenced by my presence and participation in these events.

[6] My observations were restricted to Hindu religious performances. However, much singing occurs in the Sikh temple, and in Islamic Sufi worship.

[7] Navratri can also be celebrated as a cultural performance or popular entertainment especially its "disco" version or if Hindi film stars are the guest performers for the occasion.

CHAPTER 3

Currying the Big Apple
Creating an Authentic
Pan-Indian Ethnic Aesthetic[1]

A cab driver in Philadelphia . . . induced me to
talk about what I do. After mentioning that I
currently study displaced people, especially
East Indians in the Caribbean, he perceptively
responded that the proverbial American melting
pot had been spiced by a bit of curry itself! . . .
Like curry, a spice consisting of many other
ingredients combined to form a distinctive taste
when mixed into other things, South Asians of
various backgrounds contribute a certain flavor
to the palate of the host society. (Korom,
1995:3)

. . .

I was overwhelmed by the number and variety of Indian faces. South Street Seaport looked very different from the last time I saw it in '85. Only India could have had this many Indians. Ah yes, and during the *Kasaysayan ng Lahi* (The Beginning of the [Pilipino] Race) parade in Manila to inaugurate the famed Folk Arts Theater, too. In that parade, there was a huge float depicting the early Hindu and Arab traders who came to the Philippine Islands much before the Spaniards did. For it, I danced a Gujurati *Dandya Raas* (stick dance) with my other girlfriends. But that was in 1977. Now in 1989, in New York City, I was intimidated. But nonetheless eager to see the dances, scream in delight at the fireworks, say hi to familiar faces—would I be able to recognize anyone in this mob?!! Oh, and to eat samozas, chaat, chicken tikka, and paan— yummy! It struck me that I really did not know that many people in New York. I had just arrived two months before, but everyone seemed like a person who would possibly recognize me, or my parents, or my friends—everyone looked almost familiar, sort of, kind of looked like me, someone I was just about to recognize someone I could be friends with in the future, maybe met at the Diwali party a week ago, maybe, just maybe. . .

53

. . .

As I was printing out a draft of this chapter at the NYU Academic Computer Facility, the young Sikh man who was assisting me asked why Deepavali was named such. He knew it to be Diwali, with the root of "Diwa" meaning "lamp" in Punjabi. I concurred with him since we Sindhis also used the term 'diwali'. In fact Sindhis call this day using the vernacular 'dyari', too. Overhearing our banter, a young man who was printing out his film script, enlightened us by saying that 'Deepavali' was the South Indian term, the *original* term that was taken over by the North. He half-mockingly said that at least they (the South Street Seaport festival organizers) had kept the original name. He was from Andhra Pradesh he claimed. He corrected our pronunciation of the term. After I pressed on, he continued to tell me that he did celebrate Deepavali/Diwali by going to the South Street Seaport since he couldn't be with his family in India. He really couldn't remember what Deepavali was for, but he definitely said in the South of India, it had nothing to do with Rama or Lakshmi.

. . .

In this chapter I discuss how an official pan-Indian aesthetic is asserted in the performance event of the Deepavali festival at the South Street Seaport at the southern tip of Manhattan. Though the festival is primarily a Hindu one, it is used to represent an image of the whole Indian subcontinent in the U.S.A., religious and regional diversity notwithstanding. This cultural production ostensibly portrays a secular Indianness, not only problematizing the Hindu base of the festival, but also inventing a new kind of Indianness in the diaspora. Moreover, the festival has expanded in the past nine years to include entertainments that cater not only to a multiethnic gamut of Indian immigrants, but also to a variety of immigrants of different socio-economic strata, and second generation Indian-Americans and other South Asians. The festival also caters to a non-Indian population who may not even be aware of any Indian holiday or of any Indian presence. These factors complicate the notions of an authentic Indianness, i.e., what kind of Indianness is to be performed amid this public sphere of diversity. The choice is influenced by communitarian politics as well as the minority status of the Indian in the U.S. The story of the invention of this type of Indianness parallels the patterns of immigration that have occurred since 1980.

Deepavali, or its contracted form Diwali, is part of a complex of

Hindu autumnal festivals celebrated annually in the Indian subcontinent as well as by Hindu Indians in the diaspora, around the months of October/November. The origin of the festival has many versions. How, when, where and why Diwali is celebrated is largely dependent on regional, caste, familial and community affiliations. The types of celebrations fall along the continuum of home worship services, to grand formal balls, to temple celebrations, to community programs, to dinner parties, to open-air spectacles. The origin of the festival has many versions but the most popular one traces it to those events in the *Ramayana*, the great North Indian Hindu epic, wherein Lord Rama is crowned King of Ayodhya after his 14 year exile in the forest, after he vanquished the demon-king Ravana of Lanka. It is believed that people illuminated their houses and streets with earthen oil lamps to welcome the Lord home. Thus the Sanskrit term *Deepavali* means *Deepa*—light, *vali*—string, or a string of lights.

Deepavali celebrated in the months of October-November using the lunar calendar also marks the New Year. Lakshmi, the goddess of wealth is worshipped to usher in a more prosperous year. Especially in the business communities like those of the Gujuratis, Sindhis and Marwaris, new books of accounts are opened on this day, and at night along with illuminations, firecrackers are lit, sweets and gifts are distributed, new clothes are worn and games of chance are played. Deepavali is one of the brightest and noisiest festivals in India. (Saxena, 1990:19)

DEEPAVALI IN NEW YORK INDIA

Since Indian immigrants in New York may celebrate Deepavali in the privacy of their homes, in the basement of their buildings, in small community centers, in Hindu temples, in the suburbs, or in the boroughs, why is it that for the past ten years the New York chapter of the pan-Indian Association of Indians in America or the AIA has been prompted to organize a spectacular Deepavali Festival at the South Street Seaport in Manhattan? Arun Aguiar,[2] who used to be an active member of the executive staff and spokesman of the AIA, felt that:

> If we pooled our efforts, we would be able to produce a festival that would be more varied, rich, exciting . . . *if we came out from the dark into the open in an arena like the South Street Seaport*, we would attract a lot of attention . . . promote an appreciation of Indian culture in our new homeland and would get a large non-Indian audience for the festival. [italics mine]

The AIA wanted the festival to be open to the non-Indian public, to be out of the closet if you will, in order for them to appreciate and understand "Indian culture." In the words of Arun Aguiar "we make it clear to the visitor right from the beginning that he is encouraged to take part in what is going on. That it is not a private party or private festival to which he is not welcome." Under the aegis of the thirty year-old New York chapter of the AIA and their sponsors, South Street Seaport was transformed into a space wherein on the occasion of Deepavali, (which is in India, and among Hindu Indians, primarily religious festival), becomes a public celebration of Indian ethnicity to be witnessed by a non-Indian audience also.

The Seaport festival runs the gamut of folkloric expressive genres such as folk and classical performances on various stages, arts and crafts demonstrations, merchant stalls, a food fair, elephant and fair rides, booths for voluntary associations, a fireworks display, and in the past four years, performance genres of pop culture such as disco dancing, Hindi film song-and-dance reinterpretations, rock and roll items, and dances from other Asian and Caribbean countries. There is ample room for these various events to take place, as large groups of people leisurely meander from one entertainment spot to another.

The Seaport area is reorganized to accommodate the needs of the festival. In summary, on the main performance space—the Ambrose Stage which faces FDR highway and fronts the main shopping and restaurant area of Pier 17 on the East River side, are where the classical and folk dance numbers are performed, as well as where dignitaries give their speeches. The dances begin at about 11:30 A.M. At around 5 P.M., portions of the Ramayana are re-enacted on this stage, after which both AIA officers and sponsors, as well as city and state officials and leaders give their addresses. Around the Ambrose stage, while the performances are going on, other activities take place such as the children's fair, puppet shows, traditional arts and crafts demonstrations, *henna*, face and *rangoli* painting. A fireworks display is set off at around 7 P.M. from the East River.

Crossing over FDR, away from the East River, is the Burling Slip area. Here there are secondary stages where contemporary numbers, and performances from other cultures take place. Elephant rides, booths for corporate and voluntary associations and other Indian merchandize for sale are set up here. As you go further away from the East River, further away from wide open spaces, and into the side streets such as John, Front and Water Streets, food stalls, DJ disco/*Bhangra* dancing, and carnival

Figure 3.1. A bedecked but bewildered crasftswoman from India selling her wares.

rides are set up. It is impossible to see what is going in these areas if you are near Pier 17 or even the Burling Slip area, and vice versa. The fireworks display can only be heard from here, or seen from the reflection it makes on the glass facade of buildings, that is if you are not too busy dancing or eating or riding the Ferris wheel. All in all the Seaport becomes a sensual riot—a true festival which cannot be fully absorbed in one or two visits. I have attended ten Seaport festivals from 1989 to the present. The bulk of the forthcoming discussion is substantiated by specifics of the 1990, 1993, and 1994 festivals, but makes references to other years, too. Because it expands every year, and since I have only one body, I have yet to see and participate in all the attractions that are mainstays and partake in the new ones that are introduced every year.

A big plus of having this festival at the Seaport is that the public is made aware of and can enjoy and even patronize the already established shops and restaurants at the Seaport. Not everyone is happy about the event. According to Aguiar, the South Street Seaport Merchant's

Association feels that the festival hurts their business since food from outside the Seaport is sold in the festival. However, Aguiar feels that Deepavali is one of, if not, the most successful events on the South Street Seaport calendar. Anyway, Asian Indians come back to the Seaport on ordinary days to shop, stroll, eat. Indeed, visitors from India are brought to the Seaport as part of their tourist itinerary and are told that this space belongs to Indians during the Deepavali festival. From my observations, the seaport restaurants are filled mostly with non-Indian clientele during the festival. In the Pier 17 mall's relatively cheaper fast-food area, there were ample numbers of young Indians eating burgers, pizzas and such like. But it is true, most Indians do not shop at the mall during the festival, justifying the disgruntled remarks of the South Street Seaport Merchants' Association. Indians as well as non-Indians spend their money on Indian food at the stalls, on the elephant and fair rides for their children, on the Indian crafts, greeting cards, audio-cassettes, and Hindu religious artifacts that are on sale at the Burling Slip area. Because there is no admission charge and the stage shows are free, money is made primarily from food and the artifacts sold by the stall owners.[3] Perhaps the South Street Seaport merchants will catch on and offer more Indian products for sale. This would certainly attract Indian clientele not only during Deepavali, but during the rest of the year as well. The boundaries between the ordinary, albeit consumerist and touristic Seaport and the extraordinary colorful, and populous festival are not rigid, facilitating the travel between the re-invented India and New York City and at times blurring these barriers and creating a New York India. During the Deepavali festival, South Street Seaport becomes dynamic, vibrant—a total entertainment environment of Pan-Indian cultural ambassadorship, to be consumed by both the Indian and non-Indian public. The facility is safe, nicely located, conducive to strollers, passers-by and can accommodate at least 75,000 people. According to Nalini Shah, AIA chairperson for the 1995 Deepavali festival in an interview broadcast on Indian cable TV, over 100,000 people attended the Deepavali festival in 1994, 40% of which was attended by non-Indians.

REPRESENTING AUTHENTIC INDIANNESS THROUGH DANCE

Since the AIA, according to Arun Aguiar intends to bring Indianness "out of the darkness" of parochiality, and is motivated to show a "rich and varied" Indian culture to a non-Indian populace, members of the

AIA are constantly on the look-out for community folk and classical dance groups "which depict authentic and refined aspects of Indian culture." Indeed groups can come forward and apply to participate upon the approval of the program committee. I will begin my discussion by remarking on the dances portrayed on the Ambrose stage located in the pier—the most prominent and overt space at the Seaport, the frontispiece, if you will of the festival. I consider this stage as the site upon which an official authentic Indianness is fastidiously presented.

One of the prime features of the festival is the vivid array of Indian dances performed by amateur and professional groups located in the New York Tri-State area. The program lasted from noon to seven in the evening. Some of the dances were robust, communal and rural like the folk dances depicting fisherfolk of Maharashtra in West India, the farmers of Punjab in the North Of India (Bhangra), and the stick and round dances from the Western state of Gujarat (*Garba/Dandya Raas*). Some dances interpret episodes from the Ramayana, and other devotional/spiritual themes. Other dances were graceful and virtuosic renditions requiring years of arduous classical training like those of *Kathak, Bharat Natyam,* and *Odissi*. These types of classical dances have specific and varied choreographies, postures and gestures, texts, music and histories.[4] Classical and folk forms of dance were conflated into one big reified category of "Indian dance." In the elitist criteria of the AIA, folk and classical dances are considered refined, exalted and authentic forms of Indian culture. This criteria is a residue of the anti-colonialist nationalistic historiography practiced in India. In this type of historiography, the origin of the modern Indian nation and all its exalted components such as spirituality, politics and art was from "the long and unchanging existence of Sanskritic Indic civilization." (Prakash, 1992:358–359) not from foreign sources, either from Europe nor from Islamic Asia. The origins of authentic Indianness is Hindu.

Indeed part of the nationalistic project was to recuperate the 'authentic' arts and crafts of India. Indian classical dance as we know it today is a product of that project. Richard Schechner (1985:68–69), among others, summarizes the recuperation of Indian dance by the nationalist reformers in the early part of this century from its perceived degenerate form as practiced by the devdasi or temple dancers in Madras (and other temple dancers in other parts of India like Orissa, Andhra Pradesh, etc.). The temple dancers were labeled as prostitutes by these reformers, but their dance, the *sadir nac* was believed to be a debased remnant of an ancient form. E. Krishna Iyer, who led the movement to preserve the dance, presented the devdasi dance at the 1933 Conference of the Music Academy of Madras. The dance was rechristened *Bharatanatyam*, to erase its tawdry association with prostitution and to inaugurate it as a dance (natya) of India (Bharat). The secularized dance was rescued from its perceived corrupt influences especially by high placed members of the Brahmin caste, and by respectable daughters of middle class families who danced as well as helped codify the dance. But necessary to the preservation and rescuing of the dance was to narrate its origin as if it continuously evolved from ancient, sacred, pure sources:

> They [Rukmini Devi, and other dance scholars, & masters] cleaned up the devdasi dance, brought in gestures based on the *Natyasastra* [dramaturgical treatise attributed to Bharata Muni, 2nd C, BCE), and temple art, developed standard teaching methods. They claimed that Bharatanatyam was very old. And of course, a conformity to ancient texts and art could be demonstrated: every move in Bharatanatyam was measured against the sources it presumed to be a living vestige of...The new dance now legitimized by its heritage, not only absorbed *sadir nac* but attracted daughters of the most respectable families to practice it. Today many study Bharatanatyam as a kind of finishing school. It is danced all over India by both amateurs and professionals. It is a major export item. (Schechner, 1985: 69).

Not only is Bharatanatyam danced all over India, here in the U.S.A., Bharatanatyam and the other classical dance forms are learned and performed by Indians in American as a way of learning and participating in Indian culture and aesthetics. Here on the South Street Seaport stage, it is considered an authentic Indian art form by the AIA, as well as by Indians in the US. In the South Street Seaport' Ambrose Stage, the dances performed by the best students of local dance schools were presented towards the final half of the presentation. At around 3 or 4 in the afternoon, the largest crowds assemble. Items presented during this "prime time" are both more professional, and/or more classical. Items in the beginning of the show are more "folk arts," performed by younger Indians and newer, less professional groups. The theoretical justification that informs this arrangement is based on the AIA's adoption of the Indian aesthetic hierarchies. In this hierarchy folk dances are the more primitive versions, the beginnings of classical dance. As folk dances are codified they become classical. They are mastered and taught in royal courts, temples, academies, to members of elites, royalty and the upper classes. Folk dances are the "unselfconscious, spontaneous, natural" expressions of rural folk, while the classical dances require rigorous training, and self-conscious effort (Amin-Patel, 1995). Folk dances are the infantile, rudimentary, originary of classical dances. If folk dances are "natural", "innocent," "of the soil"—classical dances are "cultural," aesthetic," "of the soul." Soil and Soul, earth and metaphysics are the twin siblings of an "authentic Indianness". It is believed that as society evolved from an agricultural to a more urbane civilization, folk dances evolve into its apotheosis of classical dance (according to orthodox Indian scholarship). The classical forms are taught in royal courts, temples, and academies to royalty and upper classes and castes, and, more recently, to middle-class people as well who are willing to pay homage and money to the guru.

Arranging these dances in this fashion, and presenting them as part of the same program, is contentious and problematic in that it robs both folk dance and classical dance of the validity of their ethno-evaluations, ethno-choreographies and history. The romanticism attached to folk and classical dance as being pure, and unsullied by foreign, corrupt interventions, valorize these dance forms as authentic expressions of Indianness.

In his astute discussion of the folk and tribal dances presented at the Republic Day parade in India, Wayne Ashley observes that the elite critics, and producers of the parade in their attitude towards folk forms:

> [Imagine] that villages were not affected by British rule and the rural
> folk are repositories of an essential Indianness capable of liberating
> urban elites from the effects of colonialism, [and thus their dances, arts
> and crafts] can restore a sense of loss by being consumed, displayed,
> and interacted with (1993:276).

Moreover, in current times, these folk dances are believed to be untainted by the vandalisms of modernity, urban pop culture and Western influences. Consequently, in the South Street Seaport Deepavali festival, in much the same way that classical dance is restored "[healed] into its presumptive past and its present cultural context like well-grafted skin" (Schechner, 1985: 65), folk dances, too are reified into the category of *Indian dance*. Thus this new, modern category of Indian dance which does not differentiate between folk and classical becomes the showpiece of authentic Indian culture here in the U.S.

The program notes indicated the names of the groups, the dance's geographic origins, choreographer's name and the length of time each dance would take. This last characteristic seemed like a considerate gesture allowing for the audience to decide and approximate when they would like to see what since there are a multitude of activities to attend to and witness at the Seaport festival. There are 20 to 30 items in this smorgasbord of movement and costume.

The choreographer is the re-inventor or re-creator of the dance—an indication that the dance is not handed down from one generation to the next and that the dancers are not necessarily 'native' to the form: They have not been born to it. As dances are learned in India, the performers have had to learn the dance, under the authoritative guidance of the specialist. For example, in the 1994 show the Kala Kendra dance school run by Anuradha Khanna presented a Deepavali pooja (worship) dance as well as a Rajasthani folk dance. Bharatanatyam was presented by the Padmalaya dance school run by Raja Rajeshwari, while Kathak performances were presented by the East-West School run by Satyanarayan Chakra. All these schools are based in New York tri-state area. All these teachers were trained in India, and are residing in the United States permanently. The participants all reside in the NY tri-state area.

The diversity in regions and genres represented in this variety show underscores the existence of sub-cultures under the canopy of what is considered Indian. The spectator gets the impression that all this diversity is present in the Indian subcontinent as well as in this part of overseas India. Yet paradoxically, despite the diversity, all these are generically Indian. True, India is divided by linguistic, racial, and religious lines, and here, too, there is a diversity of Indians, but the Seaport program seems to suggest that what binds these disparate identities is the concept of "Indianness," implying a unified cultural citizenship. Indian consciousness is made poignant because of the fact that these immigrants are in a new land, engulfed within a different and dominant culture. The South Street Seaport Deepavali organizers seem to be echoing this phenomenon of cultural reflexivity that occurred when British India sought independence from the empire.

Let me pause here to briefly explain how Indian nationalists in India configured the independence project. It was more pragmatic to cohere as a nation of Indians than to rebel against the British by regions or by religious affiliation. Whereas the British sought to exploit the linguistic and religious divisiveness within the Indian subcontinent through their policy of "divide and rule," Indian nationalists gained momentum through their "unity in diversity" program. Thus, a new, pan-Indian identity was touted for the emergent nation-state being imagined and fought for from the middle of the 19th century. The nationalists and the Indian revolutionaries needed to convince themselves and their imperial rulers, that the intra-ethnic differences were overcome, (or at least needed to be overcome, or to present themselves as having overcome differences) so that "India" could be united under a cohesive and independent self-rule.

Indian nationalists during the independence struggle saw themselves as united in their being different from the British, and by extension from the West. Here are Gyan Prakash's remarks on the most salient characteristics of Indian nationalist historiography that reiterate the official rhetoric of the anti-colonialist configuration of India as a unified nation-state:

> [Nationalist historiography was committed to the idea] of India as an undivided subject, [possessing] a unitary self and a singular will that arose form its essence and was capable of autonomy and sovereignty . . . So when politicians spoke of a nation in the making, they were referring to the task of making the masses conscious of a nation already in existence as an objective reality. (1992: 360)

To Indian nationalists, the gloriousness of Indian culture had "variety" as one of its prime appeals—primarily appealing to the westerners' lust for difference, for categorizing, for separating. There is an inherent contradiction in the impulse to show difference and unity simultaneously. Indeed, this contradiction is the result of the nationalists' framing their concept of nationhood and politics on a Western model. The urban university system, as well as being educated in British schools allowed for these leaders and reformers to emulate ideas of the modern state, i.e., democracy, industrial, scientific and positivistic progress, and a centralized government. Though culturally, these nationalists' needed to present an exalted Indianness as gloriously different from the west, politically they were Western.

Here and now, as Indians living in America, this colorful nationalist cultural identity is recuperated and proclaimed for ethnic distinctiveness and visibility in a predominantly white Euro-American society via the South Street Seaport Deepavali Festival. To the non-Indian gaze, the colors of the folk and classical dances are distinctively *Indian* colors. Bright, vivid hues of burgundies, saffrons, magentas, chartreuses, and turquoises. More importantly, there is a need to show that we can transcend our intra-ethnic differences and cohere as a united Indian front against your dominance, and why not enjoy the richness of our varied

Indian colors, in the meantime? The non-Indian need not know about the communal, class, and caste conflicts that abound, and that are at this point splitting the India and the South Asian subcontinent apart, as well as dividing the South Asian community here. The aesthetic display assuages "the potential fissiparousness of all ideas of difference" (Appadurai, 1990:16) for the non-Indian, and also for the Indian in New York city. As Kirshenblatt-Gimblett observes:

> Polyglot programs, besides offering variety, generally represent an imagined community in which diversity is harmoniously integrated, where difference is reduced to style and decoration, to spice of life. Cultural difference is then praised for the variety and color it adds to an otherwise bland and dull scene. (1991: 421)

This colorfulness underscores, nevertheless, that the Indian is different from the non-Indian. The colorfulness of Indianness that is being presented seems to suggest to the audience both Indian and non-Indian that their life as they are living it now is "constrained, lacking in vitality, misdirected, boring, and trapped in the present" (Kirshenblatt-Gimblett, 1988:65). It is a present that is bland, flaccid, prosaic compared to the exoticism of Indianness in the homeland, and the Indianness that is being reproduced in the South Street Seaport Deepavali festival for both the non-Indian and the Indian outside India.

The over-mechanized, and task-oriented present thus, opens up the wound of nostalgia. Nostalgia for a pre-industrial homeland is aroused by the performance and participation in these folk and classical dances. These dances seem to be minimally influenced by Euro-American Western industrial culture, and, in fact depict a pastoral, or at least non-urban lifestyle. These immigrants and their children who perform, and learn these dances here in a large metropolis may never even have performed or even seen these dances in India. Ironically, Indian Americans may have seen these dances first on the U.S. stage here at the Seaport festival even, on Indian cable TV in their New York homes, or through a video cassette borrowed from a shop in Queens. As a way of retaining ties with the homeland, rediscovering roots to Indian culture, socializing with other Indians, these immigrants learn, and perform these dances in public. Of course, like in the parades and performances in India, the dances are performed in the context of a Euro-American proscenium-style stage, and not in the farm, on a river bank, town square or temple. They are always and already inauthentic in this respect, removed from their everyday, workaday, "natural," functional, local setting. These dances are placed on exhibit up on stage for a specular, aesthetic display, for an ethnically mixed Indian, as well as a non-Indian audience. Adjustments have had to be made to effectively display these dances such as facing the audience instead of each other; annotations are given by an emcee before the dance is performed to explain what the dance is depicting, or are included in the brochure; people of other ethnicities, who live in the U.S. perform the dance—learning it from an expert, who was trained in a school of performing arts in one of the urban centers of India, New Jersey, or upstate New York. Improvisation, an essential feature of most folk dances, and even of Indian classical dance is eliminated because of time constraints. The music is reproduced on audio-cassette rather than with live instrumentation. Microphones, lights, and other modern equipment are used to enhance the performance of this "authentic" culture. Thus Kirshenblatt-Gimblett describes these performances that have to adapt to European or Western production values, and be set off from the flow of life of their indigenous settings to hold the interest and capture the gaze of new audiences as becoming "mute folkloric artifacts," rather than active performative processes:

> [Folkloric performances] freeze. They become canonical. They take forms that are alien, if not antithetical, to how they are produced and experienced in their local settings, for with repeated exposure, cultural performances are routinized and trivialized. The result is events that have no clear analogue within the community from which they purportedly derive and that come to resemble one another than that which they are intended to re-present. (1991:420)

Indeed, these dances do become mute artifacts if their reference point is the subcontinental regional community they are purportedly from. But if these dances are taken as transformations of these Indian dances using the styles of particular regions, they begin to narrate a different story of adaptation to cultural change. In these dances, Indian ethnic identity is marked by how distinctly non-Euro-American/non-Western these performances look in content and form, though their context Westernizes them. These dances are reconstructed, choreographed and profoundly modernized. They *signify* a bucolic India. This signification is the reason that folk and classical dances can be placed in the same category of "authentic" Indian dance despite their disparate aesthetic philosophies, histories, and choreographies. They are distinctly

non-Western dance forms, and thus become essentialized, and homogenized as Indian dance forms. The region or community from which the
dance seems to derive its form becomes secondary, merely a stylistic
variation. What is emphasized is the fact that these dances come from the
nation-state of India. This essentialization and homogenization ignores
the rural/urban divide, the class biases imbedded in the practice of the
dances, and the aesthetic merits of the dances. The non-Westerness becomes the dances' most salient and important feature. These dances become markers of culture rather than manifestations of creativity in their
own right, or depictions of the lifeways of these particular folk. In the
contest between culture and art, these dances become ethnographic artifacts rather than vibrant aesthetic pieces[5].

However, I do not see these dances as "mute artifacts." The choice of
what kinds of dances are to be performed, the criteria for what is authentic, and the privilege given to more well-known and professional groups
speak volumes of the new pan-Indian ethnic aesthetic that has emerged
as a result of representing Indianness in the U.S.A. A new type of Indian
dance emerges as a result of the diaspora. These dances, be they classical
or folk, are distinctively non-Western, depicting a varied, spicy, and colorful traditional Indianness.

At least until 1993, the Seaport show's organizers emphatically stip-
ulate that Hindi film songs and dances are strictly prohibited in the program of the Ambrose stage, (in consequent years, other venues were
created for this in the seaport festival) even though Indian immigrants,
Indian Americans and other South Asians are avid in their affections for
this form of expression. As is discussed in Chapter 4 of this book, Hindi
film song and dance genres are considered by the intellectual elites as
corrupted by Western popular culture, as well as being a corrupt popular
form for the uneducated masses to begin with. Though the Indianness expressed through the popular medium of the Hindi film dance is a Pan-Indian identity, it is looked at with disdain by the organizers of the Seaport
festival.

Let me illustrate this disdain with an anecdote. In 1991, I had joined
as chorus for the Epic Theater Company's[6] rendition of folk songs from
India for this festival. Though I cannot sing for the life of me, my good
friend and community artist/director Sudipto Chatterjee[7] "needed bodies
to fill the stage." (One other criterion for the Ambrose stage performances was that they should not be solo pieces since folk performances
are primarily group performances. Also, the organizers do not want to
encourage performances for self-aggrandizing purposes. There are other

venues for solo performances at the Seaport festival, to be discussed later). One of the songs we sang was taken from a Hindi film popularized by the star of the 1980's of supernova proportions Amitabh Bachchan[8] entitled "Rung Barse Bhige Chunarwali" from the film *Silsila* (1981/Yash Chopra). The song is rhythmic, lively, and ribald. Needless to say, the audience was most pleased by this choice. They sang along and danced with much enthusiasm, encouraging us to perform with even more gusto. Despite the rousing applause from the audience, Chatterjee was reprimanded by the program chair Divya Shah later on for including the song. Chatterjee argued that the song is originally a folk song which was appropriated in the film. Shah rebutted by saying that the audience was responding to its popularity as a film song and not as a folk song. As far as Chatterjee was concerned, he and his group had fulfilled the criteria. Chatterjee has not performed again for the AIA.

A class bias is at the root of this disdain for the Hindi film song/dance form, especially if we take into consideration that the organizers/progenitors of the AIA are highly educated, affluent members of the community who are in close contact with white American culture. When these progenitors of the AIA came to the U.S. in the mid-sixties and seventies, they were few in number, and were of mixed regional affiliations. What brought them together was their Indianness, socio-economic status and regional diversity, notwithstanding. Importantly, they were heavily influenced by the official nationalistic rhetoric, many having been educated in the universities of post-colonial India, came here to pursue further studies in the Western institutions of the U.S. Thus, these progenitors' impulse to present an identity that is distinct and that portrays a refined picture of Indian culture was a way of resisting erasure from the dominant culture in the early years of their sojourn in New York. As Madhulika Khandelwal astutely remarks "Many [of these immigrants of 1965 to 1975] saw themselves as ambassadors of India, representing a unified culture and a *refined* image of their homeland in a Western country." (my italics) (1991:72). For those having been influenced by the nationalist notions of India as spiritual, exotic, the land of ancient wisdom and civilization, notions shared by US and European Indo-philic intellectuals that I mentioned in the previous chapters, the Hindi film dance is comparatively vulgar, hybrid, kitschy—the underside of Indian culture, best tucked away in the dark parochial boroughs (of Queens, perhaps?), or performed by those 'other' Indians whom I discuss shortly.

So caught up in their proselytizing mission to display an authentic, refined and pure Indianness (Korom, 1995) the AIA seems ignorant of the fact that incorporated into what they believe to be "the untouched and frozen-in-time" rural India that they imagine, are the very highly commercial, technologized, and modern film songs they revile.

Research done by Wayne Ashley on Kerala folk music (1993: 294 to 295) and Peter Manuel on the extensive borrowings by Indian regional musics from film music and vice-versa (1993:138–145) attest to the fact that the rural folk dance avidly to film music, shamelessly borrow the melodies for ritual chants and devotional hymns, and guiltlessly resignify filmi lyrics using local idioms. Similarly, the urban film music industry reinterprets folk melodies according to the narrative needs and aesthetics of the film. These unabashed borrowings between the urban metropolises and the "bucolic" rural areas indicate that "the culture making processes are far more dynamic and hybrid" (Ashley, 1993:294),[9] and anyway "village folk [as well as film music producers!] don't worry about whether [a borrowing] is a 'appropriate' or not; they do whatever they like" (Bannerjee in Manuel, 1993:140). Alas, the bourgeois need to categorize, to separate the pure from the impure, to "authenticate" all that is true, good and beautiful in Indian culture, repudiates the dynamism, contemporaneity and agency of emerging folk forms, be they urban or rural.

THE ORIENTALIST PROJECT CONTINUES AS TOURIST PRODUCTION

Defensively asserting that an official Indianness is non-Western simply continues the orientalist project. As defined by Edward Said in his incisive analysis of European imperialism, orientalism is defined as a:

> Western [corporate institution] for dominating, restructuring, and having authority over the Orient . . . through a style of thought based upon an ontological and epistemological distinction made between 'the Orient' and . . . "the Occident" (1979: 5, 6).

The difference is based on the belief in European cultural superiority, and on a concurrent belief that however great some non-European cultures were, they are now depraved, and in need of intervention, resuscitation, study, preservation, and possession. So European culture *is* while the Orient *was*, and is now Europe's Other. Europe, the West, becomes the point of reference, in definition what the Orient is and is not. Therefore if the West is "modern," scientific, rational, superior, the East is traditional, mythic, inscrutable, inferior. Not to say that orientalists did not admire the traditions, mythology, and "the wisdom of the East." But all these cultural attributes, these essentialisms were located in the past of the colony in question, rendering the colonies incapable of agency in the present. This dichotomy "[served] to denigrate the present, deny history, and repress any sensibility regarding contemporary political, social or cultural autonomy and potential in the colonized world" (Dirks, 1992:9). Thus part of the "civilizing" project in the Indian subcontinent for the colonizers as well as the nationalist reformers was to hark back to a past of ancient and glorious Indic culture. Here at the South Street Seaport, New York City, United States, the Indian elite of which the AIA membership is part, mimics the colonial impulse to authorize "pure" classical and folk dances as authentic expressions of Indianness for an audience which includes also non-Indians (Bhabha, 1984). Rather than the British being the orientalists, this time, the orientalists are the well-meaning but slightly misguided colonialized Indian elites in New York City who "consciously manipulate performance forms . . . in an attempt to present an "official" version of Indian culture to the rest of the American public" (Korom, 1995:4)

According to Kirshenblatt-Gimblett "tourism is the great Orientalist project of our time . . . [It] reproduces colonial relationships, only now the quarry is not sugar cane, coffee, and big game, but wilderness and primitive culture" (1988: 63, 64). And if I may add the quarry includes the expressive folkloric genres of Indian culture that are deemed to depict India's soil and soul as understood by the elites of the New York Indian community, for example. Part of this orientalist project is to organize the Deepavali festival as a tourist production. A certain kind of Indianness is packaged, and then displayed for the consumption, scrutiny, and enjoyment of the visitors. These visitors or travelers are looking for representations of an ethnic culture which they can take home in their memory, or to take home in the form of a photograph, an artifact bought: evidences of having "visited" an exotic place from which they return enriched by new, if superficial knowledge concerning the lifeways of another people. The artifact is folklorized—a process in which the most romantic, and exotic aspects of the traditional culture are stereotyped for display. Also the artifact consumed by tourists is simplified. Religious/philosophical content is de-emphasized, giving precedence to the exotic, colorful shapes and lines of the object (Graburn, 1976:3–10).

To make the experience of Indianness "real" for the visitors/travelers in the South Street Seaport Deepavali festival, activities allowed them to enact some aspects of Indian culture. For example, master craftspeople from India were exported. There were carpet weavers, sandalwood carvers, gold leaf painters, glass bangle makers, puppet-makers, among others. They demonstrated their skills and sold their wares. Free brochures containing relevant detailed information authored by the craftspeople themselves were distributed. Visitors participated in the colorful folk art of rice paste pattern-making called *Rangoli* under the guidance of a specialist. Kathakali make-up was placed on children. In other years, Kathakali make-up (used by dancers in Kerala, Southwest India) was replaced by the local, commercial face painting. Visitors could have their hands intricately decorated with Henna, which has become all the rage in mainstream culture beginning in 1997. There was an elephant ride, a number of Indian arts and crafts activities for children, fair rides, etc.

Of note was the depiction of a Hindu wedding ceremony talked through by a real Brahmin priest. He was very comfortable with the audience and very aware of his role as translator of this indigenous ceremony. The ritual was enacted by a couple. In 1990, it was a non-Indian couple who reenacted the wedding. In the following year, a young Indian couple participated. In 1994, another Indian couple celebrated their 25th wedding anniversary through this performance. The priest enacted the ritual while informing and demonstrating its significance to the public. On one of the smaller stages, reiterating the significance of the wedding was a lavish costume pageant depicting the different brides of the Subcontinent. Up until 1994, the ceremony was conducted at noon. To reach a wider audience, in 1995 the ceremony was moved to 3:30 P.M. A more detailed discussion on the significance of the performance of the wedding ceremony and parade of brides (and grooms) are undertaken in the chapter on the NYU students and their performance of Indianness (Chapter 5).

On smaller stages near the boardwalk, and the apron of the pier, a different type of performance takes place. Here song- and dance-lecture demonstrations, and a puppet show were presented. In these areas, the audience was encouraged to participate in the dances. Whereas in the mainstage the audience's participation was that of passive spectator, in the small stage:

> We (the AIA) went through great pains to educate the audience about what they were seeing or what they were witnessing. . . . Sticks, teachers and partners were provided to reach out to the audience and attract

people to join the dancing . . . (a singer) was providing very detailed explanations about the songs they were singing. (Aguiar)

The choice of the items in the program as well as in the whole festival event was the result of desiring a "very centrally planned, centrally controlled festival where the organizers are very choosy about the kind of activities that go on; and about the kind of people that take part in those activities" (Aguiar) on the part of the AIA.

Besides looking for ethnic, class, and spiritual purity in the songs and dances, the AIA members are prompted to choose items that are easily interpreted and understood by the spectators who may not necessarily know about India in order for the festival to become a form of tourism. This consideration recalls Ben Amos' description of tourist art as communicative system:

> Tourist art . . . operates as a minimal system which must make meanings as accessible as possible across (aesthetic) boundary lines. [This occurs through the] reduction in semantic level of traditional forms, expansion of neo-traditional secular motifs, and the utilization of adjunct communicative systems (in Graburn, 1973:9).

Indeed, the festival is replete with traditional objects. Brochures, verbal explanations by the emcees, visitor and audience participation, the various demonstrations are the adjunct communicative systems that help the tourist—Indian and non-Indian alike—to understand the concept of a certain kind of Indianness. These varied regional cultures are strange even to most Indians. The Indian has had to make space for it, take time out to come for the festival to be Indian. Whereas in the homeland, Indianness as a term for one's identity is taken for granted, or may not even be used to define oneself, here in the U.S. one's distinctiveness from the host society is defined as Indianness—"Those who do not think of themselves as Indians before migration become Indians in the diaspora" (Van Der Veer, 1995:7). Even if these expressive forms belong to Indians, it is still exotic to them. They are tourists to these forms.

For Indians outside India there is no supporting cultural context in the dominant society to appreciate these forms save the community functions that they participate in or the classes that some people attend. Reviews of Indian performances have been done by critics such as Deborah Jowitt and Uttara Asha Coorlawala only on occasion. Indian art and culture are slowly and sparingly becoming part of the U.S multi-cultural school curricula and the mainstream imagination. Images of Indian dance, arts and crafts are just beginning to proliferate the non-Indian media. Popular music icons like Madonna, Gwen Stefani, and others have begun to wear bindis and sarees, and to henna their hands as part of their public display of self. The long-run success of Asif Mandvi's one man comedy *Sakina's Restaurant* is an encouraging step towards South Asian representation and competence in mainstream theater. These examples are fine but sparse compared to the extent that African-American, Hispanic-American and to a much lower degree even Chinese-American images have nuanced mainstream media. Effort must be made by the Indian artist and audience, producer and artist to perform and understand these expressive forms. One such effort of outreach was organized by 1995 AIA president Smiti Khanna to publicize the South Street Seaport Deepavali Festival:

> Smiti Khanna of the AIA actually dressed up a group of little girls in ethnic wear and gave them lighted diyas [earthen lamps]. They landed up in the New York Times office and put tikkas [dots of vermilion powder in the middle of the foreheads] on the editors. Asked what this was about, Khanna told the editors to come the South Street Seaport and see for themselves. The result has been glowing accounts about AIA's annual Diwali bash [in the *Times*] (Melwani, November 1995:13)

Indianness is a world separate from school, from work, and even from leisure activities of the American mainstream. Because Indian performance forms are so different, it occupies a sub-cultural, almost counter-cultural world amidst a dominant Western society.

In the Seaport festival, there is nothing explicitly exhibited, performed or represented anywhere about India's heavy industry, urban lifestyle, or even of the life of the Indian immigrant in New York! At least not as part of the Ambrose Stage main showcase. Because these aspects portray India as a modernizing nation, and presents Indians as being also westernized, these aspects do contradict the orientalist consumption of Indianness. As Annanya Bhatacharjee acerbically observes, the South Street Seaport festival presents a museum of Indian heritage to be consumed by the young for the preservation of culture, and consumed by the old to reduce the separation anxiety that accompanies migration. Consequently, there is a "restriction on the kinds of organizations which can participate, such as feminist, gay/lesbian or working class, a careful selection of the kinds of activities that are permitted and invited"

(1992:36). Earlier, Aguiar did assert that the "AIA is very choosy about the kinds of groups and people who can participate." For tourists, all that is good, beautiful, benign and classy about Indian culture are performed. The politics of exclusion of leftist, and "alternative" groups and voluntary associations in public presentations of Indianness are discussed in greater depth in Chapter 4. The tourist production of Deepavali is the presentation of an official Indianness in the U.S.

Despite, however, the official agenda of the AIA, I must mention that there are other stages within the Seaport festival where other more contemporary expressive forms are presented which I will elaborate later. Sakhi for South Asian Women, the advocacy group against domestic violence, were able to perform a Gujurati Garba dance based on a Gujurati folk song with lyrics expressing the power and emancipation of woman. Sakhi, as well as other, left-of-center groups can request tables to distribute materials and provide information about their advocacy and activism. I have discussed Sakhi at greater length in the forthcoming chapter.

Returning to the South Street Seaport as a tourist production, another symptom of the pervasive touristification of the religious festival is seen in the abbreviation of the burning of the effigy of Ravana. As part of the Deepavali celebration in India, an effigy of the ten-headed demon-king Ravana is burned. Ravana is enemy to Lord Rama having abducted his queen Sita. The effigy is burned to signal Rama's victory over him. Ravana has ten heads because he is believed to be of superior intellect. The effigy, made of paper and tinsel, is supported on a bamboo splint framework. Originally, in India the effigy is packed with fireworks which explode as the flame meets the fuse.

The South Street Seaport effigy, constructed by a local artist, is displayed prominently at the pier's apron as a reminder of its traditional pyrotechnical function as well as religious symbolism of evil vanquished. The effigy is set afloat on the water as the totally separate fireworks display is underway. The effigy does not burn; it certainly does not explode. Because of city fire restriction laws, in the New York version of the Deepavali celebration, Ravana's effigy had become an art piece, a prop for this theatric extravaganza.[10] After 1993, Ravana's effigy was not included in the festival.

Yet another, even more poignant symptom of touristification of this religious festival occurred in the 1994 celebration in which a space was created wherein young Indians were royally costumed as the deities of Ram, Laxman, Sita and Hanuman, sitting magnificently and benevolently

Figure 3.2. Have your family's photo taken with Divinity! A Ram Darbar photo opportunity.

on thrones, after their return from their fourteen-year exile in the forest. The production design of this *Ram Darbar* or Ram's Hall or Court was akin to the high contrast color gaudiness and kitsch glitter of Indian calendar art. For a mere five dollars, a full-body photograph can be taken with these deities. The response to this exhibit was enthusiastic. The artifact of Godliness of an exotic kind for the non-Hindu, and of the familiar for the Hindu could be grasped, consumed, and taken home as a souvenir. It was a thrill to be convinced that one is standing so close to the Gods, can touch them even, and be exhibited with them while the photograph was being taken. Godliness is on exhibit at the Seaport, as well as can be exhibited in miniature as a photograph at home, shown off elsewhere and everywhere as proof and memoir of participation in the Seaport festival, in the Hindu religion, and in Indian ethnicity.

A related transformation that occurred as a result of the touristification of the festival is that its religious function is practiced not as religion but as an ethnic artifact. There are religious references which I will shortly address, but what was given prominence was the celebration of ethnicity. Since the actual Deepavali does not occur on the day of this public celebration, Hindu Indians perform their religious worship in the privacy of their homes, in the Hindu temples, and in community centers. In fact, in 1995, AIA president Asmita Khana declared that the festival was purposefully scheduled on a Sunday so as not to interfere with the private celebrations of Diwali and the demands of the work week. In the South Street Seaport celebration Hindu and non-Hindu Asian Indians come to celebrate their Indianness. Ethnicity by national origin and heritage gain precedence over religious affiliation.

It should be noted, too, that a Hindu festival of Deepavali is used to represent Indianness. Indianness is being equated to Hindu and vice versa. India does have a Hindu majority, but the celebration of the festival here in this magnanimous way only underscores Hindu, or more correctly, a Northern Hindu hegemony. No Indian would consider Baisakhi, a Sikh festival; or Eid, a Muslim festival; or Christmas, or any South Indian festival a valid one to represent Indianness (though the term "Deepavali" is a South Indian term). In India itself, Deepavali is celebrated all throughout the regions and in different communities by Hindus, as are festivals of other religions. Its importance varies amongst the different states and regions. Non-Hindu neighbors participate as visitors, as merchants of sweets and delectables, as fireworks-makers. The festival spills over. This spilling over occurs in New York, as well as in other overseas Indian settlements. A northern Hindu festival is reified as an official, public, secular and by extension a universal representation of Indianness in New York.

WHITE RAMA: ON BECOMING ASIAN INDIAN IN THE U.S.

Performers in the folk dances also included non-Indians. In 1991, participating in a devotional number was an east Asian woman and a white American woman. For the past five years in center-stage of the Kathak items produced by the Satyanarayan Chakra Dance School, a white American woman danced with technical perfection. Though the dances are very Indian, these forms are not only for Indians. The involvement of non-Indians in these performances indicates that culture is not the exclusive property of Indians. Performance forms are mutable and can be shared across cultures. More importantly, this sharing of forms underscores the presence of non-Indianness in the public sphere where, for the time of the performance, these non-Indians become Indians, or at least play at being Indian. This mutability of forms also show that Indians themselves are present in a non-Indian public sphere. This participation was most poignantly and problematically presented in the theatrical depiction of an excerpt of the Ramayana.

In 1994, as well as in subsequent years up until 1998, a dance-drama depicting that portion of the Ramayana wherein Sita is abducted by the demon-king Ravana only to be saved by her husband the Lord Rama, Laxman, and the army of monkeys led by Hanuman was enacted quite startlingly with white Americans portraying the protagonists' roles of Rama, Sita, Laxman, and Hanuman. An accomplished Kathakali Indian actor played the role of the villain Ravana much to the delight of the audience. Save for the expressiveness and grace of the woman playing Sita (the same woman who was at center-stage of the Kathak items that I mentioned earlier), the actors who played Rama and Laxman were stone-faced, and bland. The Kathakali actor was outstanding, playing to the audience with great charisma. He was lively and humorous, hardly demonic, much more the buffoon.

On a simplistic level the cross-racial casting is a toast to multiculturalism and a testimony to the universalism of the story much like the success of Peter Brook's multi-cultural but controversial experiment of the Mahabharata[11]. In fact, in 1994, Manhattan Borough president Ruth Messenger made much of the universality of the theme of the triumph of good over evil, the triumph of light over dark, depicted in the Ramayana in her speech. And since this ideal is shared by both Indians and Americans, we indeed have much in common—there is no cause for divisiveness, or disharmony, is the official rhetoric.

As discussed by Bhikhu Parekh, the Ramayana narrative itself has especial appeal for the Hindu Asian Indian immigrant, because Rama is exiled from his home in Ayodhya, to which he yearns to return, and ultimately does with much fanfare and welcome. The Asian Indian can identify with this trope of exile, displacement, struggle, victory and eventual return. What is more, the exiled Rama has constantly to battle with the greedy, hot-tempered, and hostile rakshasas or demons of the forest and with Ravana—the native inhabitants of the foreign land, the not-home-land (1993:17–19). The story of the immigrant's dilemma of leaving the familiar and romanticized homeland, and living in a hostile and strange hereland finds resonance in this mythic epic.

On a more problematic level, the official story of Hinduism, encapsulated by the Rama story, smacks of the Bharatiya Janata Party's communal claims to Rama Rajya Hindutva (Rama-ruled Hindu state), justifying the razing of the Babri Masjid in what is believed to be the

Figure 3.3. Lord Rama and his brother Laxman frantically search for Sita in a multi-culti casting of an ancient Hindu epic.

birthplace and homeland of Rama in Ayodhya and other violences. More on the BJP is discussed in Chapter 4. The Ramayana story as told in Hindi speaking North India, the official narrative of Hinduism, marginalizes, nay, erases other vital forms of Hinduism. In South India, Ravana is considered a devotee exemplar of Shiva, and is deified as a fierce defender of Lanka against a Northern feudal lord and invader (*Lord* & *King* Rama to the devotees of Northern Aryan Hinduism). The narrative of Rama's triumph may even be a mythopoetic account of the rise to imperial strength of the feudal states of the North central Gangetic basin, the Western region of what is now known as Gujarat and Rajasthan, and the Northeast region of what is now known as Bengal and Bihar during the Gupta period of Indian history (c. 300 to 415) (Larson, 1995:78, 267). The phenomenon is all the more uncomfortable when the originally brown-or blue/black-skinned Rama (traditionally described as 'dark as the underside of the thunder cloud'), and his entourage, are performed by white men. True, there may not be a single Indian man or African-American in the dance troupe to play or able to play the roles of Rama or Laxman. The choreographer, Satyanarayan Chakra, chose from the student body that he has. What would be interesting is to see whether he would consider an Indian with dark skin, or even an African-American to play Rama, to be more true to the complexion of Rama. It would be more "natural" to choose a white Caucasian-American to depict these beloved deities of Northern Aryan Hinduism. Though I shudder to think of the Aryanization of Hindu deities, having Rama, Laxman and Sita portrayed by non-Indian Caucasians is very much in keeping with the nationalist's exaltation of the Aryan race from which the Europeans, and Indians from the Brahman caste were seen to originate (Prakash, 1992: 356) and in the orientalist division of civilizations as the *advanced* European-Aryan, and the *backward* Oriental-African (Said, 1979:206).

According to colonial history, as well as culled from conversations I have had, Northern Indians are deemed to come from the more advanced European-Aryan races, are of lighter complexion, may even have lighter-tinted eyes, more angular facial features, and are taller while the Southern Indians, as indigenous Dravidian natives of the South Asian Subcontinent are darker in complexion, have rounder facial features and are smaller built.

Indeed in the Ramayana story, the central episode is the battle between the gentle, law-abiding Aryan Rama and the primitive Southern (Dravidian) Ravana (Parekh, 1993:18). In reality, the Indian racial features runs the gamut of hues and shades, facial features, and physiognomies. In the mythic stereotyping, the Northern Indian, though he may be of brown complexion is believed to be closer to the Caucasian than is the Southern Indian according to colonial history as well as according to popular belief. Rama is depicted in popular iconography as blue-black, or dark-complexioned. Having to live within the racism of white supremacy in the United States, the Indian in America cannot even find solace anymore in his dark gods. Or worse, he begins to identify himself as well as the gods, as white—a very ugly mutation of post-colonial imperialism rearing its head. Indeed, "light" does triumph over "dark," and especially on the mainstage of the South Street Seaport Deepavali Festival.

. . .

A Bengali academic married a Greek man with blond hair and blue eyes. She took him to Calcutta to visit with her family. Part of the visit was to go to one of the temples. Women and non-Brahmins were not allowed into the inner sanctum. Respecting that restriction, the Greek held himself back while the other men proceeded to enter the sanctum. The officiating priest waved him over, encouraging him to enter. The priest justified this by saying that the man was after all a true Aryan, anyway!

. . .

Growing up the darkest in complexion of all the women in my home, I learned early to accept and maybe even be thankful for the fact that I "had good features" meaning a high nose, large enough eyes, and medium-sized lips, i.e., no Negroid features despite being kari (or dark-skinned). I would never be considered "sweerni"—fair-skinned and therefore, beautiful but at least I could be "saf"—clean. I had to learn to apply facial bleach, remove all my superfluous black hair on my arms and legs, lighten my head hair with henna, avoid the Philippine tropical sun so I would not be more browned than I already was, and choose hues and shades of my clothes that would lighten my complexion. One of the advantages of staying in the States, my mom and other aunts were thrilled to discover, is that my complexion, especially on my feet, had become fairer. The ladies still lament, though, that my hair is still much too black. Shouldn't I consider highlights, at least?

. . .

The irony of the white Rama is most jarring when seen in the light of the AIA's triumph in negotiating a separate category for persons of Asian Indian origin in the U.S. census count. Up until the early 70's inhabitants from the South Asian subcontinent were considered 'persons of Indo-European origin' and were regarded as Caucasian (but not necessarily as 'white'). In Maxine Fisher's study of the AIA, she contends that the:

AIA became convinced that government recognition of Indians as minority would confer economic benefits on the immigrants—irrespective of their parochial background—in the areas of employment, housing, education and eligibility for loans and health services. (1980:117)

To this end, the leadership of the AIA was successful in advocating that Indian immigrants be reclassified as Asian Pacific Americans with a separate category of "Asian Indian" in 1980 U.S. Census, and that persons of South Asian origin be granted minority status. Being labeled as "Caucasians" of darker complexion only served to disqualify Asian Indians from reaping the benefits of affirmative action, while being discriminated against anyway because of a darker skin color than white. The AIA reasoned that being defined as 'Caucasian' makes us "invisible" in the bureaucratic structure, with no representation, and therefore Asian Indians are easier to avoid being dealt with.

This understanding of the South Asian's racial dilemma of being Caucasian but not white was fortified in the Bhagat Singh Thind's case of 1923 that I mentioned in the preceding chapter. It was decided by Justice Sutherland that Mr. Thind could not be granted citizenship because his South Asian racial features and physiognomy will always scream his racial difference from other free white persons. Unlike those of European descent, his assimilation into the white melting pot would be impossible (Hing, 1993: 229). Of course since then, immigration law has changed and citizenship has been granted to legal immigrants. However, the case of Bhagat Singh Thind tells a poignant tale of how South Asians are perceived racially.

In this excerpt of the statement submitted by the AIA to the Federal Interagency on Culture and Education (FICE) in January, 1975, the AIA asserts that in granting minority status to Asian Indians now will protect us from racial discrimination in the future:

> The language of the Civil Rights Act clearly intends to protect those individuals who might be disadvantaged on the basis of appearance. It is undeniable that Indians are different in appearance; they are equally dark-skinned as other non-white individuals and are, therefore, subject to the same prejudices . . . Indians are disadvantaged, we believe, for reasons of racial discrimination. (in Fisher, 1980:129)

In the AIA asserting that we are neither white (European Caucasian) nor black (African American), but are brown (Asian) brings into question what constitutes racial categories, and does give limited value to different racial histories, and geographic origins. In fighting for recognition and for creating a voice in U.S. society, the AIA should be congratulated, but on the other hand, it reveals that the racial politics of the AIA completely adheres to and succumbs to being defined by this spurious, and contentious official U.S. discourse on race. As Annanya Bhatacharjee writes, these racial categorizations are based on biological and cultural essentialisms. The device of the census has only now devised a category for people of mixed heritages or cultures. Previously the census "fails to capture the complex relationships between place of birth, ancestral origin, language, physical characteristics, and cultural affiliations" (1992:34) and migration histories of the past 200 years.

Though morally bankrupt, it is expedient to categorize ourselves as non-white, non-black, minority Asians, even if some of us, though of Indian heritage may have never even been to India, much less Asia. Our physical appearance underscored by our heritage places us in this limited category. We are always made to confess our past, to define ourselves based on where it is assumed we are coming from, what we have left behind, rather than where we are at, are going, or can become. Admittedly, it is indeed expedient, pragmatic—a "worldly discourse of diplomacy, negotiation and officialdom" (Bhatacharjee, 1992: 34) but this kind of discourse fails to even question the inherent immorality of racial discrimination. Yet, I must submit that with this formal recognition, however, we can form coalitions with other Asian Americans organizations to be heard, to negotiate power and resources, to stand up against racial discrimination, even while accepting it as an unchangeable reality. Officially we are non-white, and will use this category to our advantage, but, as I have discussed earlier, in our daily aesthetic and mythic preferences, within our community, and familial and social relations we will continue to prefer light over dark, and will designate ourselves as white.

For the past three years, the AIA has included dances from Southeast Asia, especially those that seem to be influenced by Indian or Indo-Islamic aesthetics. Consequently, Indonesian and Southern Pilipino dances are favorites. I must add, that in the 1995 festival, Reggae and other Caribbean dances and steel orchestra were introduced to encourage and accommodate the burgeoning West Indian population of Indian origin. These non-Indian (but Indian-influenced) dances were given one of the smaller stages to perform in. Though this positioning indicates a secondary status within the festival, at least, it is the initial attempt to form coalitions with other non-white minority groups through performance.

EATING INDIANNESS

Another prime feature of the Deepavali festival is the Food Fair. Various restaurants, eating establishments and private individuals sold delectable morsels of regional Indian cuisine from rented stalls. By 1994, since the population of the festival participants had doubled, private individuals ceased to be part of the food fair. They could not keep up with the demand. Consequently, the food stalls were manned by different restaurants, and commercial food distributors in the tri-state area. The victuals ranged from full-fledged meals to bite-size appetizers to sweetmeats. There was a stall that sold Indian frozen food packets for the urban bachelor or bachelorette to take home.

Efforts were made by the food merchants to display their food in an aesthetically pleasing as well as in an appetizing way. In one stall, *mithai* or sweetmeats were stacked to form mini pyramids in different colors. In another, peppers of different hues crowned some deep-fried appetizer fritters (*chevda*). Part of the appeal of a particular South Indian food stall was the expert way in which the chef grilled rice crepes (*dosas*). He delicately poured the rice-flour mixture on a hot-plate and the visitors watched the patty sizzle. It seemed to delight them. The man was doing brisk business as a result of this exhibition. The food fair was yet another performance of diversity. The diversity of the food available mirrored the variety of dances presented on the mainstage. The message is clear. India is diverse; all these are Indian.

> The idea of an (overarching, crosscutting national) "Indian" cuisine has emerged because of, rather than despite, the increasing articulation of regional and ethnic cuisines. As in other modalities of identity and ideology . . . cosmopolitan and parochial expressions enrich and sharpen each other by dialectical interaction. Especially in culinary matters, the melting pot is a myth. (Appadurai, 1988: 22)

Enjoy Indian multiplicity. Eat her diverse foods! It was an interesting experience for the visitor:

> (To have) Indian food in the context of an Indian festival . . . it would be a much much more rich experience than just going to an Indian restaurant with a created Indian ambiance. Here was a genuine community celebration taking place with the community itself eating all that food. Here was a chance for a gourmet to savor this kind of food which the community itself is relishing. (Aguiar)

Though, too, the atmosphere in the Food Fair was as contrived as any restaurant, the fact that the non-Indian could see Indians wolfing down the food validated the authenticity of the event. Indeed, the food fair thronged with hungry people—gourmet, Indian, non-Indian eager to take mouthfuls of what is perceived to be a more authentic Indianness.

Instead of spending hundreds of dollars on air fare, instead of trekking to the rows of Indian restaurants on East 6th Street and 2nd Ave., and 29th and Lexington Avenue in Manhattan, or Jackson Heights in Queens (not to mention the restaurants in New Jersey!) it seemed more logical to partake of this little bit of India on a bright and breezy Sunday autumn afternoon at the Seaport in New York City. Even for Indians, partaking of the food in so public a place is a proud participation in a pan-cultural heritage. Though the food is not the usual fare that one has at home, its distinctive Indian flavors remain. Flavors that are the result of the blend of spices like coriander, cumin, fenugreek, asafetida, cardamom, cloves, cinnamon, mustard seeds, turmeric, and others sautéed with a generous amount of chopped onions, garlic and/or ginger tingle the tongue and produce a distinct and unmistakable pungent fragrance.

Though the spices may have been imported from the South Asian subcontinent, bought in Indian grocery stores here, the food grown, and cooked here reminds one of India. It is cooked the Indian way. Even if at least one meal eaten at home must be Indian of the particular region that one is from (Saran, 1985:104), the kind of food available at the festival is unusual, rich, and mostly Northern Indian/Punjabi/Mughlai cooking with limited number of Southern Indian delicacies. But in general, these foods are arduous to prepare at home given the 9 a. m. to 7 p.m. workday that most Indians experience. Thus the array of Indian restaurant food is a welcome and convenient novelty and, as my companion, an avid gourmand shared with me, "I don't miss India at all, I can eat anything I want here [in NYC, U.S.A.]". Eating Indian food is like ingesting Indianness, being nourished by it, having it flow in one's veins. Eating Indian food makes the Indian feel that he or she is still part of the homeland or of Indian culture, at least! (Gardner, 1993:7).

One's affection for this type of food, also reminds one that he or she is Indian because despite being in America, where food can be quite 'bland' in comparison, one's taste for Indianness has not diminished. As Una Chaudhuri elaborates:

> Food is, in the first instance, a material element of cultural identity, and one . . . that is widely recognized as such, both from within and without an ethnic group. Yet the mechanism by which this materiality is connected to identity is notoriously, even mysteriously, subjective: namely, taste. Thus food, for all its cultural determinism, seems to be a prime instance also of the transferability of cultural meaning. (1991:198)

Conversely, not eating Indian food, developing a taste for other kinds of cuisines marks the immigrant as cosmopolitan, or Americanized or Westernized. Of the few Indians who ate at the fast food center in the mall, most of them seemed young. They preferred the youthful pizza and burgers than the cumbersome curries at the food stalls. Many anecdotes abound about how much easier it is to eat a soup, salad or sandwich for lunch while at work. Not only because lunch time is limited. But because the smell, look and logistics of eating Indian food is different than the mainstream. However, an Indian dinner is preferred, especially if it is homecooked by one's mother or wife. Not to say that Indian males here do not cook. In fact, one of the changes in gender roles occurs in the area of cooking. Traditional South Asian gender roles dictate that the women of the household are in charge of cooking. When Indian males come here without their female relatives or spouses, necessity dictates that they learn to cook if they want a home cooked Indian meal. True, restaurants that cater to South Asians abound, making affordable Indian food available. However, food cooked at home is considered fresh and healthier.

Indian food dominating the gastro-economics of the South Street Seaport during this Deepavali seems like sweet revenge for the Western/European exploitation of the Eastern/Asian geography for the glory of a Christian God, labor, markets and *spices* during the age of exploration and colonialism! Especially in New York City, there are at least 150 Indian restaurants of which a majority are doing brisk business. Their clientele are both Indian and non-Indian. Of course, New York City and other U.S. metropolises do boast of a vast and varied multicultural cuisine. It does seem that former colonials have mastered and adapted the colonial model of restaurant entrepreneurship, and other attendant profitable institutions of travel and tourism as a way of fulfilling their American dream. As travel writer Pico Iyer asserts in his discoveries of the east increasingly moving in on the west that "the empire had struck back":

> My featureless neighborhood in Manhattan had now, I gathered become Koreatown, with Little India just around the corner . . . in LA, fifty Thai restaurants had sprouted up along Sunset Boulevard almost overnight, and my first night back in town I was taken to a sing-along Japanese country-and-Western joint. . . . I was greeting the New Year in downtown San Francisco, in a Cambodian restaurant just down the street from a . . . mess of Vietnamese cafes. (1989: 359 to 360).

Food for profit turns tables against a history of colonialism. Immigrants can earn a living through the food industry because Americans have acquired a taste for their cuisines plus there are enough coethnics to enjoy the food. The proliferation of multicultural cuisines is a way of introducing new cultures to the host country.

VISIBILITY AND CITIZENSHIP

Though problematic, orientalist, and classist, the magnanimity of the South Street Seaport Deepavali festival is also a manifestation of revenge against Western domination, racial discrimination, and cultural invisibility. It requires immense effort and diplomatic savvy to acquire funds from private sponsors within the community, to win grants from the arts councils and governmental endowment institutions, and to mobilize at least150 volunteers to support, and run the festival. A testimony to the AIA's political clout is the acquisition of the space of South Street Seaport and its environs in the first place, and to be able to every year to expand their activities occupying more streets in the Seaport area. The Mayor of New York, Manhattan Borough President, and other community leaders do come, and give their speeches proclaiming the great contributions of the Indian community to the U.S. society. The festival has become large enough to warrant, in Arun Aguiar's expert opinion a full-time, fully -trained professional cultural/artistic producer. Furthermore, he emphatically states as chairman of the 1994 festival organizing committee:

> I must raise, for the widest possible discussion, the imperative need of
> our community to make hard decisions about professionalizing our ac-
> tivities. If doctors, businessmen, and other Indian-American people
> who have made it in America in several avocations [sic]—in spectacu-
> lar ways—back our aspiring artists and arts administrators to the hilt,
> we can give this country the greatest flowering of a new culture it has
> ever seen. (1994:4)

Professionalizing, institutionalizing, and expanding the festival are ways to penetrate and make an impact in the mainstream of U.S. life by utilizing the official discourse of ethnic difference, multiculturalism, and bureaucracy. This is starkly manifested in the last portion of the 1994 Ambrose stage program wherein the U.S, and Indian national anthems were sung. A young Indian girl played the anthems on her flute, while the other musicians played on the tablas and the harmonium. The image of a young Indian American playing on her flute recalls to mind the pastoral frolics of the flute-playing Krishna, and the jauntiness of Yankee Doodle Dandy.

This conflation of icons is a poignant image of intercultural fusion. Upon the encouragement of Arun Aguiar, the audience sang along. After the U.S. national anthem, the crowd was prompted to declare "Long Live America!" and "Jai Hind (Victory to India)" after the Indian anthem. This conclusion to the Ambrose stage show indicates the multiple levels of citizenship, and therefore allegiances that confront the Indian in America.

In the public sphere, where her society is multi-cultural, multi-racial, the Indian is an *Asian Indian*, originally from the nation-state of India, and using that ethnic/racial distinctiveness to resist the homogenization of Euro-American culture. She also has allegiance to the United States as a nation-state since she reaps the economic benefits of living and working here, even if as a minority. In the public sphere, the Indian identity is vigilant to express itself as distinct from the west, and is simultaneously worthy of Western consideration. A reified, colorful, pastoral, commodified identity is used to curry favors in a cultural/political barter. The underlying political/cultural proclamation is: "I will give you my authenticated identity, exoticness, my difference, my non-Westerness, and in exchange, you give me the rights, benefits and privileges of a U.S. citizen."

ANOTHER INDIANNESS BUBBLES FORTH

The theme of revenge is reiterated even within the festival itself. Though the Ambrose stage is the most prominent stage for the presentation of official Indianness, referring specifically to a Hindu Indian culture, other stages in this festival proclaim an even more variegated, and vernacular Indianness, which I can call as a *Desiness*. These performative genres that I describe as Desi do not make claims of belonging to the one nation-state of India, but to a South Asia as a whole. Forthcoming chapters in this book discuss in detail this aspect of Indian identity in the United States. Here I give brief remarks to illustrate how despite the regulation and relegation of a vernacular Indianness to the margins of the festival, its appeal is infectious.

In an attempt to include more participants in the festival, in 1994 the AIA expanded the festival to include a talent show, a smaller stage for Hindi film dances, and a DJ who mixed reggae, hip-hop, *Bhangra*, and disco-Hindi film music. In 1996, Bally Sagoo, a famous DJ who re-mixes Hindi film music to upbeat dance club music took centerstage. In 1997 and 1998 the Bronx-based rock and roll band Taj performed at the Ambrose stage.

I will first focus my remarks on the changes that occurred in the

1994 show and then proceed to discuss the other changes. The 1994 festival seemed to be bursting out of its seams much to my delight, much to the dismay of the organizers, and much to the chagrin of non-Indians who felt that Indians were getting to be too westernized. It is interesting to note that the rules of inclusion become less stringent as the stages become more participatory. As the events become more participatory, their locations become less available to the public gaze. In one of the smaller stages near John Street, which was behind the audience watching the Ambrose stage, across FDR highway, solo numbers, Hindi film renditions, inter-cultural numbers were presented. When I asked one of the volunteers what was the difference between the John Street stage and the Ambrose stage, she declared that the latter was "for more religious, and cultural dances" while the former was for more "popular, filmi and foreign items". One number of note at the John Stage was a performance which combined *Kathak* with tap *KaTap* performed by Janaki Patrick, and the Kathak Ensemble. Ms. Patrick is a non-Indian who has studied with the great *Kathak* master Birju Maharaj. Jazz was combined with Northern classical music, as tap dance was combined with *Kathak* steps. In a typical call and response section, the jazz singer scats, then the Indian classical singer vocalizes. Tap and *Kathak* were not combined in one body, or in one choreography. Instead, the *Kathak* dancer responded to certain jazz rhythms using *Kathak* steps, as did the tap dancers respond to Indian classical rhythms. The performance ended with all dancers, and singers, scatting, tapping, stomping, vocalizing in a not so seamless crescendo, to jazz/classical music. Such an experiment could happen on this particular stage.

In 1995, this *KaTap* experiment was transferred to the mainstage since it was well-received and well-done. The performance was deemed worthy of the official gaze. It had after all, Indian classical music and dance, and professional Caucasian participants. The jazz aspect was a break in tradition, though jazz artists have been known to fuse Indian classical music and instruments (and other genres of music) in their compositions. What Indian classical music and Jazz share is their propensity for improvisation, and marked interdependence and rapport between singer/dancer and musician. The feature of improvisation was taken into consideration in the 1995 show but with a time limit. Other folk and classical dances did not have this privilege.

An even more bold experiment occurred on the stage of the Talent Show in 1994. It ran non-stop from 12 noon to 6 p.m. Any one could sign up to perform as long as they brought their taped music. There was no pre-judgement on who could perform. A great risk was taken as to the competence of the participants in this free-for-all performance. When I asked the master of ceremonies later about whether he was worried that the participant may not have talent at all, he confidently said "What is talent? You take from the video—it is accessible, copy it—make it your own—that is talent!" This idea of mimesis is elaborated in Chapter 4. He went on further to say that the talent show encouraged Indian children to begin learning to dance Indian dance, and that they begin to learn their culture. He believed that children should be encouraged to perform without restriction. He would prefer for them to "use their energy in these things," rather than in drugs, gangs, and sex. As I discuss in a forthcoming chapter, the Hindi film dance is not as innocent as the emcee hopes; participating in this cultural activity is a form of sublimation of potentially harmful activities. Rather than running rampant with their urges, better to enact them on stage, in front of a voyeuristic audience. It seemed that all those who were not able to fulfill the elitist criteria of the Ambrose stage, could express themselves in this democratic Talent Show. The talent show was broadcast live on Indian cable TV. The crowd thronged to watch these renditions of Hindi-film dances. This stage was strategically placed just before the food stalls so anyone who wanted to eat, had to pass that stage. From the numbers being presented, I surmised that the level of expertise was competent. Though the producers encouraged that in the other stages numbers should not be done solo, here on this stage, a number of popular Hindi Songs were reinterpreted several times by a variety of solo performers. Most of the choreography was taken from the film dance as seen on the home VCR. But I must say that each reinterpretation did carry its own weight in style, competence and grace. The performers infused the set choreographies with their individuality.

I did note, too, that in the talent show, the majority of the performers were young and female. In the forthcoming chapter, I have elaborated on the significance of this gender and age configuration.

In the 1994 festival, the participation of the audience was highest in the last performance space surrounded by buildings at the Seaport area, in an inner alley, right next to the food stalls. Though you need not venture to this stage if you did not want to, the music rhythmically blared loud enough to catch the attention of anyone who was eating nearby. Female disc jockey DJ Dora, spun out a variety of hip-hop, funk, reggae, Hindi film and *Bhangra* tunes. Her accent and intonation indicated that DJ Dora was of South Asian origin from the West Indies. Most of the participants were young second-generation Desi-Americans dressed in

Figure 3.4. Dancing is infectious, even for this woman vendor!

the typical garb of African-American rap/hip-hop culture of loose, baggy jeans, oversized shirts, and unlaced athletic shoes. The demographics and attire of these participants indicate their adherence to and affiliation with other non-white ethnic communities from the public schools that they attend. It also indicates the pervasiveness and appeal of hip-hop culture amongst the second-generation Asian Indian/Indian American youth. Alcohol and cigarettes were sold nearby while bodies danced vigorously, arms raised, cheering voices and squeals of delight were heard every time a popular tune was spun. As the evening progressed, more and more people of different ages joined the party. The dancers were oblivious to the performances in the other stages, while the spectators of the other stages were avoiding this stage "because it was just too crowded!" One non-Indian *Kathak* and yoga aficionado lamented after returning from her food jaunt and witnessing the somewhat decadent display of ecstasy, that "Indians in America have become too westernized, they are losing their spirituality!" To me, the spirit of the dancing Shiva and the hedonist Dionysus seemed alive, well, and with it, at this party.

For me, it was the most fun and infectious event in the 1994 festival. Needless to say, all the participants in this performance space were Desi, i.e. of South Asian descent rather than only of Indian descent. And looked like they were enjoying themselves immensely. They did not have the distanciating glazed look of awe and reverence that the spectators in the Ambrose stage had. In this performance space, another type of Desiness is embodied, not merely displayed. True, the young Desis were exhibiting themselves to each other, dancing the latest hip-hop choreographies, and other contemporary gestures. The big difference was that in this performance space, there was a kinesthetic involvement in a current communal life through contemporary dance and music. At one point, DJ Dora had to stop the music abruptly, and reprimanded a group of young men for fighting. She said:

> Now stop this. This is a *religious occasion*. We must all keep harmony,
> OK? We are here to enjoy ourselves, right? So let us dance, and keep
> peace—alright? (my italics)

Religion, harmony, peace and enjoyment were conflated by this pop shaman's declaration. In this performance space, categories, hard and fast rules, flesh and spirit were fluid, malleable, integrated—a gestalt. The party proceeded as usual after that, even while the national anthems were going on, even while the fireworks were released.

In 1996, UK-based disc jockey Bally Sagoo, renowned for his bhangra and Hindi-film song disco remixes was the guest artist in the Ambrose stage. He is internationally famous in the South Asian Diaspora dance hall scene. He has been credited for introducing to young South Asians everywhere traditional folk songs, and classic Hindi film songs by re-structuring them as dance club music. He made various Indian musics hip, and appealing to a young contemporary South Asian audience, as such. His remixed music is thus, distinctively Desi. Including him as guest artist in the Ambrose stage is an indication of the AIA's acknowledgment of the change in aesthetic tastes and expressive behaviors of the new generation of Indians and other South Asians in the NYC tri-state area. It is also a wise strategy to encourage the participation of this particular population of Desis, ensuring the continued existence and success of the South Street Seaport Deepavali Festival. Bally Sagoo's remixes and concerts are also very popular in the elite discotheques in the urban centers of India. While Bally Sagoo spun his music on the Ambrose stage, the audience members danced in front of the stage's apron.

Sagoo's performance is realized in the dancing bodies of the audiences, not in their passive reception of his music. Thus, the Ambrose stage was transformed into a dance hall.

Another attempt by the AIA to acknowledge the changing demographics and tastes of the audiences is the inclusion of the Bronx-based rock and roll band *Taj* led by American-born Indian Muslim Rizwan Ahmad. As denouement to the festival, after the fireworks display, Taj performed a rip-roaring half-hour of rock songs in the 1997 and 1998 events. The band comprised of an African American, a Latino American and another White American. Ahmad, the Indian American as the main singer and songwriter was the locus of the group. The band belted out original compositions which combined lyrics both in Hindi and English, melodies from Hindi films, rhythms from reggae and rap, and sentiments of American Rock and the Desi in the Diaspora. An example of this syncretism is seen in the following lyrics of the song *My India:*

> *My Daddy was a King*
> *My Mama was a Queen*
> *From Delhi to Madras*
> *Bharat Mata Ki . . . Jai!*
> *Ooo I love you my India*
> *I Like what I see*
> *Ooo I miss you, My India*
> *Get closer to me*
>
> *Been around the world*
> *But I never have seen*
> *A girl as fine as my Indian queen*
> *She make me wanna dance*
> *She make me wanna sing*
> *With her long black hair*
> *And her dark brown skin*
> *I have seen them in Kenya*
> *And Geeyaanaa (Guyana)*
> *And don't forget about the Sri Lanka*

Much to the delight and surprise of Rizwan Ahmad, audience members of all ages, from parents to young children came to the front of the apron of the stage to dance, cheering on the band, and applauding unabashedly. The sound of the music is very different from Bally Sagoo's remixes, and from other bhangra tunes that Desis are used to hearing, especially in the Desi parties that they enjoy. Rock music, is, in and of itself non-mainstream, rebellious and to some, very jarring. The look of the band members is countercultural with their long hair, flamboyant clothing, and boisterous movements that depict an unbridled sexuality and exuberance. Though Ahmad claims that he emulates the look of the dark complexioned, long haired, and all-attractive Hindu deity Krishna, the culture rock music represents can be dismaying to the Indian immigrant who strives to achieve a sober conformity to mainstream America. Ingrid Van Shipley, the chair for the 1997 and 1998 programs confessed that the other AIA officers were hesitant about including this kind of performance in the festival repertoire. She defended her choice by saying to them that they should "Keep an open mind, we need to show something exciting and different, especially for young people." On the Ambrose stage, in the Deepavali festivals of 1997 and 1998, Taj seems to suggest that young Desis can be counterculturally American, and yet within the countercultural sphere of American rock music, infuse an novel and daring Desiness. Thus, rock music is appropriated as a Desi expressive form.

Indeed, the group performed at the tail end of the festival, after the fireworks display when the bulk of the audience is leaving the South Street Seaport. Placing Taj at this point of the program indicates the hesitance of the AIA to present this radical genre as an artifact of Indianness. It is not clear whether the hesitance stems from the fact that this is a rock band, or that Taj is an *emerging* rock band. Fame and commercial success—attributes of American mainstreaming—may push Taj onto centerstage in future festivals, counterculture, notwithstanding.

Another example of another kind of Indianness bubbling forth despite the official rhetoric of the AIA board is practiced by the AIA officers themselves. Ironically, in 1994, when the AIA had their post festival dinner a week later for the volunteers, participants, and the officers, (at Akbar Restaurant out in Long Island), we were entertained not by folk or classical dances, but by Hindi film songs performed by some of the members, and even by the president of the AIA itself. Song requests were obliged. Applause was generous. After dinner, we all got up to dance to *Bhangra*, hip-hop, and funk. I guess these aficionados and managers of *Culture* display the pure and good *Authentic Indianness* in public while in private, away from the gaze of the multi-ethnic, non-Indian U.S., love to groove to a more decadent and hybrid drummer and tune. It became quite clear that the process of authenticating Indianness was an arbitrary, regulatory exercise in political barter with the host society.

In describing the aesthetics of black diasporic expressive forms,

Paul Gilroy seems to reiterate my observations of the participatory performances I have just described:

> The clubs, parties and dances where these creative negotiations between original and supplementary performances take place are governed by a dramaturgy which prizes the local, immediate and seemingly spontaneous input above all. Leaving behind the passive role of spectator to which they would be assigned by Western convention, these audiences instead become active participants . . . the audience's association with the performer dissolves Eurocentric notions of the disjunction between art and life, inside and outside, in the interplay of personal and public histories. (1993:39)

The participatory forms that insist themselves upon the South Street Seaport Deepavali festival are eloquent counterarguments to the official, Arya/Europhilic kind of Indianness that the AIA purports. Influenced by interactions of young Desis with the Black and Latino youth cultures of America and to some extent London, and the immersion of the Indian's cultural life with American and Desi popular culture, the bhangra dance, rock music, and the Hindi film dance, even the innovations with tap dance through KaTap are vital negotiations of Indianness in the United States. The AIA's South Street Seaport Deepavali Festival provides a venue for these negotiations.

AN INSIDE STORY OF DIWALI:
A BRIEF VISIT WITH THE SINDHIS OF REGO PARK

To further show the contrast between official Indianness presented in the public sphere and vernacular Indianness performed away from the public gaze, I will describe briefly the celebration of Deepavali by a regional community in Queens. Whereas, the Seaport festival seeks to show a united, Hindu, though variegated Indian face for its mixed audience, the Sindhis of Rego Park, Queens celebrated Diwali by performing a vernacular culture via an array of Hindi film songs and Sindhi folk songs, by cracking jokes in Hindi and Sindhi, by invoking the Sindhi Hindu deity Jhoole Lal in prayer, song and poetry.

A brief description of Sindhi culture and history before we go on. Sindhis—both Hindus and Muslims—trace their origins to the Sind province, which is now in Southwest Pakistan, Northwest of India. After the South Asian subcontinent was partitioned during its independence from the British, huge migrations out of Sind by Hindu Sindhis took place. These Hindu Sindhis were primarily urbane business people. They settled all over India but have strongholds in Mumbai, Pune, and Bangalore. As seafaring tradesmen, they also dispersed all over the globe, forming large business communities in West Africa, Southeast Asia, London and New York. Sindhi Hinduism has remarkable similarities with Islamic Sufism and Sikhism having been fomented in the Thar desert where Hindus, Muslims and Sikhs cohabited. One of the primary Sindhi deities is affectionately known as Jhoole Lal or the Undulating One, since he is believed to float on the back of a fish on the Indus river. Jhoole Lal is also worshiped by Punjabi, Siraiki and other Pakistani Islamic Sufis, and Sindhi Muslims as a miracle-working saint in Pakistan today. Thus, Sindhi folk songs, devotionals, and ecstatic dances to Jhoole Lal are shared by both Hindus and Muslims. One upbeat devotional in particular to Jhoolelal is sung in the various Sindhi and Punjabi dialects entitled *Damadam Mast Kalander*. The late master musician Nusrat Fateh Ali Khan included this devotional as well as others to Jhoole Lal in his prolific repertoire. Damadam Mast Kalander's energetic beat and catchy rhythms invite people to participate in song and dance. Damadam Mast Kalander is known as the quintessentially Sindhi song in various Desi circles since it bears the characteristics stereotypically attributed to Sindhis—upbeat, lively, fun-loving, pleasure-seeking (mast, as in delight) given to jubilance even in prayer, boisterous, extravagant, hospitable, family-oriented, and devoted.

Sindhi Hinduism is a vibrant melange of devotion to various deities, but with particular affection for Nanak Shah, the founding father of Sikhism who advocated peace and harmony between Hindus and Muslims, Krishna and Rama—the incarnations of Vishnu the Preserver of the Cosmos as well as the gamut of both Shaivite and Vaishnavite deities who are benign, and are providers of fecundity. As business people, Sindhis are also avid worshippers of Lakshmi, the Goddess of wealth and abundance, especially during Diwali.

Mr. Gope Chandar and his family, out of *sheva* or service to the community have been producing the Diwali show, since 1990.[12] There is no charge for the show for, after all, "Not everyone can afford $100 tickets to a Diwali ball but people still need to celebrate Diwali" is Chander's motivation. A public school auditorium is rented, letters are sent to all Sindhi businesses in New York using addresses in the Sindhi directory to participate in the program either as sponsors or as performers.[13] A very modest announcement appeared in the Indian periodical *India Abroad*,[14]

Figure 3.5. The Mast Mast girls fusing modernity with Sindhiness

inviting Sindhis of New York to come to the performance. Indeed, the 500 seat auditorium of P.S. 206 was packed to brimming with Sindhis who live in Rego Park and its environs.

While the Seaport Festival sought to depict a variety of folkloric and classical Indian performances, the Sindhi show sought to provide a variety of entertainments from the popular expressive forms that are accessible and enjoyed by the audience. It is not surprising that the latest Hindi film songs were danced to or sung by the participants. As I mentioned earlier and elaborate further in Chapter 4, the Hindi film song and dance, being one of the most prominent, though phantasmagoric visual depictions of India's landscape, culture, and good-looking people, these song and dance sequences via video and audio-cassette, Indian cable television, and the flamboyant concerts staged by visiting film stars, are some of the first teachers to overseas Indians about Indian aesthetics and culture.

Let us look at one particular dance in which three young girls sexily slither and swirl to suggestive lyrics of the then popular Hindi film

song—*Main Cheez badi Hai Mast Mast* (I am an object of great pleasure . . .) (from *Mohra*, 1994). Other Hindi film song lyrics are as suggestive, waxing eloquent the individualistic and therefore, modernistic
ecstasies of romantic love, physical attraction, and sexual satisfaction. In
this particular number enacted on stage, the participants are hip in their
black miniskirts and short leather jackets, and black hose. It is quite ob-
viously, a sexually suggestive performance, enjoyed by the audience, as
well as the performers. The mother of one of the performers told me that
her daughter agreed to participate in the reinterpretation of this song and
dance sequence because the song, costume and dance were "modern."
That is, it was not traditional, or folkloric, yet allowing her to display her
self to her community in the guise of a Hindi film song and dance. Indeed, through the hybrid music, the contemporary costuming, the sensuous Hindi lyrics, the disco/filmi choreography, participants can perform
a lively, libidinal, current Indian identity. I must add that the song is
based on Nusrat Fateh Ali Khan's reinterpretation of a devotional to
Jhoolelal. The Hindi film song version that these young girls danced to
reverts the devotion from the deity to the self. Indeed, a very modern interpretation of a traditional song.

As I mentioned earlier, though Indianness expressed through the
popular medium of the Hindi film dance is a Pan-Indian identity, it is officially repudiated by the organizers of the Seaport festival. As we look at
the profile of these immigrants who attended Chander's show, we see that
they have come to the U.S.A in the eighties. Most of them are Queens residents who either own their own businesses, or work in Indian companies
as support staff, low-level to mid-level managers (Khandelwal, 1992).
Since the community has burgeoned in the past decade, it is very convenient for the new immigrant to live and laugh amongst other immigrants
without having to contend with that much difference on a personal level.
Vernacular identity need not be sacrificed for an official one.

Vernacular identity is also expressed in the Sindhi show by the use
of Hindi and Sindhi annotations throughout the show, whereas in the
Seaport festival all print and verbal annotations were in English. Since
the audience was adept in these South Asian languages there was no need
to use English in the Sindhi show at all. Everyone was greeted by "Dyari
jo dia jo vadayun hujan" or "Congratulations (felicitations!) on this day
of lights!" rather than "Happy Deepavali." Sindhi folk songs were sung.
The most salient aspects of Sindhiness were manifested in the last portion of the show in which the Sindhi deity Jhoole Lal was invoked in robust prayer. The audience was encouraged to come on stage to celebrate

Figure 3.6. Asking for abundance from the Sindhi deity Jhoole Lal during Diwali.

their Sindhiness in dance. The final portion consisted of asking blessings from the deity as the audience extend their veils to accept these blessings. This invocation of the Sindhi deity contrasts with the invocation of U.S allegiance (Long Live America!) and Indian nationalism (Jai Hind!) in the South Street Seaport festival and the singing of the national anthems of both countries.

Throughout all the numbers, the spectators were coming and going, talking to each other non-stop. They gossiped about other members of the community, identifying who has come, speculating why the others did not, how attractive this person is, who is engaged, giving birth, having marital problems. The audience members identify who the parents of the child on stage are, how talented the performer is, how much he or she has grown since the last time they saw them, and basically gossip about the participants' family and social life as they perform. During the performance, I was invited to play cards with a group of ladies, I was told about the family history of the producers, and in turn was placed

Figure 3.7. The Rego Park Sindhi audience take over the stage during Dama dam Mast Kalander

within the genealogy of this one big Sindhi family upon declaring who I was, who my parents were, who I was acquainted with in that space. In this private sphere, the personal/social takes precedence over the political/cultural.

The Sindhi Diwali show is not a tourist production. For that matter, very little of official Indian traditional culture is present in the Sindhi show. The local, vernacular identity is manifest in the enjoyment of upbeat, hybrid popular music, by laughing at jokes in Sindhi and Hindi, by coming and participating in a community affair, and by dancing and singing. Sindhi regional culture is geographically not part of the current Indian nation-state. By virtue of these Sindhis being Hindu, and migrating to India after Pakistan was formed, they claim political citizenship to the Indian nation-state, but personal/social citizenship to Sindhiness. Sindhis are bound together by claims to an original homeland which they cannot visit unlike other Indians who do have Indian homestates to return to. Sindhis, whether they have ties to India or not are bound by a

Figure 3.8. Asserting youthful masculine presence on the Sindhi stage

sense of living in a Sindhi community here in New York, in Rego Park (as well as in different parts of the globe). Diwali is thus, used to express a very distinctive identity, an identity that is rebuffed in the Seaport festival but which proclaims a loyalty to a particular regional culture, and a certain kind of Hinduism.

In the private sphere, the vernacular identity is in the realm of pleasure, emotion, particularity, that resists the homogenization of official culture. Besides allegiances to the nation-states of India and the United States, allegiance is also paid to community and to folk religion. The private sphere is a personal terrain, where life is lived with sameness, rather than with difference. It is where identity is expressed not as distinct, but as familiar, familial, where identity is shared. There is not much anxiety to perform a traditional show amidst co-ethnics, since cultural boundaries are not threatened by difference (Hylland, 1992). Thus, the Sindhi is proclaiming: "Let me sing and dance with my friends, family, my Sindhi community. Let me celebrate—me!"

Unlike the reified public identity touted by the Indian elites at the Seaport festival, the private identity in the private sphere is *not*, to paraphrase Rushdie (1992), wrought out of an obligation to "define oneself—because one is so defined by others—by one's otherness". It is, instead, a current, processual, dynamic identity that involves life as it is lived by the Sindhi, who is also Indian, living in America, amongst other Sindhis, amidst sameness. Indeed in the Seaport festival, Sindhiness is invisible. I witnessed only two instances of Sindhi expressive forms in the years I attended the festival. Some Sindhi teenagers whom I recognized from the Rego Park show performed Punjabi folk dances or Hindi film dances at the Seaport festival in 1994. The Epic Theater Company that I mentioned earlier, sang the jaunty Damadam Mast Kalander as part of their repertoire. There was only one stall of Sindhi food in 1990. I asked a number of Sindhis as well as folk dance teachers as to why there were no Sindhi folk dances performed, and they say that they have not seen any Sindhi folk dance, and that they could probably invent them if they see a video of it. Videos are not available of Sindhi dances because of the Pakistani Islamic ban on dance, and the current geopolitical crises that the Sindhis in Pakistan face. Moreover, Indo-Pakistani political relations are hostile, trickling down to the populace's aversion for each other. Sindhi Hindus do not claim Sindhi folk dances that are seen on Pakistani cable TV as Sindhi, but as Pakistani. Thus, Sindhis seem to perform their pan-Indianness rather than their Sindhiness at the Seaport festival.

Though Sindhiness may be invisible at the South Street Seaport Festival, Sindhiness prevails in various forms in the United States. Gope Chander has been able to produce an ample number of cassettes for sale and distribution of Sindhi songs. He has just started a Sindhi show on Indian Cable TV every Sunday at 6 in the evening wherein he and his family sing Sindhi songs. There are two active Sindhi associations in the NYC tri-state area—Long Island Sindhi Association and the Sindhi Association of New Jersey, whose primary agenda is social activities for Sindhis and fundraising for various charities. In 1997, as part of the celebration of Indian and Pakistan's independence, the Asia Society commissioned the Sufi qawal Qurban Fakir of Bhit Shah, Sind and his troupe for a four day run of devotional songs composed by Sind's premier poet, the sufi Shah Abdul Latif. Two international Sindhi organizations have been formed. The World Sindhi Institute seeks to revive and conserve Sindhi language and arts, and to empower the political stance of Sind. Sindhi Samelan organizes an annual conference in various parts of North America (1997 in Toronto, 1998 in San Jose, California, and in 1999 in Orlando, Florida) to encourage Sindhi Hindus to form a community, and to enhance knowledge of Sindhi culture, language and religion. In the sphere of Sindhi Hindu devotion, The Sadhu Vaswani Center in New Jersey holds an annual conference wherein devotees of the Vaswani guru lineage gather to pray and socialize. At least every other year, Dada Vaswani visits New York as part of his world tour. Though his followers include many non-Sindhis, the bulk of his congregation is Sindhi. The main headquarters of this center is in Pune, India, where a prominent Sindhi Hindu community thrives. The Satyanarayan Mandir, the Sindhi Hindu temple in Woodside, Queens, houses, together with the Jhoolelal deity, other deities of the Hindu pantheon.

These Sindhi international organizations and international family ties sustain the Sindhi diasporic community *amongst themselves*. Sindhi families from different cities of the world are linked in intricate bonds of endogamous arranged marriages. Though Sindhi Hindus may be dispersed in far flung cities all over the globe, it is not surprising to discover familial and/or familiar ties in any one city that I visit. It is in the more overt public sphere where there are non-Sindhis, other kinds of South Asians, and non-South Asians, that Sindhis do not have (or may not need?) representation. If representation in the Pan-Indian community is sought, efforts will have to be made to create authenticated Sindhi performative forms for Pan-ethnic display. Sindhi folk forms already exist in Pan-Pakistani cultural events. Sindhis who consider themselves Indian and Hindu may have to ease their biases against claiming these "Pakistani" forms as theirs also and look to these forms as artifacts of Sindhiness rather than as artifacts of Pakistani nationalism.

OF FESTIVALS AND FIREWORKS

Coming back to the South Street Seaport festival—as is appropriate with most festivals, this one climaxed with a meticulously choreographed display of fireworks by the Garden State Fireworks, Inc. The fireworks were the pyrotechnic interpretation of the Ramayana story that was being narrated on the main stage. Thus far this is the third version of the Hindu epic in this ostensibly secular festival: the Ramayana story that is staged annually, the Ram Darbar photo opportunity in the 1994 festival, and now the fireworks, which is also a festival mainstay. The choreographer's intention was to take into consideration the tastes and preferences of the Indian and create patterns which would appeal to that audience. Indeed, some of the patterns did look like they could be recreated on Indian

sarees, and other costumes. Here are some excerpts of the creative innovations of the choreographer to retell the Ramayana story using fireworks:

The Exile in the Forest:

> Numerous shades of green emit from a variety of roman candles, rang-
> ing in size from 15mm to 50 mm, creating thick foliage. Above beauti-
> ful variegated bombettes represent flowers of the forest while Fancy
> Peonies with Palm cores and Elegant Chrysanthemums fill the sky.

The Great Battle at Lanka:

> Red and yellow magnesium blended together with various electric
> tailed star shells, multi-break cannonade shells, flashing staccato ef-
> fects and titanium reports create a true "Battle in the Sky".

The Return to Ayodhya and Celebration of Peace:

> The sky will open up millions of twinkling strobe lights, representing
> the flickering oil lamps set out to light Rama's path. Rising comets,
> multi-colored exhibition candles, fancy variegated color and noise
> shells and a thunderous barrage of titanium reports celebrate the vic-
> tory of good over evil, and light over darkness. (1993: 41)

The audience seemed to be mesmerized by the fireworks display.
Heartfelt ooohs and aaahs were heard all throughout the pier. Only if the
spectator stands in front of the Ambrose stage would she or he hear the
narration of the Ramayana story. The spectator only knows of the fireworks' choreographer's intent if she or he reads the brochure. Otherwise
the display from other vantages in the seaport is appreciated for its
forms, colors, and surprise. To me this is the best interpretation of the
Rama story, only because it is so innovative, abstracted, obscured and
unhegemonic. It titillates the pyrophilia in the spectators, and reminds
them of the displays that some Indians may have experienced in the
homeland, and also during other non-Indian holidays like the very American July 4th holiday. Having our own fire spectacle to mark our festival
of lights, here in New York, makes it comparable, equal in clout and importance to the national holiday of U.S. Independence. The Hindu myth
conflates with the American Dream.

Let us pause a moment to contemplate on the comparison Roger

Abrahams, a prominent social scientist, makes between the nature of the festival and the fireworks display:

> Perhaps the firecracker carries the message of festival most fully as a noisemaker that demands attention as it consumes itself. And, in the firework show, it becomes the most dramatic and temporary of all festival arts, made for the moment of display only, destined to self-destruct, come apart, and disappear. Like the firecracker, festivals 'go off'; they are exciting and exist only for the seized moment (in Falassi, 1987: 180)

This comparison seems to apply to Deepavali especially as the meaning of Deepavali is light. Fireworks are playful, spectacular fire and lights. Like the firecracker, the event is a temporary affair but it is seared in the memories of the onlookers. Though this event must come to an end, there is the promise that the festival will happen again the next year. Next year, the Asian Indians can gather in this well-defined space and time and celebrate their belongingness to a community, returning the following year to a New York India not only temporarily but definitely in this flamboyant and vivid manner:

> Festivals are ultimately community affairs. Indeed, they provide *the* occasion whereby a community may call attention to itself and, perhaps more important in our time, its willingness to display itself openly (Abrahams, 1988: 181).

From 1989 until the 1998, the festival officially ends by 8:30 in the evening (people eat and dance in the inner performance spaces until 10 or 11 in the evening). The crowds are exhausted but a little richer for the experience of a re-invented India on Deepavali, savoring a bit of curry in the Big Apple. Through the South Street Seaport Deepavali Festival, the Asian Indian finds a way of defining his/her ethnic identity amidst New York's highly pluralistic environment, in a new homeland. Asian Indians are presented with Pan-cultural artifacts of Indianness which they can use as a way of defining themselves to non-Indians, and to other Indians of different regions, and use to negotiate their place in the United States (Slymovics in Van der Veer, 1995). True some of these representations are contentious, orientalist, and sometimes misleading, but they are nevertheless expedient, tools and strategies for adaptation. Aspects of Indian identity that do not fit the definitions of authenticated Indianness are enjoyed in private, among other Indians, among co-ethnics, in the festival's peripheries. Forthcoming chapters will illustrate aspects of vernacular identities which are negotiated and dramatized in other public performances.

NOTES

[1] I am indebted to Frank Korom for his valuable comments and suggestions on an earlier version of this chapter presented at the 1994 Association of Asian Studies conference in Washington D.C. My gratitude to Brooks McNamara for his encouragement and evaluation of the first thoughts on this topic drafted in a paper submitted for the Popular Entertainments class at Performance Studies Department, NYU.

[2] This is taken directly from interviews and conversations I have had with Mr. Aguiar since 1991 to the present. Though he is not active in the executive board of the AIA, he is still one of its staunch supporters.

[3] The AIA exacts a small fee from the stall owners as rent. The AIA raises funds for the event from leading community philanthropists and various corporate sponsors, as well as governmental funding agencies. All staff work on a voluntary basis. However, professional participants and performers are given a modest honorarium.

[4] For example, Kathak is from the north of India, most prominently from Jaipur and Lucknow. It is based on Hindustani music and has strong Persian and Islamic influences. Its most prominent choreographic feature is its chakras or turns, its erect stance and rapid footwork. Bharat Natyam is from the South, specifically Madras, and its stance consists of turned out bent knees, straight back, pronounced hand gestures, crisp facial expressions, vigorous rhythmic footwork. Odissi from the East, specifically Orissa, is prominent for its interpretations of Jayadev's erotic poetry between Radha and Krishna, and its tri-bangha (three bends) stance in which the dancer's body is bent at the neck, the waist and the knee. In Odissi, the locus of movement is in the dancer's mobile waist.

[5] This is parallel to the debate on what is displayed at the Met vis-a-vis what is displayed at the American Museum of Natural History. European art pieces are not part of 'natural' history, in the same way that African tribal masks are not part of Art unless they are in a Picasso painting!

[6] This is a community theater company based in New York City which produces plays primarily in Bengali.

[7] Sudipto Chatterjee is an active theater, and video practitioner in the NYC Bengali community as well as in Calcutta. He is one of the founders of the Epic

Theater Company. Currently, he is part of the administration and faculty at the Undergraduate Drama Department at NYU's Tisch School of the Arts.

[8] Amitabh Bachchan owns the cable TV channel *Eye on Asia* in the NY Tri-State Area. He has appeared in over 100 Hindi films from 1970's to the present.

[9] More on the hybridity of Hindi film music in the chapter on "Performing Hybridity at NYU"

[10] Since 1993, another festival called Dussera is organized by another voluntary organization to celebrate the victory of Ram over Ravana out in Long Island. In this production, the 50 feet effigies of Ravana and two other demons are spectacularly set to flame.

[11] cf. Dasgupta, Gautam. 1987. "The Mahabharata, Peter Brook's Orientalism" in *Performing Arts Journal* 10, 3: 9 to 16. & *The Drama Review*. 1986. Section on Peter Brook's *Mahabharata*, 30, 1: 52 to 101. & Meduri, Avanti; Philip Zarilli & Deborah Neff. 1988. "More Aftermath After Peter Brook" in *TDR* 32, 2: 14 to 19.

[12] I have had two conversations with Mr. Chandar, and his daughter in 1994. And have witnessed his shows since 1993 until 1996. I have also seen he and his family perform in various Sindhi occasions, religious, secular and political.

[13] interview with one of the participants

[14] *India Abroad*, November 3, 1994.

CHAPTER 4

Underneath My Blouse
Beats My Indian Heart
Hindi Film Dance, Indian Womanhood, and Nationalism[1]

> Indians all over the United States celebrated the 47th anniversary of India's Independence Day—Aug. 15, 1947—with *traditional fervor.* The events were marked by speeches and *nationalist songs* . . . New York's Governor Mario Cuomo issued a proclamation declaring Aug. 15 India Day. The India Day parade in New York city (was) held on Aug. 21. [Emphasis mine] (*India Abroad,* August, 19, 1995:42)

. . .

As I was packing my video camera it suddenly struck me that I was going to the Independence Day parade by myself. I suddenly became frightened and began to sob. I was terrified of being found out by the community that I was not Indian enough. Oh because I had short hair, was wearing khaki pants, was born in the Philippines,—and I was without a man. I am thirty-five years old, and very single. What kind of Indian woman was I?

. . .

The Jewish shopkeeper in Rego Park from whom I bought batteries for my cassette recorder asked me if I was Indian. I said yes, tentatively, not wanting to explain that I was born in the Philippines, actually. He enthusiastically went on to tell me how much he loved to watch the Indian movies of Raj Kapoor and Nargis. He began to sing a song from *Shree 420.* I, in good spirits by now, sang along with him—*Ichuk dana, beechuk dana, dane upar dana.* After giggling, he explained to me why Indian movies were so popular in Israel. They were so romantic, he proclaimed, with the songs and dances, and no nudity. What's the use of seeing a woman fully naked? There is no mystery. And what's more the whole family can come and watch the movie. Indian women are more beautiful because they are modest, he reassured me.

To the strains of nationalistic slogans "*Jai Hind, Hindustan Zindabad*" and a popular Hindi film song "*Tu Cheez Badi Hai Mast Mast,* " hundreds of young Indians led by New City Mayor, Rudolph Juliani [sic], Indian Ambassador Siddharta Shankar Ray, Miss Universe 1994 Sushmita Sen and filmstar of yesteryear, Asha Parekh, marched down Madison Avenue in Manhattan to celebrate the 47th anniversary of India's independence here August 21. (*India Abroad*, August 26, 1994:42)

The spectacle of the Indian Independence Day celebrations produced by the Federation of Indians in America (FIA) is an example of a vernacular expression of nationalism by Indians in the diaspora. The parade which passes along Madison Avenue through about twenty blocks of midtown comprises many floats paid for by merchant associations, commercial establishments, and socio-cultural voluntary associations, and various marching bands. It culminates in a food fair and cultural program in which local talents and invited celebrities perform their version of "Indian culture".

The FIA is the umbrella organization for ninety-three parochial, merchant, sectarian, and service-oriented voluntary Indian associations in the New York tri-state area which seeks to represent a pan-Indian population and image, one rising above the regional and religious boundaries (Khandelwal, 1992). Besides promoting ethnic solidarity, the FIA also seeks to introduce Americans to India in a congenial setting (Fisher, 1980) The FIA's main activity, since 1981, has been to organize the India Day Parade and the cultural program in Manhattan ostensibly to celebrate India's independence from British sovereignty. According to 1994 FIA president Probhir Roy, the parade is a prime opportunity to publicize India as the "best place to visit and best place to invest" and to display and assert political clout in the U.S.A. These four-fold motivations— commemorating India's independence; representing a united Indian community; asserting the Indian presence in the current political milieu; promoting tourism and investment in India—are part of the official rhetoric of other similar voluntary associations in marking Indian holidays here in the United States.

As I discussed in the previous chapter, these associations' cultural ambassadorship is laudable and a heavy responsibility. I continue in this chapter to emphasize how the event of India Day becomes an opportunity for Indians not only to socialize, network, and have fun, but also to vent their frustrations, and express their ambivalence about being Indian and the pleasures of being Indian in America. The parade and the celebrations surrounding it become yet another arena wherein various expressions of Indianness are contested and negotiated.

On August 21, 1994, against the urban-commercial backdrop of Madison Avenue, various floats lumbered by blaring loud, mostly Hindi film music while displaying with aplomb their commercial and cultural affiliations: merchant associations from the New York tri-state area, Indian restaurants, shops retailing Indian foods and spices. These businesses proclaim their mercantile power and their contribution to the U.S. economy. Their presence indicates a big market for their goods. Most of their customers come from the South Asian communities in New York, New Jersey and Connecticut. Religious organizations included Asian Indian Ministry, ISKCON, Bochasanwasi Swaminarayan Sanstha, Muslim Federation of America, Sri Chinmoy Centre, and some other Hindu organizations. This array is a testimony to the robust variety of religious sects in the tri-state Indian communities.

To enliven the parade there was much dancing, shouting of *"Jai Hind,"* and waving of the Indian flag in various sizes. A group of teenage girls whirled flags to the rhythms of a Hindi film song with a disco beat. These girls would later appear on stage dancing to a folksy filmi dance. There were others who lip-synched Hindi film songs, waved at the onlookers, passed out fliers in English and in other regional Indian languages. Some people marched, others strolled, many meandered. The parade ended on 23rd and Madison Avenue amidst Indian food stalls. This is also where the cultural program took place. Needless to say, dignitaries like the NYC Mayor, or the Governor, and candidates for political office looking for the Indian vote as well as members of the Indian consulate, marched down Madison Avenue, and made speeches extolling the Indian community's great importance and contributions to U.S. society. On that weekend of Aug. 21, 1994, the Empire State Building was lit saffron, white and green, the three colors of the Indian flag. Probhir Roy proudly attests that the FIA persuaded the Empire State Building's management to light its tower for free for that weekend where usually it costs $10, 000 per night. Roy bragged that no other ethnic community has been able to do that. One of the most prominent icons of New York City was used to acknowledge the Indian presence. Within the politics of visibility, the Indian community does have some clout after all. On this summer day, Manhattan witnesses Indianness in America.

There is much to tell about the India Day celebration in New York, but I restrict my discussion to three salient themes gleaned from three years of observation and attendance in the parade—1991, 1992, 1994, especially focusing on the 1994 parade. First is the relationship between the celebration of nationalism and the preponderance of Hindi film songs and reinterpretations of Hindi film dances. Second is the fact that the performers for the cultural show are primarily female, usually young adolescent or pre-pubescent girls. The celebrities who come to grace the occasion are full-grown adults while the community participants are mostly young girls. Why is that? And what is the relationship between these young girls, Hindi film songs and dances, and Indian nationalism?

The third theme is a bundle of sub-plots feeding into the two main themes. One subplot involves the ambivalence of the parade's organizers in including in 1992, and subsequently excluding in 1995 and 1996, SAKHI, the advocacy group against domestic violence, and SALGA—the South Asian Lesbian and Gay Alliance from the parade. Whereas young pre-pubescent girls are encouraged to dance, these highly politicized women are excluded from the parade. To complicate the matter of sexuality, I have contrasted the expressive presentations the dancing girls, and SAKHI with a description of the Bharata Janata Party's float in the1994 parade and how this float represents the ideal woman of the Hindu fundamentalist nationalist. How does this ambivalence bear upon the shifting definitions of the Indian woman, and on Indian sexual politics in general?

Related to the communal politics of the subcontinent as well as to the communal tensions in the Indian and Pakistani communities here, another subplot involves the shooting of Gurmukh Singh by a Pakistani during the1993 India Day celebrations. What narrative of nationalistic machismo was enacted in this incident? How is nationalist fervor of the independence project reinterpreted in the USA?

The third and last subplot is a personal one. Despite not proceeding in the path of marriage and family of a traditional Indian woman, what is my involvement, my place as a woman of the Indian diaspora in the India Day Parade? And by extension in the Indian community in the USA at large? These themes are enmeshed in the forthcoming discussion on the final portion of the cultural program that I witnessed in 1994. I consider this portion the most theatrical enactment of vernacular nationalism.

Unlike the mainstage at the Deepavali Festival at the South Street

Seaport, the main source of inspiration for the Independence Day numbers are Hindi film song and dance sequences. According to Manhar
Patel, chairman of the cultural program in 1994, despite his encouraging
participants to present folk or classical numbers—the more respectable
artifacts of Indian culture, they insisted on film dances, and were in fact
competing to perform the two or three Hindi film songs which were currently very popular. Out of the nine items approved, six were Hindi film
song and dance reinterpretations. In 1992, 12 out of 16 items were Hindi
film song and dance reinterpretations. Even if the title for an item
promised a folk dance, the music was from films in the particular regional language where the so-called "folk" dance was said to come or
were Hindi film folk tunes. These song and dance interpretations were
performed by girls mostly between the ages of 12 to 16, costumed in folk
dresses or classical garb. Their parents are members of the associations
that are part of FIA.

TOO MUCH MASALA[2] IN THE HINDI FILM

To comprehend this overwhelming influence of Hindi films on immigrant lives, it is important to understand the ubiquity of the industry itself. Film in Hindi, one of the official national languages of India, has
captured 20% of the Indian market while regional films are restricted to
their linguistic regions. The Hindi Film Industry is a big, booming industry based in Bombay, India. As of 1990, the statistics show that the daily
film viewership reached thirteen million. On the average, 750 to 800 Indian films in various regional languages are produced a year, out of
which approximately only 50 become hits of which 10 are Hindi films
(Pendulkar, 1990). With an average of 100 million tickets sold every
week, (Iyer, 1989:245) the industry is the sixth largest employing over 2
to 2.25 million people. The annual box office receipts are approximately
550 million dollars. These films are exported to over 100 countries.
Major markets are Saudi Arabia & the Persian Gulf ($50,000,000.00),
Asia ($9,283,000.00) and Eastern Europe & the former USSR ($12,
000,000.000). Overseas, too, these films are viewed by 12 million expa-
triate Indians, and other South Asians, and Indo-Caribbeans via video
cassette or in cinema houses. (Lent, 1993, p. 240).

The usual formula for a Hindi Film to become a hit according to
Barnouw and Krishnaswamy "called for one or two major stars, at least
half a dozen songs, and a few dances . . . the subject matter, with increas-
ing concentration was romance" (1980:155).

To elaborate further, the formula consists of the following. There should be at least six song and dance sequences ranging from love songs, comic numbers, cabaret and/or disco dances, and a religious song. These songs as a rule are not sung by the actors themselves but by playback singers while actors lip-synch. The songs are choreographed for the actors to dance and interpret, thus requiring the actors to move well. The strong hero has a well-groomed, well-dressed 'beautiful' heroine preferably played by superstars whom he has to win, quarrel with, tease, and break the resistance of or triumph over. Sometimes, the families object to the romance, or a villain or a pack of hoodlums disrupt the pastoral bliss of our couple whom our hero fights in elaborately choreographed fight scenes and invariably, and sometimes single-handedly, outsmarts the bad guy. There must be a comedian and some sketches with his cohorts, maybe the sickness or death of a close family member of either main character. Emerging from all these excessive travails and tribulations the hero and heroine *must* live happily ever after. These tacit stipulations for the hit Hindi film are called *masala*—spice. There are variations on the themes such as those having a patriotic or historical or religious flavor but usually the more masala, the better. Like good Indian food, the masala must be blended well[3].

Let us focus on the important convention of including songs and dances in a popular Hindi film. Whereas in the United States and in other giant film producing nations, the film musical has died only to resurrect on the live stage (Jarvie, 1986:176), these Hindi film 'melodrama—musical spectacles', prevail and flourish in the sub-continent and its diasporic sites. The song and dances sequences outlive the films of which they are a part. For example, the very popular All India Radio and Vividh Bharati in India broadcast these songs. Audiocassettes, and now compact discs of a film's songs are released months before the movie is out so that the audience may familiarize themselves with them before seeing the movie. Indian audiences wait for the songs to come alive on screen and then judge how well these songs are rendered (Barnouw & Krishnaswamy, 1980, 157-8) or to use the Hindi-English colloquial term, "picturized".

Within the structure of the film itself these song and dance sequences serve a narrative function, helping to release tension, playing out sexual contact between the hero and heroine without portraying actual coitus or related activities. Song and dance sequences are also used to arouse pathos or bathos. A song and dance can move the story from one point in the plot to another. The sequence can cause romance to bloom, can strategically distract a villain, can change the fate of the characters. Underlying all this action is the classic Indian aesthetic concept of *Rasa*-- the arousal of sympathetic delight and pleasure in the spectator evoked by technical and emotive expertise of the performer through the theatrical devices of dance, song, costume, scenery, and poetry. In the *Natyasastra* (2nd Century BCE—2nd Century CE), the Hindu dramaturgical treatise which is believed to have been formulated by the sage Bharat Muni upon the command of Brahma, the Lord of Creation, the human populace is to be spiritually uplifted through song and dance, drama and poetry. This classical tradition, extends into popular performance where it is transformed (or as some elitist critics would have it, corrupted) in the Hindi film. Indeed, Hindi film aesthetics borrow and innovate from folk and popular Indian theatric spectacles such as Jatra (Bengali), Nautanki (Rajasthani), and Tamasha (Marathi), and Parsi Theater (Gargi, 1962), as well as from commercial films of Hollywood, art films from Europe, and other international cinemas.

I do not want either to apologize for or legitimize the existence of popular genres by referring to the *Natyasastra*. Rather I want to underscore the historical and aesthetic-theoretical depth of including songs and dances as fundamental to Indian cultural, and not, as in Aristotle's dramaturgical theory of poetics, as mere appendages to the "higher" aspects of theatre, namely plot, character, and thought. Indians, as well as other South Asians—Desis, if you will, not only like songs and dances, Desis especially like film songs and dances. It is at that point in the film that the spectator experiences a most charged and total theater.

When television became widespread in Indian middle class homes in the seventies, one of the first and most popular prime time shows was the MTV-like *Chitrahaar* which depicted song and dance sequences spliced from various Hindi films. Though there are independent musicians and musical compositions, India's popular music industry consists primarily of Hindi film songs.

In New York, with the greater availability of home video machines, and the new audio-visual technologies of Digital Video Discs and Laser Compact Discs, many rented video cassettes, and video discs only have song and dance sequences, expertly edited together for the homeviewer, and sold by Indian video shopkeepers. Sometimes these are edited together according to theme, subject matter, period or superstar performing the number in the film or playback singer rendering the songs: Love songs are a popular theme, so are comic songs; songs played on the piano or with piano as prop form one category; the disco dances of certain movies or superstars are another. The songs and dances enacted and sung by the stars of supernova proportions are readily available. ITV, the Indian cable TV channel in New York has an hour of these song and dance sequences every day, over and above the two or three full-length features that they broadcast. On the weekends, other channels, as well, broadcast these 'melody hours' in different regional languages.

Most importantly, the song and dance sequences via video are one of the first teachers of overseas Indians about Indian aesthetics and culture. The film dances are watched and watched again, re-choreographed or are imitated pat, put on a live stage and performed during Indian festivals, commemorative days, and community affairs for overseas Indians. The reinterpretation of songs and dances from Hindi films is the most potent marker of Indian ethnicity in the diaspora. Hearing a familiar and well-liked song accompanying the deft dance movements of a young compatriot is sufficient to create, at least, an ersatz experience of community, or to coin a Turnerian phrase 'a liminoid experience of communitas' (1986). As an overseas Indian, myself, I grew up performing these dances. I "expressed my Indian ethnic heritage" and learned about India through them. It was for me the most effective and affective way to participate in the Indian community in the Philippines. In New York, I dance film songs sometimes, to entertain friends at parties, break the ice, gathering a little recognition as an artist in the process. At times I have absolutely nothing to say to other diasporic Indians since they are concerned with their children, husbands, and mortgages. But dancing together to Hindi films helps us relax and enjoy each other's company and bodies in melody and rhythm despite our disparate intellectual and life interests. As Kiren Ghei has observed in her studies of Indian immigrant teenage film dancers in the Los Angeles area:

> Forming one aspect of this rich public life are immigrants' and first generation Indian Americans' interpretations of Indian popular cinema. Film music and dance typically appear in "cultural programs" which are usually the centerpiece of a larger event celebrating a religious or national holiday celebrated in India (For example, Diwali or India Independence Day). (1988:3)

In the New York tri-state area, there are at least ten theatres that screen Hindi Films – two in Long Island, two in Queens, a few in New Jersey. In the last 10 years a number of theaters have shown Hindi films in Manhattan but have closed down due to lease agreements and the short run of Hindi films. As there are only a limited number of films that are screened, these theaters have not yet lessened the popularity of video watching. Still, family social life is enhanced by a trip to the cinema. Especially on the weekends, these theatres are full. Tickets can be purchased in advance from Indian retail stores in Jackson Heights and Richmond Hill in Queens.

Also, several entrepreneurs have produced 'Star extravaganzas' in which a number of superstars are imported to the U.S. and other cities of North America from Bombay to sing and dance to the Hindi film songs that they enacted on screen. These performances cater to an audiences of not less than 15,000. Nassau Coliseum in Long Island, New York, the Patriot Centre in Washington, D.C. are examples of venues for these mega-events. Not only Asian Indians attend these events, but so do Pakistanis, Bangladeshis and Indians from the Caribbean attend these events. These productions are lavish, hi-tech, with at least 100 people in the production crew. A single performance runs for five to six hours. The ticket prices range from $15.00 to $150.00. Needless to say the venues are packed. Since 1992, two or three shows are produced each year in the New York area (Melwani, Sept. 1995:27 & 29).

From 1993 to 1998, a Hindi film group dance competition entitled *Naya Andaaz* (New Style) was produced by a group of young professionals in New Brunswick, New Jersey. The competition was open to South Asians in the tri-state area and judged by a Hindi film star, established artists and prominent members of the Indian community. The purpose of this competition was to encourage young Indian American amateur performers to reinterpret Hindi film songs creatively or to innovate choreographies with an Indian idiom to any kind of music. This competition received overwhelming responses both from audiences and participants. At least 1000 people attended this event. Fifteen items were chosen from the thirty entries. In 1996, the organizers added a separate competition for children under 15 (Lobel, 1996:4). Some of the winning numbers in the past years include a 'folk dance' choreographed to the tune of "Hothon Main Aise Baat" from the 60's hit film *Jewel Thief* in1 996 and a clever reinterpretation of "Ama Dekh" on in-line skates in 1994. It is not surprising that Parag Amladi concludes that "Our public culture in North America is thoroughly dominated by (Hindi film) cultural form." (Sept. 1995:22). As a result of this immersion, many professional classical and folk dance teachers have had to teach their students Hindi film dances just so to keep them as students, and to hook them to learn the more traditional forms. In 1992, Dheeraj School of Dance in Richmond

Hill, Queens includes the choreography and the teaching of Hindi film dance in its curriculum.

There is one more point to be made regarding the Indian film industry. All films produced for showing in India have to be screened, approved and rated by the Central Bureau of Film Certification. The Censorship Act of 1952 excerpted here stipulates that the public needs to be protected from being corrupted by immoral acts shown on the screen.

> It is not advisable that a film, shall be certified suitable for public exhibition, either unrestricted or restricted to adults which:-
>
> C) deals with relations between the sexes in such a manner as to :
>
> 1. lower the sacredness of marriage
> 2. suggest that illicit sexual relations are ordinary incidents of life and are not to be reprobated.
> 3. depict—rape, premeditated seduction, or criminal assaults on women; immoral traffic in women; soliciting, prostitution; procuration; illicit sexual relations; excessively passionate love scenes; indelicate sexual situations; scenes suggestive of immorality.
>
> D) exhibits the human form, actually or in shadowgraphs;
>
> 1. in a state of nudity; or
> 2. indecorously or suggestively clothed;
> 3. indecorous or sensuous posture

Sexual acts, nudity, rape, and prostitution are all banned as morally corrupting. Consequently, film producers who aim to have their films released and viewed by the largest number of people, must innovate to get around these rules. The challenge, therefore, is how to include 'adult' material in a film produced for general patronage. The challenge is met in rather creative ways, and primarily through the choreography, suggestive lyrics, costuming and erotic mis-en-scene of the song and dance sequences.

Censorship, especially in post-Independence India seemed to have inherited the residue of Victoria's England, reinforced by Islam's strong prohibitions concerning the public display of sexuality. Moreover, the excessive restrictions are directly related to resurgent post-independence Indian cultural awareness. Sexual expressiveness, and anatomical exposure are considered a Western export by the new nationalists (Barnouw & Krishnaswamy, 1980:53). The standards of modesty imposed were necessarily those of the burgeoning middle class who were educated in Christian missionary run schools as well as resistant to the sexual boldness that the west was perceived of as possessing. Official Indianness was equated with spirituality, refinement, sobriety. The West was sexually promiscuous, irreligious, outspoken and the youth, women, and masses of Indian people needed to be protected from these Western barbarisms (Chatterjee,1993:626, 630). 'We don't have sex, please, we're Indian' seems to be the message of the high-brow colonialists. But we do sing and dance! The FIA president Probhir Roy lamented that the filmi dances in the cultural show were "cheap entertainment . . . but necessary to attract a bigger crowd". Debates and discussions amongst the intellectual elite in India condemn the Hindi film as catering to the lowest common denominator of mass taste. Shamefacedly, the English-speaking, middle class apologize for its 'garishness', 'vulgarity', 'gaucheness', 'sentimentality', i.e., the excesses of the Hindi film melodrama-spectacle. Their standards of criticism are based on a Western film aesthetic that emphasizes plot linearity, realism, and a subdued acting style. (Thomas, May-Aug., 1985, pp. 118 to 119). Chidananda Das Gupta believes that the Hindi film acceptance is limited to the lower classes in India and abroad:

> [The Hindi film acceptance] is confined to pre-industrial, mainly agricultural societies that have thrown up large urban lumpens in the process of industrialization and urbanization, generating marginalized migrants to the cities whose adaptation to a technological society has yet to begin or is at its earliest stages. (1991:251)

Dasgupta is hopeful that this preoccupation with the Hindi cinema is "destined to disappear as the socio-economic scene is transformed into that of an industrially developed, socially and geographically mobile society." (1991:252). I wonder how Dasgupta would react to the Indian-American's love of Hindi films! I imagine he would be distraught, disgruntled that people in 'an industrially developed, socially and geographically mobile society' have appropriated a 'lumpen' cultural product as a way of expressing Indianness. Avanti Meduri, a proponent of

Bharat Natyam and a dance scholar quite eloquently describes her dis-
comfiture at how during a classical performance of Bharat Natyam in
Madras two young teenage girls measured the impact of a particularly
poignant moment by comparing it to a love scene in a film:

> "Shh. . .Shh . . . Look, that is how Amitabh looks at Rekha in the film
> *Silsila.*" (Amitabh and Rekha are the romantic pair of the silver
> screen). I was quite literally shattered. I looked around me and realized
> that I was the outcast, *the initiated spectator* who had neither value nor
> connection with the changing world. What possible future can there be
> for a classical art form that a new generation cannot relate to except in
> the *literal terms* of the movies? ([Italics mine], 1998:18)

In the aforementioned declarations, Meduri and Dasgupta betray
their class and caste snobbishness, somehow assuming that the Hindi
film is 'literal', occupying a low position in the evolution of art. As has
been discussed in the Deepavali chapter, part and parcel of the nationalistic project was to reform India, and redefine Indianness based on the criteria of European notions of what it means to be civilized, positivist,
rational, spiritual.

In more contemporary intellectual circles, there is much interest in
Hindi commercial cinema as a valuable area of study because of its prolific and widespread popularity and impact internationally. Mammoth
encyclopedic studies and discussions have been conducted in the past
decade by film historians and scholars such as Ashish Rajadhyaksha
(1994) and B.D. Garga (1996). The National Film Development Fund in
India seeks to fund and subtitle well-done popular films for international
audiences. A number of international film festivals have included a number of Hindi films. In 1997, the Asian Art Museum of San Francisco initiated a popular Hindi film series. In late 1998 to early 1999. The Asia
Society in New York pioneered a series entitled *Bombay Blockbusters:
Popular Hindi Cinema* to acknowledge the importance of this film industry and to educate American audiences about Hindi film aesthetics and
culture. In 1998, a twelve part documentary was broadcast on Business
Indian TV. Entitled *Power of the Image*, it analyzed various aspects of
popular Hindi cinema with interviews of stalwarts in the industry, as well
as thematic analysis by social science experts. Similar series have been
produced by Channel 4 in London.

As I discuss in this chapter, it is through the stylizations of the song
and dance sequences and its consequent reinterpretations on North

American/New York stage by middle-class Indians that a vernacular nationalism can be depicted.

GYRATING TO A NEW NATIONALIST TUNE

Let us return to our India Day cultural show in 1994 which occurred after the parade, at about five in the afternoon. One of the marvels of this cultural variety show was the performance of a young seven year-old girl whom I name Preeti[4] who catapulted to status of STAR. Not affiliated to any particular association, she was, in fact, "discovered" by Mr. Manhar Patel's son in a performance at a wedding reception, who then suggested her name to his father. She appeared right before the introduction of the guest stars and grand Marshall of the parade "filling in" until they arrived. She therefore, had the formidable task of holding the audience attention, assuaging our impatience at the delay. Not only did she hold our attention, she dazzled us.

Her depiction of the popular and controversial song "Choli ke peeche Kya Hai"—" [Guess] What is underneath my blouse"—is a conflation of sexuality, nationalism, rusticity, disguise, and talent. The song she danced to sparked considerable controversy in India because of its sexual innuendo and explicit earthy dance gestures that jar reserved middle-class erotic sensibilities. The censorship board wanted to stop release of the movie *Khalnayak* (Anti-Hero or Villain) of which the song is a part until it was edited out. After much negotiation between the producers and the censorship board, the song remained but in the meantime, the controversy and the audio release of the song alone were used as publicity hype before the release of the film. The movie was ultimately released with the song intact because the Central Bureau of Film Certification in India took the overall context of the song in the movie into consideration (*India Abroad*, August 27, 1993:31 & August 22, 1994:42).

The context of the dance in the film is that the heroine as a policewoman tries to lure the villain by masquerading as a prostitute. So you have the good, well-bred girl playing bad for the greater good. The prostitute or courtesan genre is prevalent in Hindi films with unforgettable examples like *Umrao Jaan, Pakeezah, Amar Prem, Mughal-E-Azam*, among others, where the heroine/courtesan has a heart of gold, i.e., the tart with a heart, even wholesome as she gives vent to her socially degenerate aspects in suggestive song and sensuous dance. The courtesan provides pleasure and entertainment to men through her talent, beauty and sexual expertise without the burden and tedium of matrimony and

domesticity. Sumita Chakravorty (1993) summarizes the significance of
the courtesan genre:

> Part of the motivation of filmakers [to evoke the female vision through
> the image of the prostitute] is no doubt to recapture the 'magic' of a de-
> ceased institution and a lost art (the poetry and classical song-and-
> dance traditions preserved by the courtesans over the centuries).
> Courtesans thus provide a sense of continuity with the past that is
> glamorous and erotic, even if laced with pathos. . . . She is a romanti-
> cized Other whose cultural contributions the dominant society has al-
> ready been acknowledged but whose sexuality remains outside its
> normative horizon. (pp. 304 to 305)

Choli ke peeche is a parody of prostitution and heterosexual seduction as the heroine slips in and out of her masquerade. Moreover, since
she is playing at being a prostitute in the line of duty of her police work,
her womanhood, and her reputation are at risk for her profession, for her
dharma. She becomes quite heroic in the process, not a victim to be
saved by a macho hero; rather, she *is* the macho hero. This is a welcome
departure from the male-centered films that inundate the industry. In
Khalnayak, the heroine, aided by a real prostitute is cued about the right
moves and encouraged to perform her role more convincingly. Since her
disguise is in the call of duty, this gives her license for seduction and display. The duality of her licentiousness and chastity, badness and goodness, debauchery and heroism, shimmer in the dance. It can and does
provide much pleasure.

The music, the costuming, and some of the choreography are mimicries of Rajasthani folk traditions, syncretized with Hindi film music
and dance aesthetics. According to Peter Manuel's research on cassette
music in India, Rajasthani folk music is popular amongst the youth because of its somewhat ribald and explicit lyrics (1993:183). The familiar,
and exotic simultaneously lure the audience. Although the dance is new
in that it was in a recently released film locating the audience experience
in the novelty of the present, it also harks back to a folk tradition that is
'timeless, untouched by modernization/Westernization'. Ironically, however, we know of the dance and the song because it was transmitted to us
through the modern technologies of cinema, video, audio cassette, and
cable TV. The song balances between timely and the timeless: The audience feels as if they are at once in modernity, in the present, and also experiencing an ancient heritage, an old tradition from the interiors of the

homeland. The majority of the audience at the India Day celebrations have seen this movie on their VCRs, on Indian cable television, or seen it sung or danced at other functions like wedding receptions, parties or at the very least, heard it on audio-cassette. In this age of mechanical-technical reproduction, the song has seen many incarnations in the bodies of performers in a variety of community shows. The song is redundantly present in our lives.

It cannot be ignored that the superstar Madhuri Dixit who performs this dance is a gorgeous and extremely talented performer and financially successful to boot. She has appeared in a number of films playing roles that run the gamut of emotions, character types, costumes and disguises. In her other dances, she is able to look luscious without being vulgar, in-love and refined, expressive, wholesome, and sometimes even wacky. In this dance she has added an edge of crassness in the broadness of her movements, in the volubility of her facial expressions, in the forceful gyrations of her hips and pelvic thrusts. She expertly exaggerates the stereotypical earthiness associated with the prostitute. But we know it is only an act because in the course of the dance she expresses fear and confusion to her cohorts and to us, unseen by the villain, when he gets sexually aroused by her dance and asks her to come join him. She is able to show that as Madhuri, the actress, and as the law enforcer in the film's narrative, she is separate from the role of prostitute—she is *not* the prostitute. Nevertheless, the dance's upbeat rhythm, suggestive lyrics, and teasing gestures impress upon the audience a forbidden, delectable sexuality enrobed in a 'filmi' imitation of the Rajasthani folk dance and the respectability of the law enforcer gone undercover.

What happens to this blatantly erotic dance when a young girl of seven, whose sexuality is still ambiguous, or at least unrealized performs it for Indian Independence Day? Interestingly enough much of the sexuality remains intact in the gyration of her hips, her flirtatious facial expressions, in the sheer self-control of her body in performance. Her reinterpretation of the dance is not superficial mimicry, her mastery of the spirit of the dance is seen in the choreography, stage presence, eye contact with the audience, in her embodiment of the dance. To accommodate the demands of the stage and her milieu and shaped by the demands of middle class morality, her costume is made more modest—whereas, the actress in the film revealed her fleshy midriff, navel, and curvaceous waist, Preeti wore a blouse that covered her whole torso. Her modest costume underscores the immodesty of showing too much flesh even in so young a body. Though the audience do remember the sexy costume of the movie star, Preeti is not yet one. The context within which she performs is different from that of the movie. Preeti is still the child of middle class parents, and must therefore conform to that mold. In the instrumental portions of the dance she has innovated what looks like Bharat Natyam steps to fill the gaps left by the absent chorus. Whereas in the movie, the camera can focus on the actress' s facial expressions, the scene and scenery, or the other actors, on a live stage, all eyes are fixed on the performer. Thus the film dance is translated for a live audience in New York City.

Removed from the narrative context of the film, the song on this stage takes on another story. The audience is endeared by the child mimicking and altering the dance of an adult Indian woman, who is a superstar playing the role of a policewoman disguised as a prostitute. Overlaid on Preeti's somewhat innocent and therefore unavailable body is the not-so-innocent text of the song, the sexy choreography, the narratives of the film, seduction, disguise, and, most importantly, the child's destiny into Indianness. This destiny into Indianness is related to her growing up into an Indian woman, a child-bearer of more Indians. As the child moves, what shimmers in this free space of performance is the fact of her being a child now and the potentiality of her adult womanhood in the future, the fact of her being child now and a child-bearer in the future. Contained in her tiny dancing body is what Susan Stewart (1993) calls the "future-past" of Indian culture. As the emcee of the show proclaimed in admiration of Preeti's charming performance "She is only seven now and look how beautiful she already is, what more when she is seventeen!!". 'Watch out for her, you young Indian studs out there' seems to be his subtext. The girl-child in this dance is not only a future child-bearer, she is also already erotic, a source of delight and pleasure.

As a miniature of Indian culture—she is portable, she can be held, she can be had by the spectators by the sheer act of looking. Moreover, what the audience can have with this "optical tactility" is the glamour of Madhuri Dixit, the superstar. They recall Madhuri's performance in the fantasy that is the Hindi film as they watch the child. It is likewise for the little girl. Through her mimicry and alteration of the dance there is a "palpable, sensuous connection between (Preeti's own) body and the perceived (and remembered body of Madhuri)" (Taussig, 1993). In dancing *Choli ke Peeche*, audience and performer acquire the glamour and talent of the Hindi film, its star, its multi-layered narratives, and a vernacular Indianness.

What is interesting is that when Preeti is asked who taught her the dance, she proudly, and to some extent rightfully claims that "I did it *myself*'. No other human body taught her the dance. Preeti herself put in the tape, watched it, re-wound it and imitated some of the steps, innovated others. It is her relationship with the domestic technology of the VCR, her initiative in accessing the dance, and her personal discipline that have facilitated her learning of the dance, her learning of Indianness. Her mother explains the meaning of the lyrics since Preeti, born in the United States, is not conversant with Hindi. Preeti having seen dances on video, on the screen and on the New York stage, takes bits and pieces of gestures and choreographies she has seen to complete her dance.

According to her mother, Rakhee, she would like Preeti to take Bharat Natyam or Kathak lessons since she recognizes that her daughter is gifted. This is a typical practice amongst middle class immigrant families in the U.S. Corroborated by my own research of Indian immigrant children in the San Francisco Bay Area (1989), as well as by Ilana Abramovitch's fieldwork on Indian residents of Flushing, Queens (and many others like Lobel 1996, Henson, 1994), Indian classical dance classes initiate Indian children into "lessons [of Indian] culture and grace . . . [a] marking of Indian identity" (Abramovitch, 1987:21) in a respectable way. However, when Preeti chooses to use the 'high culture' Bharata Natyam steps to merely fill in the gaps of a 'low culture' filmi dance rather, in her innocence of class differences between these aesthetically diverse genres, she is repudiating the official discourse on what is 'respectable'. Without having to depend on the precarious socio-political structure of the *guru shishya* tandem, the little one independently creates her own version of the filmi dance.

It is most convenient that these videotapes and audio-cassettes saturate the home life of Indians. Unlike Bharata Natyam and other Indian classical dances, the choreography of the film dance is easy to imitate, not requiring years and years and lots of money to learn. Preeti's guru is the dancing film actress who is accessible via video technology rather than some high-flown and expensive master of Indian classical dance. Much like the arduous rounds of repetitious movement lessons in classical dance, the Indian child, in the comfort and safety of her home can , in about four or five days, with some practice and attention, by rewinding the video-cassette again and again and again while imitating the choreography embody the dance and by extension the culture. According to Rakhee, Preeti choreographed a dance while they were en route to Atlantic City's Taj Mahal casino where she was to perform. She heard the song all throughout the three hour car journey with Rakhee explaining the words in English. Her number was sixth in the program, giving her about 45 minutes, ample time, to observe the other dancers and their choreographies, retrieve steps from her memory, incorporate these gestures into her own interpretation of the dance, and practice backstage.

From what I witnessed of the video recording of this dance, Preeti performed excellently. Because of the film dance's accessibility, Preeti can appear almost every other week in a community performance, wedding reception, or any other such show. Her mother rather unconvincingly lamented that she needed to control Preeti's performances so that she can concentrate on school, though according to her grades and her teachers, she is doing very well academically. Performing thus, is a cheaper and more democratic way of learning culture. She can perform this artifact of culture during Independence day without the burden of classist and classical bias[5], without having to wait for a guru to authorize her debut. Preeti becomes the author , as well as authority of her dance, her talent, her expression of Indianness. Preeti, thus celebrates India Day by saluting her own independence and practicing a democratic aesthetic.

This independence and authority transferred onto and celebrated by the performer is corroborated by Kiren Ghei's research on teenage dancers in Los Angeles. I summarize an interview she conducted with one of her subjects:

> When you have a dance class, there's a planned dance practice, there's a planned time, date, . . . the teacher's there to say this is how you do it, and that is how you're going to do it. But here [on your own], you've got to say, well I'll just do it after I finish my homework or whatever. You sit there and go, I'll do it , turn on the tape and you do it on your *own* . . . where in the class, you sit there and wait for the teacher to tell you, well 'we're going to do this dance this time, and *this* is how we're going to do it'...there's no one to tell you 'practice your dance', you've got to do it on your *own*. (Ghei, 1988:7)

Using Michael Taussig's definition of the mimetic faculty as the "nature that culture uses to create second nature" (1993:233), I can say that the child's self- taught mimicry of the dance naturalizes her talent, naturalizes her Indianness. Her ability, her talent to copy well, to perform the dance with such confidence and self-sufficiency persuades us, comforts us that Indianness is indeed, second-nature. As our miniature star

Figure 4.1. Pretty Preeti flaunting her infantile citizenship through Hindi film dance

sparkles on stage, we are reassured that Indian culture is intact, that it is alive and well in the body of our children and will continue, even on Madison Avenue, New York City, United States of America.

Preeti, being born here in the United States, in this generation, appreciates the occasion of Indian Independence in a very different way than do her parents or the show's organizers. Her elders remember the independence struggle, or at least, are products of the post-colonial Indian nation-state. Their lived experience of Indian nationalism can be narrated to Preeti in the form of stories so that what Preeti knows of India or Indianness, includes not only what she sees on video in her suburban home in New Jersey, U.S.A, and what she dances on stage in New York City but what she has been told by her elders as well. The vivid portrayal of dancing superstars, romance and sexuality are fodder for her allegiance to India and for her understanding of what it means to be Indian. She therefore, expresses her 'infantile citizenship' to India in her reinterpretation of an ahistoric, media-produced and reproduced, popular Hindi film dance (Berlant, 1993). To her the Hindi film song and dance is as nation-alistic as the poetry of Tagore, the chant of *Vande Mataram* or, even singing the national anthem solemnly. It is equivalent to shouting out '*Jai Hind! Jai Hind! Jai Hind!* which she does after her dance. The crowd re-sponded likewise with much exuberance, and understanding!

The insistence of the emcee that the talent is somehow passed down to the child because her mother dances may hold some logic. For indeed, if mom notices her daughter performing and performing well, she will encourage her by providing her daughter the tape, VCR, costume, trans-portation to and from performance sites, i.e., the socio-cultural-eco-nomic milieu to dance. After all, her daughter is fulfilling and continuing the genealogical line—a matrilineal one at that—of talent. Her daughter dancing may even be the vicarious fulfillment of her own personal aspi-rations to perform, aspirations which may have been curtailed by the obligations of marriage and family life. Indeed, it would be immodest for Rakhee to perform *Choli ke Peeche* precisely because the sexual explicit-ness of the dance would glaringly exhibit her sexually realized adult body. The thrill of sexual potential is made flaccid by its fulfillment.

.   .   .

> In a wedding reception I had attended in 1995, I was asked to perform a dance. While I was figuring out which song to dance to, one of my dear woman friends firmly told me that I was not to dance to *Choli ke Peeche* under any circumstances. She reasoned that it would be too much for a grown woman like me, who is still looking for a husband to dance to such a song, in front of all these strangers. It would not look good. People would think I was loose. Nevertheless, the song came on as it is standard music to dance on. My other married friends, my girl-friend and I all danced to it, enjoying its rhythms, and flirtatiousness. My friends formed circle around me, allowing me to perform the dance for them, veiling me from the malicious gaze of people who didn't know me, who may have misunderstood me.

.   .   .

The thrill of sexual potential is made flaccid by its fulfillment. Better that her daughter Preeti, in her chronological innocence mimic the adult ges-tures of the dance. Preeti's pure and young body is comparable, allegori-cal to the idea of India being pure, young (Berlant, 1993), and virginal-

the newly carved out 'infant' nation untainted by the lusts of Westernization, bureaucratic inefficiency, governmental graft and corruption, im-
balanced global politics and economics, communal violence, to name
just a few of its post-colonial troubles. A young child dancing a Hindi
film song on independence day is a tale-telling of Utopia. Of course the
Indian paradise is not devoid of eroticism.

DREAMS CAN COME TRUE

The fortune of being away from India is underscored by the fact that the
movie stars and celebrities feel privileged to make an appearance
amongst Indians outside India. The film actress Meenakshi Seshadri,
who was 1993's grand marshal in the parade fulfilled her promise to return in 1994. Meenakshi is not only glamorous, successful, and beautiful, she also keeps her word. After Preeti's dance, she attempted to share
her mystical philosophy of true independence by explaining that "Liberation is not just for a country or a people. True liberation is, even while
you are still human, you are liberated from being human". Indeed, as a
movie star, she is already much, much larger than life. By virtue of her
profession, economic status, and social position she can be liberated
from the trials and travails of being merely an ordinary human being. The
audience presence in the United States, in the metropolis par excellence
of New York City, experience her three-dimensionality. The celluloid
goddess is present, in the flesh, rapping about how happy she is to be
loved by all.

The phantasm of the movie star bleeds into the reality of the audience. Her live presence somehow cuts her down to familial and familiar
size. Meenakshi is both giant and life-size. Giant-size because she is
screen idol, life-size because she is in our presence, in our life. She is our
big sister from Bombay who has come to visit. Audience and star have
forged a relationship, which in turn seems to promise to Indians here that
they, too, by virtue of this bond are extraordinary, liberated from being
merely a human trifle. Indians across socio-economic classes in New
York are more apt to see, take darshan, i.e., be blessed by exchanging
glances with a divinity, of these mythic beings here than they would in
India. Hindi Film stars are more apt to give live performances in North
America than in India. This reassures the diasporic Indian that we are indeed privileged over our siblings who have been left behind. The fantasy
of America being the land of opportunity coalesces with the film star
come alive, in the flesh from our dream-world of the Hindi film. It

reassures us who are here that America is truly a place where our dreams come true, albeit the dream is produced and directed in India. Moreover, we are also reassured that we have not been forgotten by these exceptional Indians who come to visit us. The stars in turn are assured a transnational audience.

An even more personal relationship is forged between the 1994 parade's grand marshal Miss Universe, Sushmita Sen and the audience, who made an appearance after Menakshi. Strictly speaking she is not a Hindi film star as yet, though she has expressed ambitions to be one after her reign but she shares the same mythic status as a film star, may be even more so because her fame is international (nay, universal- cosmological). "Does anyone want to know anything about me?", she asks, assuring the audience that she will answer every personal question. The fissure between glamour and reality, image and object, is sutured in her intimate proclamation "I just love all of you!", both in English and in Hindi, (reinforcing Meenakshi's insistence that we are all special earlier). Though the proclamations are unrealistic, corny and sentimental their subtext hints at these celebrities' availability to everybody—class, caste, religion no bar, if even for just this half hour, even for just this flash. The result is subjectivity and democracy. With the physical presence of these imports from the homeland, the nostalgia for that imagined place represented by these mythic beings turned real is healed. In these celebrities' presence here, in their evocation of solidarity with the populace, India is here in America. Both star and audience are transformed in their meeting. Ah! Only in America!!

The narrative of cultural genealogy is most poignant when celebrities and the local talent all dance together to another popular Hindi film song towards the end of the show. Three other young girls (Preeti included), and these two young women Sushmita and Meenakshi form a sorority as they all improvise, and interact with each other, displaying and celebrating the libidinal potential and sensual actuality of their bodies in dance. As the young girls, who are part of our ordinary milieu, dance at par, touch and embrace these mythic ideals, mythic idols, we are reminded of, made to believe in the girl-child's potential to grow up into one of these beautiful embodiments of Indian womanhood. Indian culture flourishes as the child grows, as the culture *becomes* her, as she evolves into a Meenakshi or Sushmita. As adult women, these young Indian girls have the vital capacity to produce more Indians, assuring that the culture will prevail in the bodies of their children, no matter that they are growing up in the United States or living in India. Indianness is literally reproducible from the wombs of these Indian females:

Figure 4.2. A complicit sorority of celebrity and womanhood.

The womb [is] the mimetic organ par excellence, mysteriously under-
scoring in the submerged and constant body of the [woman] the dual
meaning of reproduction as birthing and reproduction as replication.
(Taussig, 1993:35)

Needless to say the lyrics of the song, the hip and pelvic gyrations of
the dance, the familiarity shared between audience with the performers,
reiterate the girl-child's heterosexist fate of marriage and consequently
that of biological family. It is not surprising that the song these women
danced to is a song about a young girl lured by the romance of marriage,
popularized by no less than, yes, Madhuri Dixit. The production of Indian culture becomes conflated with the reproduction of Indian children.
As long as one's heart (that is under her blouse!) beats to the pulse of
Hindi film music, Indianness transcends geographic limits. This born
again patriotism as described by Arjun Appadurai (1993) is *transnational*, transported by the very long multiple arms of electronic media,
travel and communication. Like Krishna's multiple presences in the

Raslila, India/Indianness appears simultaneously everywhere there are Indians celebrating Indianness.

BAD INDIANS

Amidst the din of the heterosexual fervor manifested in the Hindi film songs and dances, yet another sororal performance of a different sort occurs simultaneously, on a different stage. Voices proclaim the underside of the ideal of the heterosexual Indian family. In the 1994 parade the South Asian Lesbian and Gay Alliance (SALGA) were not allowed to march because, according to the FIA President Probhir Roy, having such a group in such a parade is "out of place". SALGA was considered a misfit, because they placed their gay rights agenda over and above the celebration of India's Independence. In the 1994 parade, Roy had requested them to carry posters that saluted Indian democracy which they apparently refused, arguing that their organization also catered to non-Indian homosexuals of the South Asian subcontinent. Also, they did not apply to join the parade on time. SALGA's bureaucratic laxity provided a good excuse for Roy's and the FIA board's homophobia[6]. To rectify their exclusion, SAKHI, an all-woman advocacy group against domestic violence, invited SALGA to march with them. This act was considered disrespectful and anarchic by the FIA. Roy likened it to bringing along an uninvited guest to a party without informing the host. To me, SAKHI's inclusion of SALGA expands the concept of the Indian family to include into its fold all other expressions of identity whether it is mainstream, alternative, populist, or official. SALGA and SAKHI had a demonstration while the performance on the mainstage was going on to protest the violence of exclusion performed on SALGA by the FIA. Indeed, underneath SAKHI's blouse beats a heart that embraces the recalcitrant, the different, the abused, the out-of-place[7]. Roy's 'party' became even more colorful with the arrival of these bohemian guests.

The attempt of the officials of FIA to exclude the SALGA, is their adherence to what Anannya Bhattacharjee (1992) describes as the bourgeois "habit of ex-nomination". Originally coined by Roland Barthes (1988), the practice of the habit of ex-nomination by the bourgeois is based on the propagation of the myth of a single universal human nature. Its universalism is so pervasive, assumed and taken for granted that it need not be named or marked, it is natural, it is in place:

> All that is not bourgeois is obliged to borrow from the bourgeois.
> Bourgeois ideology can therefore spread over everything and in so

doing lose its name without risk: no one here will throw this name of bourgeois back at it. It can without resistance subsume bourgeois Theatre, art and humanity under their eternal analogues; in a word, it can ex-nominate itself without restraint when there is only one single human nature left; the defection from the name 'bourgeois' is here complete . . . Bourgeois norms are experienced as the evident laws of a natural order (Barthes, 1988:139, 140).

Thus the bourgeois FIA does not want the Indian community to be marked as even more different in the mosaic of the NYC multicultural society by being problematic, "imperfect", i.e., unnatural. By allowing groups like SALGA to march, we admit to the host country, and other minority communities that we are not a model minority, are not free from abuse, racism, disease, and god-forbid! alternative sexualities. SALGA ruptures the bourgeois norm of the heterosexual family, and that is what the FIA is ashamed of. SALGA thwarts the notion that Indianness necessarily includes the production of Indian children, the reproduction of pure and innocent Indianness, unsullied by late twentieth century social and gender identity realities. SAKHI sought to break this habit by including the not-so-innocent SALGA.

In the 1994 celebration, snubbing the group that announced its alternative libidinal potential did not discount it, hide it, or extinguish it. SALGA, in fact, was mounted on a valorized stage of controversy with SAKHI as stage manager. As the debate continues, more and more members of the community will begin to know that they can be Indian and alternative, and mainstream, and populist, homosexual, and unfortunately, a battered woman, too. All this hullabaloo added up to publicity, good or bad depending on your point of view. Roy lamented that the 'American' press—the *New York Times* (Aug. 22, 1994:B2) paid much more attention to the exclusion of SALGA than to the fact that the parade included representatives from the varied regional and sectarian Indian communities. Roy's point is well-taken. It is an achievement well worth noting that in the same parade, in the same 'party', in the same 'family', Muslims, Christians and Hindus could celebrate their Indianness together. But it is still a sad fact, that the famed 'Indian tolerance' did not operate in relation to alternative sexualities![8]

It is not surprising that SAKHI welcomed SALGA's marching with them. As an advocacy group defending the rights of women in the South Asian community, their activist agenda embraces other oppressed and abused groups. Though the FIA considered both groups unacceptable because of their 'undisciplined' guerrilla (read non-bourgeois) methods of interacting with the FIA, Roy admits that SAKHI does good work for the community in helping out battered women.

The ambivalence towards SAKHI has been astutely discussed by Caitrin Lynch (1994). SAKHI appears as a threat to the bourgeois community because SAKHI locates the cause of domestic violence in the out-dated values of a traditional patriarchal South Asian culture. Therefore, says SAKHI, the culture needs to be changed. To Indians in the diaspora, faced with too many changes and dislocations already, this is a threat to an Indianness which has been romanticized as perfect, an Indianness that can give much comfort to the displaced immigrant. The change SAKHI advocates is to take place within the family where the women as wives, mothers, and child-bearers enact traditional roles. Moreover, SAKHI is perceived as primarily comprised of young, unmarried women (though there are many married members), who criticize, question and expose the lie of heterosexual marital bliss. Thus, to Roy and his associates, and to some members of mainstream Indian community, SAKHI appears to be "home wreckers", "man-haters", and even lesbians, all felt to be anti-Indian.

What does the *Choli ke Peeche* dance, film stars and the dancing girls and the exclusion/inclusion of SALGA/SAKHI have in common? Besides their saturation in two varieties of sexual politics, each in their own ways rebuke and refute the official rhetoric of the ideal Indian woman. The kind of Indian womanhood that is imported in the persons of Meenakshi, and Sushmita, that is performed in the dances by the young girls, that is enacted by the SAKHI joined by SALGA is a lively, upbeat, assertive, and libidinal one. This Indian woman seems very unlike the woman redefined in the nationalist project of post-independence India as elaborated by Partha Chatterjee (1993) in his analysis of the role of women in the Indian independence movement:

> The home was the principal site for expressing the spiritual qualities of the national culture, and women must take responsibility for protecting this quality. No matter what the changes in the external conditions of life for women, they must not lose their essentially spiritual (that is, feminine) virtues . . . [such as] chastity, self-sacrifice, submission, devotion, kindness, patience, the labors of love . . . orderliness, thrift, cleanliness, a personal sense of responsibility, the practical skills of literacy, accounting, hygiene, and the ability to run the household. (126, 129-130)

The nationalistic Indian woman of post-independence India was posited as a goddess or as a mother which "served to erase her sexuality in the world outside the home" (131).

This reminds me of the figures of Sita interpreted as passive and victimized, and the mute and benign Mother India represented in one of the largest floats in the 1994 India Day parade earlier. This float belonged to the Overseas Friends of the Bharatiya Janata Party (BJP). There were at least a hundred people in this contingent—a reflection of the unprecedented support the Hindu fundamentalist opposition party BJP has in this country, as well as it is the ruling power in India currently. The float costs at least $2,000.00., an amount that this group could easily come up with but that groups like SALGA and SAKHI can not set aside for this cause as they have other priorities. The BJP float included a tableaux from the Ramayana showing Ram, Sita and Laxman, and Hanuman triumphant over Ravana of Lanka. Raised on a dais in front of a map of pre-Moghul India was Mother India, invoking the image of India as Sita being saved by Ram from Ravana. Only now, the enemy of Hindu India/Mother India-Sita are the Muslims. According to the BJP version of Indian history which is based on the colonial version, the Indian subcontinent, comprised of a Hindu majority, has been continually subjugated by foreigners—Muslims and British. The Aryans coming into India is not an invasion. They are in fact the Hindu civilizing factor. According to the BJP rhetoric, these "foreign" Indian Muslims, are 'most welcome' to stay in a Hindu India. And as foreign guests, they must accede to the rules of their hosts, otherwise they can go live in the Muslim homestead of Pakistan. Indeed, in the mind-set of the BJP, the problems of Mother India have been exacerbated by the 'primitive' practices of Muslims. For example, a Muslim man having multiple wives who have many children, increase India's population, depleting her resources. As avid meat-eaters, the ecological balance of animal population is tipped by the Muslims' slaughter. In the area of economics, there are too many privileges bestowed on (poor) Muslims, leaving qualified Hindus unemployed. Too, historically, the Islamic Moghul emperors converted hoards of Hindus through threats, tortures and other such violences. As guests in the Hindu Indian subcontinent, the Muslims have been misbehaving, if you will[9].

The partitioning of the Subcontinent into secular India and Islamic Pakistan as separate nation-states, provides fuel to the rage that BJP foments among Hindu Indians against what they perceive to be the invasive and divisive Muslim forces (Banerjee, 1991). The BJP plays the communal card by advocating, quite ironically, a state based on sectarian affiliation much like that of Pakistan, conflating very dangerously Indianness with Hinduness. As Gerard Larson predicts in his analysis of the role of religion in India's history and current political situation:

> It is possible to detect in the BJP and its programs a political style and strident rhetoric not unlike a variety of Islamic protest movements in South Asia and the Middle East. . . . One has the sense that if the people of India elect a BJP government at the Centre, it could well be the case that [India] will begin to look more like a Neo-Hindu version of the Islamic republic of Pakistan or the Islamic Republic of Iran. (1995:287)

However, the Hinduism that is propagated by the BJP, is a version which does not take into account varieties of Hindu sects such as Shakti cults (goddess- worship), Shaivite Hinduism (Shiva), and other hybrid forms of Sufi/Bhakti/Sikh (Islamic/Hindu devotional) denominations which are alive and thriving in India, as well as in the Diaspora. Their tableaux in the parade was a blatant conflation of a certain kind of Northern Hindu monotheism (Ram as the One True God) with a non-secular nationalism. It depicted the triumph of Hindutva (a Hindu State) rather than of India, the triumph of an ahistoric, monocultural political formulation over the reality of a multi-ethnic, multi-religious, intercultural, even syncretic federation. These characters were played by young adolescents with the most solemn expressions on their faces. They seemed to carry the weight of their fundamentalist, and communal mission with a seriousness and stillness unbefitting youth. It was quite frightening.

NATIONALIST MACHISMO

What was equally frightening is the bloodletting that occurred in the 1993 parade. A Sikh man named Gurmukh Singh was shot by Pakistani Ashraf Muhammad during India Day because of an argument. There are three versions to the story as reported in the press: The first is that Muhammad and his cohorts had come to the India day celebrations waving a Pakistani flag and hurling obscenities at Indians who passed by. Singh was waving an Indian flag which was then grabbed by Muhammad and stomped on. A fist-fight ensued and Singh was shot and severely wounded. Recuperating in his hospital bed, Singh proudly proclaims that "As an Indian, I defended the flag and if I have to do it again, I will" (India Abroad [IA], Aug. 20, 1993:40). Another version involves Singh

Figure 4.3. A young Hanuman devotedly protects Mother India/Sitamata on an Overseas Friends of BJP float

being asked to intervene at the request of a 15-year-old boy, who said his sister had been insulted. After a heated exchange with Muhammad, Singh was shot. (IA, Aug.27, 1993:34). The third version puts Muhammad on the defensive, and has been largely ignored. He claims that he was approached by Indians and beaten; he then shot someone in self-defense. (IA, July 22:40). Muhammad faces a 5 to 15 year prison sentence for assault (IA, Jan. 14, 1994).

What seems to scream out from these stories is the violence that results from the kind of macho and virulent nationalistic fervor expressed by Singh and Mohammad. Though both are South Asians, the historical circumstances that brought about the split of India and Pakistan feeds the fury of a divided and politically competitive subcontinent. The scuffle reenacts on India Day in New York City, the anxiety and frustration over the unrealized project of a united India.

The Pakistani Muslim appearing on India Day "represents a fundamental anxiety of nationalism itself: of the nation as something not achieved. And as such every Muslim becomes, at a certain level, the symbol of national frustration and insecurity." (Devji, 1992, pp. 1–2). It is not surprising, then, that the former BJP president, Murli Manohar Joshi and the 1994 president of the Overseas friends of the BJP, Dr. Mukund Mody both visited Singh at St. Vincent's Hospital, wishing "him a speedy recovery" (IA, Aug. 27, 1993:34). This is the kind of event that fans communalist fires against those invasive and divisive (and disruptive) Pakistani Muslims, as interpreted by the BJP rhetoric against Indian Muslims who may have questionable allegiances to Islamic Pakistan rather than to Hindu India. This kind of event is a trump in the BJP's communal card game.

What's more, according to at least one version of the story, Singh had 'heroically' defended the 'honor' of an Indian girl, as well as the Indian flag against the crudity of a Muslim man and his Muslim cohorts. This is a very reassuring gesture for the BJP to celebrate the protection of some of the most important symbols of Indianness. Furthermore, it is important to note that Singh is a Sikh, not a Hindu. His relationship to India is potentially contentious since there is large contingent of Sikhs who yearn for a separate state named Khalistan, even if Singh himself is not pro-Khalistan. His 'gallant gesture' to fight for the Indian flag/Indian girl, not only once but 'again' if necessary, aligns his loyalties to the Indian nation-state. As one community leader proclaimed "True to his *Sikh* valor, the patriotic youth put his life on the line to protect the honor of *Indian* women" [italics mine](*News India*, Aug. 20, 1993:1) It is not clear whether the girl was Hindu or Sikh. It is important that she is described as *Indian* and *not* Sikh.

Singh is a potential ally of Hindutva where he will always be a minority, by virtue of his religion. Surely, Singh performed his allegiance to an India as he understands it, the India that was fought for by Gandhi, Nehru, and an army made up of a Sikh majority. Gurmukh Singh was reenacting the struggle of Indian Independence at the India Day parade in New York City. The main difference is that the British are physically absent, though India is still stuck in a post-colonial quagmire. The present-day enemy is Pakistani/Muslim. Singh is a pawn in the official rhetoric of present day Indo-Pakistani politics. In the rhetoric of the BJP, the shooting is a re-articulation of the Sita/Ravana story. The demon-king Ravana is played by the Pakistani-Muslim Mohammad, Sita is the Indian girl garbed in the Indian flag abducted by Ravana, and Singh, is the devoted Hanuman, who saves Sita. Hanuman is the extension of Rama's machismo. Recall at this point the young girls dancing with the flags in their march down Madison Avenue, and the three colors blazing proudly atop the Empire State Building. These images complete the scenario of a virile, violent Hanuman played by the India-loving Sikh Singh rescuing the Indian Hindu Sita/Mother India/Indian Womanhood. The price Singh pays for this macho heroism is bloodshed, "two bullets lodged in his back and jaw, and unemployment. He is lucky to be alive". (IA, Aug. 20, 1993:40)

A NEW INDIANNESS

In contrast to the BJP Hindutva tableaux, and to the Singh-Muhammad drama, what we have in the performance of these dancing movie stars, star-struck girls and activist SAKHI women is a dynamic expression of pleasure, talent, initiative, uninhibitedness, beauty, articulateness, success, wealth, confidence, and political assertiveness. Whereas Sita is swallowed up by the earth (after being banished by her husband, the good God-king Rama to quell even a rumor of infidelity)[10], these worldly women, these earth-bound women are in control of their environment, bodies, and the audience, and advocate this message to the public at large. Even though these performers may appear larger than life (liberated from being merely human, remember) they are nevertheless very alive in our lives, in the present, in our presence. Sita and her ilk seem to be quite distant, quite dead in contrast. Dancing to film music, which is upbeat, libidinal, and on occasion jarring to middle-class sensibilities, thankfully, subverts the official rhetoric as propounded by the patriarchal narratives of Sita, and the artificial and asexual construction of Mother India, and the apathy of the life-denying spiritual/nationalistic woman.

The dancing body performs the earthy pleasures of being in a community, of being Indian. Actively defying the official edict of the FIA by SAKHI, emphasizes a true sororal spirit, against oppression, even on the domestic front by facilitating the SALGA narrative of homosexuality and homophobia to be told. The Indian woman within this space of vernacular nationalism outside India is active and deliciously loud.

This indeed is a very different kind of nationalism. Through the mimesis and alterity of the popular form of the Hindi film dance spectacle, the heavy handed and closed fist of official nationalism is pried open into a wave of effusive greeting by the movie star and beauty queen, and into the playful hand gestures or *mudras* of the young girls in their dance. Gun shots are substituted by a lilting drum beat. Hindi films are distributed throughout the Indian diaspora. Through this agency, a special kind of Indian culture is learned and performed. From the enthusiastic response to film dance, film stars, and the construction of community in New York during and by means of the Indian Independence day program, I would concur with Amitav Ghosh's contention that the relationship between India and

Indians in diaspora "[is not based on] language, religion, politics or economics . . . [but] this relationship is so much a relationship of the imagination" (1990). Ghosh goes on to say that the specialists of the imagination
are writers, I say that the specialists par excellence are the spectacular and
phantasmagoric, ever-reproducible Hindi Film songs and dances .

The purposefulness and wisdom to show a united front, non-West-
ernized front to the American mainstream has been discussed in the preceding chapter. But those who define what is traditional also define what
kinds of histories, narratives, and ideologies fortify the Indian culture.
Usually these decisions are made based on the agendas of political parties. The immobile sullenness on the faces of the young adolescents on
the BJP float strongly show the deadening and reification of Indian culture. The Singh-Muhammad drama alarms us with the violence and
human waste brought about by official nationalist propaganda. Homosexuality, feminism, and other variations of sexual politics are perceived
as Western interventions, as Western corruptions. Feminist or gay activists are marked as anti-Indian by official culture. But there needs to be
room cleared for a dynamic, contemporary Indianness, and, indeed, the
vernacular, unofficial response to the call for participation on India Day
was a performance of what is most pleasurable, what bespeaks the needs
and values of certain hitherto suppressed segments of the community.
Just as Hindi film dance subverts the overly refined, Sanskritized classical dance, SAKHI, SALGA and other such groups subvert the heterosexist ideology, challenges reproductive sexuality, exposes domestic
violence. India could after all also be a 'queer nation', she could also be
Mother India in tri-color drag gyrating his/her hips to a ribald Hindi film
song! In Anannya Bhattacharjee's words:

> Indianness is not a natural excretion of a genealogical tree, but a con-
> tinual struggle along multiple modes through a negotiation of the in-
> escapable tension between secure definitions and a consciousness of
> the oppressions that such definitions rest upon. (1992:41)

MY PLACE IN THE SUN

Taking my cue from Bhattacharjee, I want to find my place in this milieu,
despite tears and fears. Having come with a video camera to the India
Day celebration, I carried a certain legitimacy as a recorder of culture, a
visual historian if you will. I was allowed a place in the front of the stage
to document the show. Guided by the stage managers to a position where
I could get a relatively good view of the stage (I did not need a press pass

as such), I was able to tape footage of Preeti's dance and look at the celebrities up close. Participants eagerly agreed to have themselves videographed. Members of the public did not seem to mind my panning the video camera. Some asked me why I was doing this, not suspiciously, but out of curiosity and maybe even just to make conversation. I told them I was doing a paper for NYU. They were pleased that I was doing something for 'Indian culture' and agreed to pose for me. They played at being movie stars for my camera. They seemed to think I was doing a favor for Indianness, reproducing Indianness for others to see, learn from, enjoy. Does this mean that there is a place for a single Indian woman from the Philippines in the community, after all? I have to chisel that niche out though—by means of my intellect, my scholarly enterprise, my voyeuristic video camera, I can participate. Clearly, I align myself to the left-off-center groups like SAKHI and SALGA. These groups have a larger ethnic sweep than just Indian. They are more Desi, inclusive of all other South Asians and the attendant issue-driven agenda that they seek to accomplish. I have, in fact, acted in an educational video for SAKHI entitled quite appropriately "A Life Without Fear" in 1993. I played the role of the SAKHI advocate who persuades a battered woman to seek help. In 1995, I also acted as moderator of a televised discussion among the groups who were excluded from the parade, and are thereby marginalized. An abridged version of this chapter appeared in the *Little India* magazine in November of 1995. Preeti's dance, Choli Ke Peeche, and aspects of this book have been reconstituted in various versions and genres, as articles, poetry, panel discussions. Since then, I have been engaged as artist, cultural worker, scholar in the South Asian community in NYC. I am fulfilling my destiny into Indianness—reproducing Indianness in my own ways, I guess. On India day of 1994, I celebrated the success of my masquerade, my own playing at Indianness by singing that popular Hindi film ditty along with the crowd.

> *Choli ke neeche kya hai?*
> *Choli me dil hai mera!*
> *Dil mai dungi pyar ko! Yar ko!*
> (Guess) What is underneath my blouse?
> Underneath my blouse is my . . .
> my heart!
> My heart I give to my lover,
> to my friend.
> (Laxmikant & Pyarelal,
> and Bakshi, 1993)

NOTES

¹ A shorter version of this chapter appears as an essay in the book *A Patchwork Shawl: Chronicles of South Asian Women in America* edited by Shamita Das Dasgupta, Rutgers University Press, 1998.

² the Hindi word for spice.

³ recent examples of hit masala films available in video cassette from any Indian store in NYC are *Hum Apke Hai Kaun* (Who Am I to You?) or *Dilwale Dulhaniya Lai Jayenge* (The One Who Loves Takes the Bride) or *Dil to Pagal Hai* (The Heart is Mad!) or *Kuch Kuch Hota Ha* (Something Happens).

⁴ I have used pseudonyms to protect the privacy of community participants. Community leaders, professionals in the entertainment industry have been named.

However, I must mention that the child Preeti preferred her true name to be revealed upon seeing an article that I had written about her dance in *Little India* magazine in 1995. She wanted people to know it was her, since she was made to understand by her mother that the article was a compliment to her talent. Her parents' friends recognized the description of her and her dance and promptly called Rakhee and her husband about the article. Appreciative that I had seemed to say that Preeti danced better than the film superstar Madhuri Dixit, I was invited over for dinner to their home in New Jersey to be introduced to Preeti's teachers, and to other family friends.

I keep her pseudonym intact here as the sexually charged discussion may cast malicious and misunderstood aspersions on the little girl's reputation.

⁵ for a discussion of the upper class bias of Indian classical dance please refer to Avanti Meduri's "Bharat Natyam: What are You?" in the *Asian Theatre Journal 5, 1:1-22*

⁶ As of this writing, SALGA as well as Sakhi, together with the South Asian AIDS Action, Lease Driver's Coalition/Committee against Anti-Asian Violence were banned from joining the 1995 parade in NYC. The official reason is that these organizations cater to a general *South Asian* population while this is a celebration of *Indian* independence. In this light, the parade should be only for *Indian* organizations. The boards of Sakhi and SALGA have expressed that this is FIA's strategy to exclude SALGA without appearing homophobic. These excluded organizations staged a protest strike during the parade in 1995.

These groups were banned from marching in the 1996, 1997, and 1998 parade as well. This time the FIA only allows its dues-paying members to join the parade. Sakhi and SALGA are not members of the FIA.

⁷ Sakhi, too has been embroiled in a controversy in which they have been accused of being exclusionary. A splinter group *Worker's Awaaz* consisting of

domestic workers and original founding members of Sakhi was formed in reaction to what they perceived as class-based misuse of power within the organization by the current Sakhi board.

[8] As of this writing, it was revealed to me by one of the SALGA members that Probhir Roy's son has confessed his homosexuality to his father.

[9] These are culled from many disturbing conversations with BJP supporters here in NYC.

[10] Sita being banished is the most popular version of her being returned to her mother—Earth's home. In other versions, she willfully leaves Rama, unable to bear his injustices, and wanting nothing of his imperialist ambitions.

CHAPTER 5

The GlamoroU.S. Bride
Snow White Dances Disco
Bhangra[1] with Desi[2] Groom
Performing Hybridity at New York University[3]

Hybrid—person or groups produced by interaction of two unlike cultures, traditions, etc. L: *hybrida*: offspring of a tame sow and a wild boar. Syn: mongrel: used for dogs; offspring of repeated crossings of different breeds; usually depreciatory or denoting mixed or degenerate breed or characteristics. Ant: purebred, thoroughbred.

Hyphen—short line used to connect parts of a compound word.

Hyphenated—noting a naturalized citizen of the U.S. believed to be ambivalent in his loyalty: so called because of his tendency to style himself according to his former and present nationalities. (1989 Webster's Unabridged Encyclopedic Dictionary)

Many of this country's diasporic Asians [reject] the hyphen in the term "Asian American"——we feel that the term incorrectly locates us between Asia and the U.S., when we are more accurately located between a U.S. which takes notice of racial difference, and a U.S. which professes to be color blind—or, as I say on more cynical days, to be Asian American means one is neither Asian nor American. (Feng, 1994:1)

.   .   .

After weeks of discussions, arguments, and more discussions, we, the executive board of the Merry Maidens' Club of Manila had agreed, at last, on the format of the 1978 annual show. Since we had something really important and controversial to say, yet did not want to appear disrespectful, but wanted to be entertaining, too, it was hard but challenging to come up with appropriate numbers for the show, with a loose but convincing story line. What really bugged us about the Indian community we grew up in was that there was just too much gossip and emphasis placed on 'what people would say', so we entitled the piece "Kathputli" or puppet, as we strongly felt we were puppets of the community's out-dated values. The story was set in a toy store owned by a tyrant owner who kept his toys jealously locked up. At night, the toys come alive and enact vignettes about restrictions placed on friendships between Indians and Filipinos, not being able to go out dancing late at night in a mixed-gender group (or go out at night, at all, for that matter!), the crass materialism of our marriage and dowry system and the low value given to love and romance. All this in song and dance variety show format using catchy Hindi film songs, current disco hits, some short and funny sketches in English, Hindi and Sindhi, punctuated at appropriate moments quite menacingly by the chant "Manu cha chawanda?" or "What will people say?" from the chorus. For a happy ending, Buddhi, our form of deux-ex-machina-source-of-enlightenment-voice-of-conscience deity, cut the puppet strings and opened up the tyrant store owner's mind, releasing his toys from their cases, and boxes. The whole ensemble danced a Broadway style chorus piece to a fusion jazz composition in a glittering grand finale scene led by a glamorously seductive modern Indian woman (the earthy version of Buddhi, his reward?—who knows what we were thinking?!) who eventually marries the once staid but now enlightened toy store owner. I guess you could call this our version of an opera, capitalizing on the kitsch and melodrama of movies, TV, and musicals; controversies of our community life in Manila, and the single-minded gall of our youthfulness.

. . .

> Interculturalism has several things, the least desirable but probably
> most powerful of which is an effect of global mass communication.
> The wholesale export of films, videos, and television programming,
> not to mention also the worldwide dissemination of images of Western
> consumer culture through print advertising, has in effect "intercultur-
> ated" the world to a degree and in a way that is obviously and pro-
> foundly disturbing . . . a flattening of cultural differences into a
> homogeneous mediocrity. (Chaudhuri, 1991:192-193)

Shruti, the South Asian Student Association at New York University is an exemplar of first and second generation immigrants nurtured by what they imagine India to be in comparison to their lived reality in the United States, specifically as university students. Besides socializing, creating a niche of prestige for themselves at NYU, and garnering campus awards, the organization is eager to "[give] the university not only a taste but an *explosion* of South Asian heritage" (Shruti Handbook [SH], 1992–1993:7) [my italics]. Shruti ambitiously promotes South Asian awareness at New York University and its environs through lectures, film festivals, social outings, and cultural programs both for South Asian students, their friends and families, as well as for the Greenwich Village community and the New York tri-state area population. Another important item in the agenda of the organization is the advocation of a South Asian Studies department at NYU. The organization believes its visibility and volubility in the social and cultural realms will "heighten a demand for [such a] program in the University" (SH:7). There is no program or department specific to South Asian disciplines, but an Asia Pacific American Studies program has been constructed by the College of Arts and Sciences since the Fall of 1996 under the direction of Dr. Jack Tschen. Courses pertaining to South Asian American interests and issues rather than to South Asia area studies are included as part of the curriculum. There is also an East Asian Studies department. To bring the South Asian (Area) Studies department into reality, funding and sponsorship are needed—NYU South Asian alumni are to be tapped for that.

Shruti produces an annual cultural show, an extravagant display of dances, songs, skits, and a fashion show that fuses choreographies and aesthetic sensibilities from the popular entertainments of both the Indian diaspora and the U.S.A. There is a pronounced absence of classical performance numbers, an abundance of Hindi film songs and dances, urbanized versions of folk dances, and redundant references to American television and movies. The Indian-American as re-presented by Shruti seems to be comprised of the ersatz elements of Indian and American popular, commercial cultures.

SOUTH ASIAN HARMONY—NOT!

The examples I examine closely in this chapter are taken from the 1992 show entitled *Harmony, Pride & Heritage: Reflections of Our Artistic Traditions* mounted in the Cooper Union Great Hall in cooperation with the Cooper Union Asia Society. Similar numbers appeared in the 1993 and 1994 shows. In fact, similar type numbers appear in the shows mounted by the South Asian student association in Columbia University, and in other campuses in the country. At first glance, the show looks like a youthful and humorous celebration of being an Indian-American, of playing with performative genres, cultural stereotypes, a display of glamour and fashion, talent and beauty. But on deeper analysis, it evidences the manner in which the students use the performance as a way to negotiate the anxieties, even the split of being of South Asian origin, but born and raised 'American'. It is a condition between being marked and unmarked, named and unnamed. The students are already distinguished as different from their parents since they are brought up in America (and for being of a different generation, surely); they are different from their non-South Asian contemporaries for having South Asian heritage. They desire for that difference to be a mark of distinction rather than a stigma. They want to belong to both the American and South Asian communities, to be indistinguishable when they occupy both those cultural landscapes. And to create a third community of hybrid Americans of South Asian origin. Una Chaudhuri argues for looking for the representation of the plurality of identities experienced *within* the hyphenated Indian rather than *between* disparate cultures especially in theatrical works. This representation can be a most effective and practical form of interculturalism if within the piece our attentions are directed to

> Unexpected, even apparently idiosyncratic reactions to cultural displacement . . . [*producing*] the *experience* of difference . . . [staging] the detailed processes of differentiation which are the as-yet unrepresented realities of modern life. Instead of rehearsing and rehashing cliches about how this or that culture is different from 'the West,' it would catch up with and show the levels and forms of actual cultural interpenetration in the world . . . [Revealing] that the awful gap of cultural difference suddenly yawns wide in the everyday experience of the individuals . . . and situates it instead in the personalist terrain I call difference *within*. (Chaudhuri, 1991:196, 197, 198)

The immigrant who finds herself in a multicultural landscape experiences the phenomenology of cultural interpenetration in her daily life, in the dynamics of her idiosyncratic reactions to differences. Especially when this individual is thrust into a situation where home is unlike the world, where food smells, tastes and looks different from what is eaten by other contemporaries, where she is darker in color than her classmates *but not black*, where she worships not only a bearded old man in a heaven or one hanging from a cross, but many deities in a variety of shapes and forms. Young people are most vulnerable to this 'identity double', because they have to leave their 'Indian' homes and go to their 'American' schools where they learn about the world, forge friendships, and sometimes have to make major decisions based on the ethnicity of who to be with, what to confess about oneself, what one can or cannot indulge in. They come back to their 'Indian' homes in the evening, or on the weekends if they are dorming. They socialize and interact with their parents, family friends who may be distinct from their school friends, go to the temple, and in general follow different rules of existence. Thus intercultural identity is processual, constantly transforming, emerging, incomplete.

In naming the show *Harmony, Pride & Heritage: Reflections of Our Artistic Traditions*, Shruti takes for granted that the audience understands that the artistic traditions are those of South Asia—'our' traditions. The irony lies in the words 'heritage' and 'tradition' because the genres chosen are unlike the folk dances and classical numbers defined as 'traditional' in the South Street Seaport Deepavali Festival that I describe in chapter 3. These numbers do not speak of the 'soul and the soil' of Indian heritage. The genres chosen are very contemporary, very urbane. Though the types of numbers are formulaic, appearing in many other performances, these forms cannot be more than a quarter of a century old. The Hindi film song and dance, the Indian costumes, and other like genres are contemporary forms, products of modernity, transnational capitalism, international fashion. Their Indianness makes them 'traditional'; their non-Westerness makes them traditional, part of a past—"treasures" from the trove of an ancient civilization.

What marks this 'new tradition' is the patterned and formulaic inclusion of these genres. Ritin Chakraborty[4], the executive producer of the Shruti show, as well as ex-officio Shruti executive board member, explains that the acts had to have an 'Indian' theme. The term included a broad range of genres:

> The acts had to have an Indian theme. They could be Americanized or classical, modern, film music but not like American music with Indian people dancing and calling that Indian-American dance, no! It could be South Asian music; could be South Asian modern music or even an English tune redone into a Hindi film song, that was fine. (Chakraborty, 1995)

Hybrid forms were encouraged just so long as they were interbreeding with Indian expressive forms. So a fashion show, for example, though not "indigenously" Indian, is choreographed using Indian costumes, Indian music, Indian models. These innovations make the fashion show a 'traditional' artistic form from India's 'heritage.'

Shruti takes for granted, too that the audience will be of South Asian descent. Possessing incredible confidence in their youthful potential and pragmatism, they have appropriated popular entertainment genres, one of the root sources of their identities, as their medium of expression and sites of identity negotiation.

Another contentious term that was used in the title is 'harmony'. It is important to note that this organization is a "South Asian" rather than "Indian". Club members and leaders want to "transcend the political and religious struggles that plague South Asia . . . and to serve as a catalyst for unifying the peoples of South Asia here on campus as well as in the general tri-state area" (SH, 1992-93:7). Members of Shruti are descended from the post-colonial nation states of India, Pakistan, Bangladesh, Sri Lanka, Tibet, Nepal, Bhutan and Maldives. Though in official diplomatic circles Tibet is defined as Chinese, here it is included as part of South Asia, thus expanding the usual "Seven Sisters" of South Asia (Cowsik, 1995) to eight sisters. Shruti also has members from the West Indies, specifically those with heavy populations of South Asians, mostly from Guyana and Trinidad. Unlike the stipulation of the Federation of Indian Associations to include only Indian organizations in their Indian Independence day parade (see Chapter 4), Shruti's inclusionary policy is based on cultural citizenship, ancestral descent and historical links to the South Asian sub-continent as well as the South Asian diaspora. Shruti officially repudiates what many members consider artificial and contentious national boundaries, ethnic and religious warfare, and communal strife. What is emphasized is not uniformity but the accommodation of differences 'in harmony'. The family extends to include the 7 sisters + 1 + others = Shruti. Shruti, "[encourages] everyone no matter what their ethnic or religious background to join and participate as full members . . . [since we] respect all the peoples of these nations as well as all those who respect our culture" (SH, 1992-1993:1). In theory, at least, anyone can join Shruti as long as you love South Asia, or South Asians, are of South Asian descent, or are part of the South Asian diaspora.

The rhetoric is utopian. It can be argued that the inclusionary zeal of these students is merely a jump onto the bandwagon of multicultural political correctness. The majority of the members are Indian, specifically Gujarati, Punjabi and Malayalee. These communities in the NYC area have achieved the economic power and infrastructure to purchase visibility, and to pay their tuition fees as undergraduates at this private institution. Naheed Islam, a scholar of Bangladeshi descent laments the loose use of the term 'South Asian':

> In the belly of the multicultural beast, I am named South Asian . . . the term has become interchangeable with [Indian]. Some Indian American groups have made a deliberate policy statement to acknowledge the inclusive nature of the term. But the easy shift of the tongue between terms makes one wonder at the commitment to ensure all our visibility and interests. I have worked with numerous political organizations claiming South Asian membership. The majority of the participants tend to be Indian American with some Bangladeshi and Pakistani members. Despite many discussions on the use of the term in sweeping generalizations and its interchangeability with India these problems [lack of representation] resurface in old frustrating ways. (Islam, 1993:244)

Indeed, the reality of South Asian immigration shows that Indian Americans are the numerical majority. However, since there is strength in numbers, to include the marginals of this already marginal category in its fold expands political clout and visibility. Still, *Indian* hegemony is feared by non-Indian South Asians[5]. The tension is palpable as South Asians try to form a community despite our glaring differences. Shruti is not exempt from the tension, and tries to overcome it. Open to all South Asians , Shruti was renamed from 'Asia Society' to *Shruti*, (the term defined as 'harmony') in a 58 to 7 majority vote in 1992. The term reverberates with idealism. This idealism is also manifested in the types of numbers that are presented in their annual show. I must confess that as an Indian myself, I recognize these numbers as depicting Indianness whether performed by Shruti member of Pakistani or Tibetan descent. I admit and succumb to the obvious hegemony. Henceforth, in this discussion, I refer to the show as "Indian".

In fact, the fissiparousness within Shruti is not amongst other South Asians, or even between South Asian and non-South Asians, but between Indians from the North and Indians from the South. The arguments and discussions around and about who the true Indians are is eloquently summarized by Chakraborty:

> I was told I couldn't talk about being Indian because I am North Indian and I was bastardized, because I am part Aryan, part Dravidian. The true Indians are the South Indians—the real Dravidians. . . . My friend Anita[6], from Tamil Nadu also got it from the other South Indians in Shruti for being friends with me and some other Northern Indians. They accused her of 'selling out' of her race to the Aryans who had

driven the Dravidian man down south, out of their homes, raping their
women.

The discourse of racial purity is used as a criterion for what can be
defined as "authentic Indianness". The erroneous assumption in this discourse is that people from the South of India are pure Dravidians, that
Dravidians represent "true India" and that the culture of the subcontinent
is impervious to history, syncretism, and change. Yet, despite these discussions and discontents, the numbers in the show even when performed
by those of South Indian origin, were largely of North Indian origins, i.e.,
Bhangra from the Punjab, Hindi Film songs and dances from Bombay,
numbers inspired by the popular versions of the Hindustani Kathak
dance. These genres have become pan-Indian expressions easily available in the U.S. due to video, film and audio technology. In the 1992
show, the one and only Shruti proponent of *Bharat Natyam* preferred to
perform in *Kathak* style a Hindi film song from *Umrao Jaan*, a story
based on the Lucknow courtesan poetess of the same name. This South
Indian dancer reasoned that this number would be more accessible to the
audience. Moreover, the show warranted a more 'popular' style of dance,
rather than a 'classical' number. The 'bastard' form of the Umrao Jaan
song owes its influences to hybrid styles of courtly Urdu-speaking cultures of the North, Islamic as well as Hindu. The film's lavish mise en
scene recalls a nostalgia for the opulence and hedonism of Moghul
courts. The actress who plays the Northern Indian Umrao Jaan in all her
arresting beauty and grace is the sultry, cocoa-complexioned South Indian, Rekha Ganesan. The Shruti performer relived quite expertly her
South Indian sister's glamour in the Shruti show via this Hindi film
dance version of a Northern Indian courtly art form.

HAVING TWO NAVELS[7]

Hindi film song and dance being one of the most prominent, though
phantasmagoric visual depictions of India's landscape, culture, and
good-looking people, reinterpretations of these song and dance sequences inundated the show. Via videos, audio-cassettes, Indian cable
TV, and the flamboyant concerts staged by visiting film stars, these song
and dance sequences are some of the first teachers to overseas Indians
about Indian aesthetics and culture. Watching Hindi films, knowing the
songs, and talking about them link the overseas Indian to India, and to
other overseas Indians even if they belong to other castes, classes or reli-

Figure 5.1. A back breaking innovation in popular Hindi film dance choreography, in a reinterpretation of an Umrao Jaan song.

gions. The film dance is watched and watched again, re-choreographed for the stage.

The choreography at the Shruti show, mostly taken from the film but since the original dance was made for the movie camera, the young artists had to innovate steps to fit the demands of a live performance. In some numbers, classical dance steps taken from *Bharat Natyam* and *Kathak* were incorporated. Often enough, the dancers in fact improved on the film versions by adding rhythmic footwork, lithesome legwork, and a democratic group choreography where every one on stage is given prominence. The audience revels in the familiarity of the song, sharing with the other members of the audience the memory of the delight derived from watching the film on their VCRs. Furthermore, the number is not performed by some unattainable superstar, but by one of the young members of the Indian community. The delight is doubled by witnessing yet another virtuosic embodiment of the song and dance sequence by people who actually inhabit their own milieu. So in the process of mimicking the film dance, innovating steps to fill the live stage, costuming, and performing for an audience who understands the same fantasy, the young artists take possession of and domesticate the film's once distant glamorous portrayal of mythic India. Hearing a familiar and well-liked song accompanying the deft dance movements of a young compatriot is sufficient to create, at least, for this moment, a euphoric experience of belonging, of community.

In an anecdote narrated by Shruti's advisor, Sudipto Chatterjee, one of the Indo-Caribbean members asked him the meaning of a Hindi film song she was dancing to. She did not understand Hindi, and was not familiar with the film. She was embarrassed to ask her colleagues for fear of being mocked as not being 'Indian enough'. Participating in the dance despite her linguistic ignorance, and her not being born in India made her feel that she was contributing to this particular type of Indianness of the Shruti show. It made her feel part of a vast and global Indian community.

These Indian Americans seemed to possess two umbilical cords, one attached to India or more correctly to a Hindi Film fantasy of India, another one attached to an Americanness constructed from popular media. Television sitcoms like *Gilligan's Island*, *Saturday Night Live's* sketch *Wayne's World*, and the Disney version of the fairy tale *Snow White and the Seven Dwarfs* were Indianized in the 1992 Shruti show. For example, in a Shruti version, *Gilliganji's Island*, the sexy starlet Ginger is renamed *Adrak*, the Hindi for ginger root. The multimillionaire character finds his equivalent in the comic stereotype of Mr. Patel, a rich Gujarati motel owner. In the sketch based on *Wayne's World*, the two spaced out buddies—one with a turban, mind you—enumerate the top ten best babes. Eight of the slots were filled by Hindi film actresses, along with Sharon Stone. The babe who topped the list of ultimate babeness was Mina, a college-going Indian American woman in a black velvet bustier. The Babe of all Babes is one of Shruti's own[8].

The audience laughs with the recognition that these sitcoms, though removed from anyone's life experiences, can be coopted and made vernacular by sheer clever wit. Snow White was envied and admired, not specifically for her beauty but for her ability to dance *Bhangra*, a Punjabi folk dance, reconfigured in to dance hall genre by South Asians all over the globe. The seven dwarfs were transformed into seven desis—*desis* being the term given to an India-born hick, in this context[9]. Their chant of 'Hi ho, Hi ho, its off to work we go' , was translated to "Ai yo, Ai yo! Eet is off to vork ve go" in a thick Indian accent, a stereotypic characteristic of a desi. One of the desis named Popatlal showed off her hip hop skill while her cohorts cheered her on in the typical way African American kids do—'Go Popat! Go Popat! Go Popat!'

There is an energetic celebration of hybridity in the affection for the fused styles of the urban and folk dances like *Disco*, reggae, hip-hop, funk, etc. with *Dandya*, a Gujarati folk dance with sticks, *Garba*, a Gujarati round dance and *Bhangra*, a Punjabi folk dance are popular amongst the youth. Garba, Dandya and *Bhangra* are brought into city life by remixing them to the pulse of disco, hip-hop, Hindi filmi music, and other African American and Caribbean popular musics. The fused styles exported from London, West Indies and India appear in Hindi films, and are also played at wedding receptions, dance parties, and community celebrations here in New York, in other cities in and outside the U.S.A., as well as in the major cities in India. In fact during *Navratri*, the nine night Hindu celebration of Goddess Durga's and her sister Ambha's triumph over a demon, includes dancing *Dandya Raas*. In Queens and in Indian communities in New Jersey, large tents are put up, sheltering 25,000 or more people dancing in unison. Sometimes these events include the guest appearances of Hindi film superstars. At South Asian dance parties, for fun or to raise money, this new *Bhangra* is the music of choice. The fondness for these types of music is apparently a transnational phenomenon, helping to form a transnational community of hyphenated Indians, grooving to the beat of the same drummer. Young Indian Americans can dance to this kind of music because its referents, though ambiguous—being neither 'purely' Indian nor wholly non-Indian—are from urban youth culture. The fusion is very much like them—Indian yes, American/Western, yes also, but really young.

DWARFS DANCE *BHANGRA*

The emphasis placed on *Bhangra* is crucial. The dance was used in the 1992 show as a leitmotif in the *Snow White and the Seven Desis* skit. Besides the Indianizing of the fairy tale, the skit is the story of the emergence of a self-conscious, reflexive hybrid identity as expressed through the dwarfs' (desis) learning to dance the *Bhangra*.

Bhangra is originally a dance performed by Punjabi men during harvest, weddings, and other such celebrations in India and Pakistan. In England, specifically Birmingham and Southall, where there is a huge population of Punjabi immigrants, pop or disco versions of this type of dancing experience an unprecedented success and proliferation into the nightclubs, and was picked up by the recording industry. Through the long arms of transnational commerce and audio and video technology, *Bhangra* was repositioned and distributed throughout the globe. Pop *Bhangra* consists of characteristic Punjabi vocal melodies set to a very lively eight-beat meter common to folk, popular and Hindustani (northern Indian—again!) light classical music with various disco-derived percussion effects in the background (Manuel, 1993:178 -179, 284). It is unlike the *Bhangra* of the villages of Punjab.

Disco *Bhangra* gives second generation South Asian youth a sense of community[10]. Prior to the emergence of *Bhangra*, these youth in Britain danced to British or American pop music and "hung out with Blacks, Whites, Filipinos". But with the spread of *Bhangra*, *Bhangra* parties, even *Bhangra* classes, "now they can hang out [and party] with other Indians" and in the process learn to dance an Indian folk dance and by extension participate in Indian culture in a fun way. The hanging out with other Indians allows for a bonding with people who share similar experiences in the crises that hyphenated youth typically experience—"we accept our confusion with East and West and can party [together]"(Sikand, 1994; Ganti, 1995; Chaddha, 1989).

This new version of *Bhangra* is born out of what Indian immigrants experienced living in white dominated cultures. British Asians identified at first with blacks, having grown up alongside black communities in Southall and Birmingham and being regarded by Britons as non-white, and therefore, as 'black' (Zuberi, 1995; 36). As expressed by a *Bhangra* artist in the London group *Cobra*:

> Asians [Indians] were lost, they weren't accepted by whites, they drifted into the black culture, dressing like blacks, talking like them, and listening to reggae. But now *Bhangra* has given them their music and made them feel that they have an identity. No matter if they are Gujarati, Punjabi, or whatever—*Bhangra* is Asian music for Asians. (Baumann, 1990, p, 91)

Let me extend this last statement by saying that Bhangra is Desi music for all Desis. Though the Indian lyrics of *Bhangra* may be in Punjabi, mixed with pidgin English, Black English, Indian English, and Hindi film song lyrics not necessarily understood by all diasporic Indians, the beat, some of the instruments, the melodies are regarded as non-white, generically Desi, and specifically of Desi hybridity. "Whereas Asians were rendered unintelligible, could not be made sense of or read coherently as raced beings, and were thus treated with absolute effacement and erasure" (Gopinath, 1994:12), dancing to *Bhangra* gives Indians a place to be. The *Bhangra* maintains its traces of blackness in its "verbal inflections . . . the ground bass of . . . rhythm and bodily movement" (Hall, 1990:230) through it remixing with African diasporic musics such as hip-hop and reggae, and its definition as non-white, racially discriminated, and marginalized expressive form. Many dance parties in New York organized by Indian associations spin a hefty number of disco *Bhangra* tunes. Even if other kinds of musics are played, these parties are called generically *"Bhangra* Parties". The term *Bhangra* has come to mean in the diaspora a dance party with South Asian dance musics. The other term used to describe this kind of party is the Desi party. In fact, since 1997, every first Thursday of the month, at a famous South American dance club—Sounds of Brazil or SOB's there is a Bhangra party facilitated by DJ Rekha and DJ Joy. On this day the club is packed and has received recognition in the mainstream press for being one of the most popular and prominent South Asian Parties in the City of New York. To celebrate various occasions like the New Year, Thanksgiving, Valentine's Day, Independence Day, Diwali, any of the American or Indian holidays, a number of Desi Bhangra Parties proliferate various clubs in the City. In fact, there are at least three Desi club parties to go to a month if a young Desi would like to immerse him or herself in Desiness amidst his or her American life.

Nabil Zuberi, a scholar and radio show host, has the following to say about disco versions of film music, applicable to Bhangra's effect on South Asian youth:

> The dazzling syncretism of Indian film music is a celebration of hybridity...we read the shrill voices, one thousand violins, and Bombay mix of Eastern and Western elements as part of an amorphous subcontinental identity to be messed with, deformed and appropriated. The lyrics don't matter much; its the in-your-face hyper melange, the camp disregard for cultural boundaries that is cause for pleasure. (1995:37)

The energetic disco beat allows for an exuberant, almost ecstatic, very physical and aerobic dancing. The dance is loud, expressive, rhythmic. The music hastens, and reaches a crescendo, making the body reach a peak of energy and awareness. When dancing the *Bhangra*, one feels very alive, very present, absolutely not erased.. Dancing the *Bhangra* together is a move towards a coalitional identity. The unindividuated WE all dance together forming one pulsating body of 'amorphous' South Asianness. It enlivens our hybridity kinesthetically. In the dancehall scenes in England, Canada, U.S. and Asia, the *Bhangra* is danced to by everyone, with partners of the opposite sex, with partners of the same sex, in groups, even alone. The dancing is free-style with some gestures copied from Hindi film dances such as hips swaying and chest heaving, Bhangra's raised arms and clapping, squats and jumps, hip-hop steps and breakdancing, etc. Everyone is on display for each other, bodies are moving in ways which may suggest one's sensual potential. People can dance really close, touching and teasing, playing out possible erotic scenarios with strangers, friends, with the same or opposite sex, with Desis of different communities.

The following description of a blues dance is comparable to the experience of *Bhangra* parties I have attended:

> A top sound system is thirty to one hundred times as powerful as a domestic hi-fi. The point isn't volume, but the amplification of the bass until it sounds like the world's biggest drum, until it becomes music you can *feel*. You feel it in your feet . . . you feel it through your partner's body. The first time you hear it, it's unbelievable, unbearable, oh my God! But you get used to it. You grow numb, through that and there's a cool, cool joy, a sedative high. Ice in the spine. No pain. (Hebdige, 1987:90)

The *Bhangra* numbers in the Shruti show also reflected this variety of participation but of course the choreography was set for theatrical performance. In the Shruti skit, Snow White's *Bhangra* expertise is described as "so exciting, so alluring, so different". The music she dances to is composed by a British Punjabi *Bhangra* artist Malkit Sing remixed by disc jockey Bally Sagoo, who I mentioned in Chapter 3 as famous for his insertions of hip-hop mixes, use of synthesizers, and other not necessarily Punjabi or Indian musical instruments such as the electronic drums, acoustic guitar, electronic organ, and the like.

Snow White in the skit is the quintessential hybrid Indian from the west, specifically from the United States. Her name is Western, indexing her Caucasian affiliations. Indian-Americans are familiar with the fairy tale whose very name indicates Snow White's aspiration to whiteness. Her name is an acknowledgement that the race relations in the U.S. do not define Asian Indians as 'black'. Quite the contrary, American Asian Indians aspire to the mainstream, to be 'white' in lifestyle, status, and even in physiognomy (please see chapter 3).

In U.S. immigrant history debates raged as to whether Indians can be considered Caucasian and not if they were black (Chapter 2). Snow White speaks in English but her dress and accent are Indian,

Figure 5.2. Snow White and the Desis bhangra!

the latter for comedic effect. Her dancing shows that she has mastered the idiom of diasporic, hybridized Indians. The desi dwarfs are characterized as tea plantation workers reminiscent of the indentured laborers in West Indian British colonial history as well as farmworkers in plantations in India. As desis, the dwarfs are not wholly Americanized but are very much like the early immigrants in the UK, the railroad and farmworkers in the U.S. West Coast in the early part of this century, and the non-English speaking Asian Indian immigrants of the 1980's in the U.S. who live in predominantly Indian neighborhoods in Queens and New Jersey working as clerks in Indian companies, as taxi drivers, or in other blue-collar jobs. Snow White stumbles upon their ghetto, and cleans up their *jhopar* or Indian shed, bringing it up to Western middle class standards.

Recapitulating immigration history, and not having developed yet any dance to represent themselves, these disenfranchised dwarfs take up the popular form of their black, Hispanic, and West Indian disenfranchised neighbors in the South Bronx neighborhood- the hip-hop in the

Figure 5.3. Fashion! Glamour! Fame! You can have it, too

U.S. (and reggae in the UK) calling it "our own kind of dancing" which one of the dwarfs, Popatlal, proceeds to demonstrate. Snow White in teaching the dwarfs *Bhangra*, hastens their evolution from an invisible desi/black identity to that of a hybrid Desi/brown identity. In this way they learn the "in-your-face hyper melange" world of whiteness, blackness and Asian Indianness, infected by the rhythms and exuberance of the music. Surely, when the dwarfs learn to dance the *Bhangra*, the free-style choreographies that the dwarfs appropriate use the vocabularies taken from the gamut of hip-hop, traditional Indian folk dances, and filmi gestures. They are no longer dwarfed by their desiness. By dancing the *Bhangra*, they have crossed-over into the playing fields of hybridity of a brown and more hip Desiness. Snow White, "the best *Bhangra* dancer in all the subcontinent", or more aptly, the best *Bhangra* dancer in all the transcontinents, liberates them from their parochiality. Through the *Bhangra*, they also become part of an interpretative community of the Desi diaspora.

BEING FASHIONABLY INDIAN

Another example of owning more glamorous aspects of Indian-Americanness can be seen in the Shruti Fashion Show entitled, *Expressions*. In a confident mimicry of the world of Haute couture, outfit after outfit was displayed as a celebration of glitter, colors, and textiles. Examples of outfits included contemporary versions of the traditional salwar khameez, variations on how the Indian veil could be used to accentuate any style of dress, Western style dresses using Indian fabrics, men's suits, silk shirts, silk sarees from different parts of India, and various evening wear. The models undulated to world beat and club music, striking poses amidst swirls of dreamy fuzz emitted from the fog machine. In response their cohorts in the audience squeal with delight as they evaluate and recognize their buddies on stage.

In this display of youth, beauty and sexual potential, fame's duration is measured in minutes. Through the excesses of the fashion show, these models enunciate how much their Indianness and Americanness are intertwined, much like the interwoven threads in the fabric of their high fashion garments. Also, they demonstrate that they can, at will, be traditionally Indian manifested by wearing the Indian dress, be American as they don Western clothes, and be Indian American, by mixing styles. In fact, many of the hybrid outfits looked like those worn by the bohemian inhabitants of Greenwich Village in New York City. They are announcing that they are Indian, that they are American, and that they are Indian American. They contain multitudes. The identity is at once compartmentalized, layered, and enmeshed.

The expert shifting between the three cultural runways of Indian, Indian-American, and American reflects the awareness of these young Indian Americans of the necessity to play and manage the impression they give. Goffman (1973) explains that the presentation of self is based on how one manages, puts together a desired impression. Dress is an important factor in constructing this impression. As costuming it can help define character. It marks a distinguishing style, a refinement of taste, a designation of class and gender. It is the mark of identity and individuality. But more importantly, it is a mark of belonging.

The fashion show deconstructs the rigidity of biculturality. The clothes displayed indicate a transnational style shared by hyphenated individuals. For example, the *salwar khameez*, loose pleated pants with a long tunic blouse and veil is originally a North Indian dress. But now all over India, as well as in the diasporic sites globally, it is used both in ormal and informal affairs, and casually because of its convenience and elegance. It is the *Indian* thing to wear to an Indian occasion, where you want to show your Indianness. The *saree's* line and structure, on the other hand, is not casual to the Western eye. It is like wearing a long gown of another distinct ethnicity. Also, the saree is mostly worn by married, and/or older women. With its 6 to 9 yards, it is more cumbersome. The saree weighs heavily in terms of social status, and traditionalism, not befitting the light-heartedness, and mobility of youth (Nag,1991:106). The line of the salwar khameez can look like a loose-fitting pantsuit or a dress with tights—it can look modern and yet have that distinctive Indian touch. The looseness of the salwar khameez also adheres to the traditional call for modesty. The female body is shielded by textile, bead work, the veil, and ethnicity. It seems invulnerable to conversion to non-Indianness. Dulali Nag defines fashion vis-a-vis tradition in her analysis of fashion amongst middle class Bengali women:

> The word *fashion* is commonly taken to mean styles of dressing that come to be accepted as desirable in a particular period. Defined thus, fashion embodies change; it is itself only by being forever transient. It is often understood to be a mark of the ideologically modern. Tradition, on the other hand, signifies the unchanging, the repetitious, the stable. It is that which transcends temporality and is thereby opposed to the quintessence of modernity—changeability. Fashion and tradition are thus apparently irreconcilable. (1991:93)

Fashion and tradition may appear to be irreconcilable but the salwar khameez is a happy reconciliation between Indianness and convenience, between tradition and modernity.

It is important to note that though there were male models who exhibited many Western style clothes, none of them wore any Indian outfits, except for shirts which were made in India or had Indian inspired prints. The cut and line were always Western. This division between men's and women's fashions recalls to mind Partha Chatterjee's analysis of women's role in the nationalist project (1993). Women were expected to keep and practice the distinctively traditional and spiritual aspects of Indianness especially in the home while the men were in charge of worldly affairs and thus were required to be 'modern'—which meant more Western outside the home. Their dress was one of the markers of this difference. One of the ways women maintained their Indianness was by wearing Indian clothes while the men could wear collared shirts and trousers, suits and such. Men might change into a their regional dress when they returned home but they wore Western dress to work. As the repository of Indianness, women literally wore her nationalism all the time. In the same way, only women wore regional dress in the Shruti fashion show. Thus even in the discourse of modernity as practiced by sophisticated NYU students, the present-day Indian woman continues to be that visible repository of tradition. But the Indian American woman does and can present herself in Western style dress as well publicly. Indian men living in the West are not given that option, they must dress Western publicly, which is too bad, because Indian men look luscious in their kurta pajamas! They have to be only a *man* rather than an Indian. i.e. be ethnically neutral, while an Indian woman can be a *woman* as well as an *Indian* in the outside world, even here in the U.S. In my conversations with some Indian men, they believed that Indian clothes for women have a broader range of appeal for normal wear as opposed to Indian clothes for men. The most appealing of Indian clothes of men were of extremely formal wear, an extra-special occasion calls for men to dress ethnic such as a wedding, a formal Desi ball, a Desi concert, and others.

Indian clothes also mark economic status. A simple, cotton salwar khameez costs at least $150 in the U.S.. A good one of the latest design, made of silk, with beadwork, can cost anywhere between $250 to $600, with the very formal ones reaching to $5000. One can buy them cheaply in India, of course because the dollar stretches a long way there. To know the latest fashions one needs to be regularly in touch with India, either as a visitor, or by having visitors from India bringing you gifts of the latest fashions or through research, reading the latest fashion magazines. The direct contact is extremely expensive. An airline ticket costs at least $1000 added to which is the cost of the gifts you must bring as a foreign returned relative. The pleasure and necessity of shopping for authentic Indian things requires a hefty sum of money. All in all, one has to be making at least $50,000 annually to afford a living, personal link to India and her contemporaneity. This salary scale and ability to bring back to India many foreign gifts are attestments to a person's fulfillment of the American dream. Reading Indian magazines and seeing Hindi films and then having what you see stitched by Jackson Heights Indian dressmakers is a viable alternative. However, the ready made dress from the homeland is the more authentic marker[11]. Some of the salwar khameezes in the Expressions show were provided by different boutiques in Jackson Heights, Lexington Avenue and Iselin, New Jersey who in turn get their clothes directly from shops in India. Most of the clothes, however, came from the wardrobes of the participants who in turn acquired them from India directly from their last visit indicating the middle to upper middle class socio-economic status of the participants.

The fashion show was the center piece of the 1992 Shruti show. In other shows across U.S. campuses, a fashion show is always included[12]. The fashion show lets members participate, whether or not they can dance, sing, or act. As long as they have something gorgeous, or innovative enough to wear, whether from their own wardrobe or acquired for them by the producers, they can walk on the stage and display themselves. After which they can say that they did participate in the show, having contributed their presence and body even for just a few moments to propagate 'Indianness'. The presentation of self in this manner reassures their participation in the theater of cultural representation.

This is a glamorous contribution without the oppressive stringency of body weight and body type that is required in the profession of modeling. Shruti fashion show performers came in all sizes, weights, and types. In the show young people played at being glamorous, acquiring for a few moments the attention of being recognized and adored for their beauty. The variety of body types, body weights, complexions and facial features that were displayed repudiates the anorexic (for the female), the wash-board belly and buffed (for the male), unattainable, Caucasian-dominated fashion industry. The eye is surprised by an array of different embodiments of charm and also persuaded that this charm can be acquired by any body type, weight and size—by you, by me, by anybody. Furthermore, the Shruti home-grown models were very available, very attainable coming from the same milieu as the audience. They are not merely images, or 'coat-hangers' for the clothes, they are flesh and blood. They can be friends, future or present lovers, people that can be interacted with, people to whom one can relate.

LOVING THE WRONG SORTS

Thus far, it seems that these young Indian Americans celebrate their hyphenation, enjoying the thrill of difference and the irreverent, hilarious cooption of the homogenizing forces of mass media. However, a more anxiety-ridden negotiation of this hybrid identity is expressed in the redundant references to being 'too Indian' or 'too *desi*,' and how this hybrid identity deals with dating and marriage. These themes are played out in the form of Hindi film dance interpretations of love songs, in the jokes that mark the short skits, in the emcee's patter, in the display of

Figure 5.4. Bride and Groom in full South Asian regalia.

dolled up selves in the fashion show, in the girl-boy choreography, and especially in the item entitled *Brides and Grooms of South Asia.*

Brides and Grooms of South Asia was a swift exhibition of traditional regional wedding costumes with a Hindi film song blaring romance and conjugal bliss in the background. Both men and women wore traditional regional wedding ensembles. On the surface *Brides and Grooms* was an enunciation of the rich diversity of South Asian culture, indicating that it is not a homogeneous monolith. It also underscored that there are indeed real differences between this kind of South Asian from that kind of South Asian. Brides and Grooms points out that even as we may all be South Asians, and can be friendly to each other, we are also subject to the ethnocentrism and xenophobia of strong regionalism—of being Gujarati, or Sindhi, or Kashmiri; or religious difference—of being Hindu, Muslim, Christian; of caste—of being Brahmin, Kshatriya, or Vaisha; and of class. The restrictiveness and specificity of various caste, class and sectarian rules of endogamy depend on one's family and socio-economic background[13]. Coming into contact with the gamut of Indian cultures in a university setting, in a Pan-Indian organization like Shruti while working together to produce a show makes you conscious of these differences such as the North Indian and South Indian divide I mentioned earlier. But working together also provides, despite the differences touted, ample opportunity for friendships with like-minded others, as well as ample opportunity for coupling. Spending time rehearsing for the show, attending club meetings, joining the outings organized by Shruti allows for increased interaction with co-ethnics[14] The Indian Americans can always justify to their parents that they need to go out to do Shruti work, that they are doing work for the *Indian* organization on campus. Despite caste, class, regional and religious differences, what these young Indian Americans do share is the experience of New York University life in the heart of Greenwich Village. However, participation in Shruti does often put a person in the situation of being torn on the one hand, between traditional values based on familial obligations and on the other, the impulse towards individuality and bonding outside of traditional restrictions. Whom you *will* marry, whom you *can* marry, whom you *really want* to marry complicate and burden the Indian American identity.

As if the tension of marrying the 'wrong kind' of Indian isn't enough, there is the greater tension arising from the fear of losing one's mythic Indianness to the other myth—the hegemonizing monolith of white American (Western) culture. Marrying the 'right kind' of Indian (for you) is believed to preserve the culture from dilution, insuring the reproduction of Indian progeny and the re-production of Indian culture (please see chapter 4). It is for this reason that the arranged marriage is still a viable option for Indian Americans. Though both Indian and American popular media wax eloquent on the individualistic and therefore modernistic ecstasies of romantic love, physical attraction, and sexual satisfaction, choosing one's own life partner for the Indian American is fraught with the fear of parental disapproval and community rejection; for them familial ties still bind and sometimes even gag.

Studies conducted by various social scientists like Agarwal (1991), Ramaswami (1995) and others[15] reveal that Indian American youth are not totally opposed to arranged marriages so long as they have the opportunity to reject or accept the potential partners introduced to them by their parents. Indian Americans do not mind being introduced to a person who has been screened by their parents regarding family background, educational level, personal reputation, but would like to exercise their privilege of having the final say, and "the freedom to get to know the person and take the relationship from that point" (Agarwal in COSAW 1993:25).

Whereas, in the Western system dating is believed to be purely an individual endeavor (facilitated by peers), in this hybrid system, parents are involved in a limited sense. In many cases, parents do exert considerable control on the choice of partners, even here in the United States. Chakraborty shared this about one of his contemporaries:

> Anita's parents told her that at 19 she would be engaged to be married to this person they had chosen. He was from the right caste, right background, was from a very good family in India. Anita said she would do whatever her parents wanted. But right now, she would do whatever she wanted, have the best time, enjoy life to the fullest. Who knows what would happen when she got married!
>
> Since her parents found out that she was having too much fun at NYU, they pulled her out and placed her in a university close to her home. They picked her up at 3:30 on Friday from her dorm, and dropped her off at 8:00 on Monday. Weekends she spent at home. (Chakraborty, 1995)

Before submitting to a life of familial and societal obligation which her arranged marriage would bring, Anita wanted the freedom to enjoy herself. Afraid that this 'excess' would destroy her reputation, habituate her to a life of hedonism, disentangle her from familial bonds, or worse, get her premaritally pregnant, her parents discipline her by force of their economic clout (who else would pay for her schooling?). However, the control parents exercise over their children is not only economic, but also emotional. Anita, like many Indian-American youth, desires even as she fears her parents' approval, opinions, and feelings about her circumstances, choice of marriage partner, and lifestyle. It is for this reason that Indian-American youth would date, but would prefer not to let their parents know if they were seeing anyone (Agarwal in COSAW1991:25 & Kadaba & Barrientos, 1993:28)). Consequently, dating is done on the sly. As Chakraborty explains:

> The community is not a safe community for dating. Even if you say you are dating someone, or are bold enough to say that you are having sex with someone it goes from student to student to student and somehow reaches parent to parent. I have seen it happen. Someone told so

and so and that so and so told someone else. It went throughout Shruti
and then to all the parents of the Shruti members, and then to the parents in the community, and then back to the parents of the one who said
it in the first place! (Chakraborty, 1995)

More efficient than modern telecommunications, gossip is not only
a disseminator of information but a potent form of social control. Gossip's potency is based on the assumption of an Indian community despite
inherent regional or class fissiparousness. Armed with this knowledge,
Chakraborty paired non-dating Shruti members as couples in the Bride
and Grooms portion. He was careful not to pair actual couples together
for fear of them being found out by their parents. It was acceptable to
represent coupling, especially in the traditional garb of the wedding costumes, but dangerous to pretend in so public a manner that actual dating
couples were married since they were not as yet. Knowledgeable of how
parents can influence and disrupt romance, the Shruti couples did not
want their parents to suspect anything. Especially for those living at
home, their parents would hear names of certain people being discussed
over the phone, amongst friends, or even discussed with their parents. "If
they saw them coming down together as a couple, it will be one more bit
of information to complete the picture." (Chakraborty, 1995). Distorting
the truth, facilitates romance; couples enjoy each other during rehearsals,
but are not exposed by the bright lights of the actual performance.

This fear of parental disapproval of one's mate was expressed in a
joke cracked by one of the emcees. She tells of how she introduces her
date to her father who quickly consults a ludicrous pseudo-scientific oc-
cult formulation to gauge the desirability of the fellow. It is called the *Indian Marriage Theorem*:

> You take a 45 degree triangle, multiply by the third of the atomic
> weight of calcium, divide by the net present value of his past earnings
> and take into account the logarithmic function of the year he was born
> and the astrological alignment of the stars.

> If this number is non-negative, your parents will say—*no.*If the num-
> ber is negative, multiply that number by negative one, making the
> number non-negative. At this point, your parents will say—*no.*

Of course, the formula is rigged to be against any date. No matter
what, father will not approve of your choice. His decision is an act of the

cosmos corroborated by math and science! The vast terrain of dating is unfamiliar, and therefore vulnerable to error, the pain of heartbreak, and the shame of divorce. The answer to your own choice of mate may, in all probability be *no*. At least, at first. Though some parents may ultimately agree to your choice, the process of acceptance is emotionally charged and complicated (Kadabe & Barrientos, 1993:29).

.   .   .

When we were growing up, Papa made it very clear to us what kind of mate he would approve of. His approval could be measured by how much he would contribute financially to our weddings:

If we married a Sindhi (from our region), he would give 100%. If we married an Indian, but a non-Sindhi, he would give 50%. If we married a non-Indian, he would give 0%.

My poor Papa, despite his own Wedding Axiom, none of his children have chosen Indian partners, and only one has married—a Christian Filipina at that. And he's had to pay through his teeth for it!

.   .   .

Another fear that Indian Americans have is that the partner their parents might choose for them will be too desi, too Indian, old-fashioned, tradition-bound, tacky. The arranged spouse might speak English with a heavy Indian accent, wear outdated clothes, be stingy with their money, and in general, be ill-equipped to live an urbane Indian-American lifestyle. The show was punctuated with jokes regarding the clumsiness of the newly arrived desi, the inability of older émigrés to adapt to an American lifestyle, the parochiality of fresh-off-the-boat illegal aliens. The self that they perceive as precious, the impulse to individual freedom and self-fulfillment, is threatened into subjugation by the perceived tyranny of tradition, obligation, and 'desiness' as described by Anita's predicament earlier—it is like carrying a screaming monkey on your back[16].

Being Indian American is being comfortable, smooth and cool amidst non-Indianness, in the exciting space of hybridity. It is dancing *Bhangra* unabashedly, wearing contemporary Indian and Western clothes one chooses, enjoying the pleasures of an urban, cosmopolitan life in New York, as well as in Bombay, London, or Hongkong, while still caring for mom and dad (and the extended families of both spouses!) , and going to the temple on occasion. Summarized as follows is the opinion of 95% of the Indian Americans interviewed by Priya Agarwal in her study of their dating preferences:

> It would be best for them to marry other [. . .] Indians who grew up here, rather than having arranged marriages with partners directly from India. They said they wanted to share the commonality of their Indian-American backgrounds as well as to avoid their partner's possible culture shock. (Agarwal in COSAW, 1993:25)

Participating in college life allows for an important aspect of being a 'cool' Indian-American. Succeeding in school despite one's freedom, despite being away from home and away from parental surveillance is greatly lauded. New York University enjoys the prestige of having top-notch schools in business, medicine and law, worthy and lucrative professions in the eyes of Indian parents. Its location in Greenwich Village is, however, a draw towards 'wildness' since the West Village conjures up images of homosexuality and other 'alternative' lifestyles, the East Village of anarchy and bohemianism; and Washington Square Park of drug-pushers and other such 'freaks—with bright orange hair, earrings and tattoos'. As Chakraborty elaborates:

> When a young typically sheltered Indian child comes to NYU, they have a tendency to flip out. It has happened to a lot of Indian kids. This guy, Salman, coming from a very sheltered home—all of a sudden can stay out late after midnight every night of the week, no one to ask him where he was. What happens? He sleeps through his classes. Couldn't make it—he was at Stern (NYU's business school)—got kicked out.

> *If you want to have that freedom here, then you must have the discipline that was bred by your Indian culture.* A lot of kids can't hack it. They see this world of freedom. They get surprised because they have this freedom—'Oh my God it's Monday night and I can go out until 12:00, 1:00 in the morning', and then they sleep through their class the next day. Then they don't hand in their papers on time. [italics mine] (Chakraborty, 1995)

If you want to have that freedom here, then you must have the discipline that was bred by your Indian culture. Yet this trait may backfire because once strong authority of the parents is withdrawn or inoperative, the young Indian American may be unable to handle freedom. The trick is to enjoy the 'wildness' of NYU and its environs, while "keeping your priorities straight"—which means, do nothing to undermine your NYU education. In Chakraborty's terms, discipline is an Indian cultural trait which must be conserved, and utilized, a trait instilled by parental control and attention which in excess, may make the young Indian-American too sheltered and unable to handle freedom. On the other hand, it can be an important ingredient for success. A too sheltered, traditional, i.e., desi (parochial) lifestyle, will not allow that balance between school (discipline, success) and worldly savvy (a free lifestyle).

Homosexuality is a particularly contentious issue. In the skit *Lost Desi in America*, the only 'woman' who is willing to dance with the unhip hick is a transvestite garbed in a salwar kameez. The desi, unschooled in the social mores of Greenwich Village cannot distinguish between transvestite and a woman. In the sketch *Vinu's Vorld* , a joke was cracked about how hanging out in Greenwich Village too long would increase your chances of and preferences for homosexual encounter. This expresses yet another kind of anxiety that the free and open American society is believed to brew in the minds of Indian Americans and their parents[17]. The vast spectrum of choice of whom you can love that a cosmopolitan city like New York is believed to offer sometimes, much to the dismay of Indian parents, weakens the traditional Indian ideal of an endogamous heterosexual marriage. Not to say that homosexuality, transvestitism, transexuality do not exist in India as well as among Indians in America though many would like to believe not[18] (see Chapter 4), but such liaisons will not produce Indian babies, future Indians who will carry with them the seeds of Indian culture.

In Shruti, there are no "out" homosexuals. In fact, according to Chakraborty, most of the Shruti members are homophobic which encourages him and his cohorts to play at being homosexual just to shock the others. He himself is considered gay because he is a theater buff as well as theatrical, organizes the fashion shows, is an English major, and most of his friends are female. He is comfortable putting his arm around his male buddies as well as discussing menstruation cycles with his female friends. He was even suspected of being part of a menage a trois, even a menage a quatro with two other females and one of their boyfriends. He told me about three of his female friends who used to fearlessly kiss each other full on the mouth in front of the other male members just to titillate and shock them.

Figure 5.5. To dance, per chance to touch? And yet be Indian!

Homosexuality (and for that matter even heterosexual dating), though very much in the closet is enacted in this playful way. Chakraborty chirpily admitted that "I loved being at the center of it all. Let them think what they like—they are the ones most insecure about their sexuality!" Chakraborty, thus is the playful and performative, androgynous Krishna making sexual and theatrical mischief[19]. He and one of his buddies were the only men who sported braids in the Shruti show. Indeed, what could be expected from newly let out young adults who can now, at last, explore different aspects of their self, especially in the fertile fields of liberal, Western collegiate education?

GROOVING IN THE THIRD SPACE

How then does the young Indian American adult carry the burden of the protective demands of his or her heritage with the confusing and complex pains and pleasures of cultural variety? An answer glimmers in the group dances that appear throughout the Shruti show, in the skits and jokes enunciated by the participants, in the strategies of discreet dating. One such number, *Antakshree*, was the show's climax. Couples danced a fusion of film dance, folk and Western styles to a medley of Hindi film songs. Like the *Brides and Grooms* presentation, real couples were not paired, but coupling was represented. Antakshree enables heterosexual contact between co-ethnics as their bodies touch, coordinate, and display their prowess and beauty to each other as well as to the audience.

The audience revels in the ambiguity and potential that the young men and women on stage can, indeed, become or are couples (even though they are not). This activity is cloaked in the protective and familiar harmonies of the Hindi film songs, the Indian costumes worn by the participants, and the fact that they are involved in performing an aspect of Indian culture. An important note about the costuming in Antakshree. As elsewhere in the Shruti shows the women wore salwar khameezes while the men wore Western style trousers and shirts. What was distinctive is that the men wore the veils that accompanied their partner's salwar khameezes around their waists. The veil is traditionally an emblem of modesty and chastity. The men using these as accents for their attire suggest that these women and men have shared, exchanged, enjoyed or would like to enjoy that modesty and chastity in sexual play and exploration. They are in effect tied to each other, partners in these child to adult games. Their dance seems to be saying :

> Hey! Look at me! At least, I am dancing to an Indian song, wearing an Indian costume, participating in an Indian organization with other Indians. Though I may choose my own partners, trust me to pick someone Indian enough for you, Indian American enough for me, not too desi, and, *not* an American (and of the opposite sex, too!!). So let us sing, let us dance, let us be Indian American.

These strategies, as well as the gamut of numbers throughout the Shruti show make the assertion of partner choice by the Indian American youth easy for parents to accept since it is represented in so visually arresting a manner. Parents of the Shruti members comprise the bulk of the audience that attend the show. The show is videotaped, copies of which are shared and passed around different households of both Shruti and non-Shruti members in the tri-state area. Through the show, parents become used to seeing their children interacting with members of the opposite sex, especially with other children who may not necessarily come from the same regional, linguistic, religious, or parochial backgrounds as they are but nevertheless with others who look Indian, and share the same experiences of their hybrid youth.

The Shruti show's portrayal of Indian American identity depicts the fluid dialog, integration, fusion, of coalescing value systems that they have been handed down by their Indian parents and that they confront as young U.S. Americans. Because of their amicability, pragmatism and contemporaneity, it is no surprise that the popular entertainment genres of the variety show, fashion show, the narratives disseminated through electronic mass media are used to navigate the rough and unfamiliar topography of cultural variety and ambiguity. The performance of Indianness in this Shruti show is "neither wholly Indian, nor wholly American—but partially both . . . [it] does not exist in the hyphen between India and America, but within Indian Americans" (Feng, 1994:3). Since this performance is "almost Indian but not quite, almost American but not quite" (and definitely not white), it fits Homi Bhabha's description of hybridity as the creation of a "third space":

> This third space displaces the histories that constitute it, and sets up new structures of authority, new political initiatives . . . it bears the traces of those feelings and practices that inform it, just like translation, so that hybridity puts together the traces of certain other meanings or discourses. It does not give them authority of being prior in the sense of being original: they are prior in the sense of being anterior. The process of cultural hybridity gives rise to something different, something new and unrecognizable, a new area of negotiation of meaning and representation. (1990:211)

The self that is expressed in this Shruti production seems to be a natural, informal, spontaneous, and dare I say, an authentic representation of what it means to be Indian in America, of being American having Indian heritage. The Shruti show is the site—the third space—where Indian Americans celebrate the difference between their Indian heritage and American culture, as well as it enunciates the differences amongst castes, classes, religions and regions. Most importantly, the Shruti show is the process with which the anxieties experienced by the interpenetration of cultures and intergenerational conflicts are confronted and differences within are negotiated.

The Shruti show is an example par excellence of an active and empowering intercultural moment. Una Chaudhuri states:

[Identity] shows itself as multivalent, subject to the shades and shadows of difference, a matter of circumstances, feelings, and perspectives—plural—not privilege [. . .] an incomplete, on-going process [. . . in the personalist terrain [called] the difference within (1991:205, 199)

The third space of hybridity exists within the selves of many Indian-Americans. The Shruti show and others like it, is the theatrical space of the third kind wherein this hybridity is enacted.

NOTES

[1] A Punjabi folk dance now adopted by South Asians world-wide.

[2] desi is a term also used for a parochial Indian. It literally means 'country-man'.

[3] Earlier drafts of this paper have been presented in the *Social Theory, Politics and the Arts* conference, Northeastern University; *Rethinking the South Asian Diaspora: The Politics of Cultural Production* workshop, Iowa University & Independent Scholars of South Asia; *Asians in America* conference, New York University. I especially like to thank Peter Feng, and participants in the Iowa workshop for their valuable comments.

[4] Unless otherwise indicated, information on Shruti's policies, and anecdotes about Shruti have been garnered from interviews with Mr. Ritin Chakraborty.

[5] In my own involvement in such organizations, I have observed that those organizations that can really be true to the idea of an inclusive *South Asian* organization are run usually by young, first and second generation American born South Asians, or young diasporic South Asians whose sense of being rooted to a geographic homeland is amorphous. Usually these South Asian organizations are issue-driven rather than for cultural advocacy such as Sakhi for South Asian Women (domestic violence) South Asian Women's Creative Collective (women's artistic expression), South Asian Youth Action (youth development), South Asian Lesbian and Gay Alliance (sexuality), amongst others.

[6] This is a pseudonym. So are all other names of Shruti members to protect their privacy.

[7] This subtitle is taken from Filipino writer Nick Joaquin's novel "Woman who had Two Navels". It is a surreal portrayal of cultural confusion of Filipinos wrought out of having two colonial 'mothers', i.e., Spain and America.

[8] The issues of gender representation have been discussed in the previous chapter. In Vinu's World, the Shruti version of Wayne's World, Mina, the top Babe who is their colleague rejects these two idiots, and saunters off.

[9] In the forthcoming discussion, the term desi is used to describe the more parochial qualities of Indianness that is reviled by young Indian Americans. I have used this term in lower case—*desi* to distinguish it from the way I have appropriated it to describe a new emergent politicized and inclusive South Asian—*Desi*.

[10] Gurinder Chadha "I'm British But..."; Nandini Sikand's "Bhangra Wrap"; Tejaswini Ganti's "Gimme Something to Dance To" presented in Sakhi for South Asian Women's Fourth Annual Film Festival Women Directors from South Asia.

[11] It is also prestigious to bring back to India as gifts cloth cut for salwar khameezes made in the US, and sold in Indian textile shops here. The designs on these cloth pieces must look non-Indian. US cotton, rayon and other synthetic fabrics are desirable.

[12] There are ample opportunities across various Indian and Indo-Caribbean communities to participate in beauty pageants, especially for young women. These contests also include talent competitions and costume displays which locate the young girls in their fulfillment of their "destiny into Indianness" that I discuss in the previous chapter. Other Asian American communities like the Filipino and Korean, also include fashion shows and beauty pageants as part of their displays of ethnicity. The celebration of beauty and talent, and traditional dress seem to suggest a similar phenomena of "destiny into Filipina-ness/Koreanness" being practiced by these minorities. In stark contrast, Chinese Americans do not practice this.

[13] Some preliminary research on the sociological variations in attitudes towards and actual arranged marriages amongst Indian American youth have been made by:

Jagat Motwani. "Arranged Marriage and Dating: A Source of Intergenerational Conflict" (paper presented at *Conference on Family*, Washington DC, May 26 to 27, 1984.

A. K. B. Pillai. "Asian Indian Family: Psychological and Cultural Adaptation" _____.

Lini S. Kadaba & Tanya Barrientos. "Balancing Two Worlds" in *Little India*, July 1993, vol. 3, #7.

[14] The prolific Desi party and club scene also helps increase social interaction between young South Asians.

[15] please see previous footnote

[16] In a spate of interviews conducted in 1998, there is much dismay expressed by young Indian American women regarding the way their male counterparts prefer to date and have sexual relations with Indian American women, but will marry more traditional women directly from India via an arranged marriage

"Though men may date the women here, they don't want to marry women who have dated or been around the block a few times" or "They think they can do whatever they want to their women here, then go back to India and get a nice little virgin" are some of the remarks gathered from young Indian Americans. (Melwani, 1998: 29, 30)

[17] I do not mean to suggest here that American society is not homophobic. Though, as I have discussed in chapter 4, living a homosexual lifestyle is believed to be an American phenomenon.

[18] please see *A Lotus of Another Color*, ed. by Rakish Ratti, 1993.

[19] Chakraborty answered my straightforward question on his sexual preferences in the negative in quite a matter-of-fact way. I suspect that he isn't for now and he himself would not be appalled if he turns out to be gay.

CHAPTER 6

It's a Drag Growing Rutabagas in the Shrinking Himalayas
A Performance (Ambi)Valence to Indianness

> *[Spivak]: If there's one thing I totally distrust, in fact, more than distrust, despise and have contempt for, it is people looking for roots. Because anyone who can conceive of looking for roots, should, already, you know, be growing rutabagas . . . And everyone has roots. Why look for them?*
> *[Ingram]: Yes. We carry them around; they're right here. (Spivak, 1990:93)*

Fiji. Singapore. Guyana. Trinidad. Kenya. Uganda. South Africa. Canada. Britain. The United States. The Indian diaspora has placed half-inch Himalayas into mailboxes all over the world. And "home" is no longer a geographical place, but the two-dimensionality of memory and nostalgia…this construction of a global Indianness is (always) already one enabled only by distance traveled; the flattening out . . . of the local values ascribed to regional identities re-veals the extent to which the Himalayas have shrunk . . . the idea of India is used as a signifier of home and identity—which can then function in diaspora to create a sense of homologous home, identity, and community. (Karamcheti, 1992:262)

And 'Indian-ness' is not a thing that exists. Reading Sanskrit scriptures, for example—I can't call that Indian, because after all, India is not just Hindu. That 'Indic' stuff is not India. The name India was given by Alexander the

> Great by mistake. The name Hindustan was
> given by the Islamic conquerors. The name
> Bharat, which is on the passport, is in fact a
> name that hardly anyone uses, which commem-
> orates a mythic king. So it isn't a place that we
> Indians can think of as anything, unless we are
> trying to present a reactive front, against an-
> other kind of argument. (Spivak, 1990:39)

What then does it mean to be Indian outside India? This question is a subset of the bigger question of what does it mean to be Indian at all—"a reactive front to another kind of argument" as Spivak puts it, though there is more to Indianness than it being reactionary whether in India or outside[1]. Outside India, in the United States, being Indian takes on other complexities of being away, of a spatial distance, of memory and forget-ting, of a different representation. This project has described an Indian-ness that is conjured from residual "memory" of an India of great names, of a glorious past and of living here in the US—a hereland that is essen-tialized as Westernized, that is at an advanced stage of industrialization and capitalism, specifically focusing on the cosmopolitan entrepot of New York City. This conjuring bears upon the ways in which those of In-dian heritage outside India deal with the world and with India, influence local politics of their herelands, and experience their life of difference in the West, specifically in the U.S., in a time in history which boasts of the facility of global communications, travel, and multiculturalism.

This concluding chapter illuminates with earnest the two-fold ques-tion of identity politics: 1) How does a minority group express, enjoy and preserve the particularities and varieties of its identity despite the pull, impulse and necessity to assimilate, and 2) what does it mean to perform this multi-faceted and problematic identity against the tragic drama of Indian communalism, in the current climate of the United States' rhetoric on multicultural policy-making, and most importantly, as a means of socio-political empowerment and resistance against racism, the homoge-nizing forces of capitalism, and Western hegemony? I discuss this two-fold questions through several salient points, broadly thematized as **Representation and/of Difference; Multiculturalism and Coalition; The Metropolitan Life and the Logic of Money; Class and Caste; and Migration & Diaspora**.

Interspersed in this final chapter is a performative response to the enactment of Indianness through poems I have written while grappling with the production of this book in its earlier form as a dissertation, while discovering what it means to be Indian for those of Indian origin outside India, and for myself. My personal confrontations with being a woman of Indian heritage in diaspora culminates in a description of a performance piece that I have conjured as a medium of syncretizing the substance and discoveries that have resulted from this study. Please note that I have begun to identify with my subjects since aspects of my life, and this book are examples of Indianness. The pronoun 'We' that I have used indicates my empathy, albeit critical and ambivalent, with the Asian Indians of New York City as well as with Desis in the Diaspora.

REPRESENTATION AND/OF DIFFERENCE

The anxiety of sameness and of possible equality often conjures a heavy weight on difference to justify racism. It is after all easier to kill off, oppress, exploit people who are unlike "you", who are not of "your own". Color, gender, class are some of the differences that are weighed against each other. Varieties within these differences are assigned hierarchies of power. But then again, to begin with, we, human beings are really different in our adaptations to life, in our lifeways, in our socio-cultural responses to living, in our individuality. If the one true way is believed by the host country to be the White/Western/European way, we, who are Other—not White/Western/European fracture that one true way with our difference. We of color, create color while dismantling that empire, yes, still.

> Difference and the salience of different identities are produced by discrimination, a process that establishes the superiority or the typicality or the universality of some in terms of the inferiority or atypicality or particularity of others ... diversity refers to the plurality of identities ... as the effect of an enunciation of difference that constitutes hierarchies and asymmetries of power. (Scott, 1992:15, 14)

If borders are unbound then that means borders are fallible which in turn means one can travel back and forth through these borders, leaving traces of culture here, there and everywhere, intermingling and creating new hybrids. The border is porous and somewhat useless in keeping difference out. Therefore, there really is no support for the hierarchies of difference between that human and this human. If borders are porous, how then to apportion resources? How then to hoard more for your own self and your own group? These concerns of hoarding and apportioning are the roots of a spurious nationalism based on models of scarcity rather than that of abundance of and the egalitarian distribution of resources. It is a nationality based on the fixity of territoriality. What happens to this fixed sense of territoriality, to the sense of citizenship when one is an Indian living outside India? Where one's living place seems to contrast one's cultural space?

Despite the Indian immigrant or the diasporic Indian having crossed the porous boundaries, having traversed the "black waters" and having lived away for many generations, amidst others, she still has a strong sense of Indianness, still bears the weight of her attachment to her Desi ancestry and heritage. Since so much of this sense and attachment is in the imagination, in memory, rather than actually lived, Indianness has to be continually defined, invented, displayed, performed. It cannot be taken for granted, it is a phenomenon. The performance of Indianness is manifested in a variety of expressive behaviors running the gamut of marga and desi hierarchies, and in the new diasporic Desi hybrid forms.

There is a broad linguistic diversity amongst Indians so we use performative genres that are not necessarily language-bound but can be embodied such as music, dance, clothes, food. The pan-Indian versions of these forms and the diasporic/international editions of these forms such as disco *Bhangra*, the salwar khameez, Hindi film songs and dances, and chicken tikka masala or lasagna keema (aspects of recipe forthcoming) are some specific examples of Desi forms.

The lingua franca of the end-of-the-century diverse Indian community in New York, in the United States, in diaspora, is the Hindi masala film especially the song and dance sequences which are enjoyed on video or heard or performed by visiting superstars or reenacted for a live audience. Other popular expressive forms such as fashion and variety shows, comedy sketches, food fairs, are also pan-Indian expressions that appear in community shows globally, in other diasporic sites of Indianness.

These expressions are also the new urban folklore forms. We can move in these forms. Our bodies are involved in the enactment of, in the production and consumption of culture using these pan-Indian expressive forms. Indianness displayed needs movement to show presence— physical, visible, robust presence. A heart-pumping, feet-stomping, pelvic thrusting, arms flailing presence. We are not erased! We cannot be ignored! This is very unlike the home-bound traditional/spiritual nationalist woman or the self-effacing, passive portrayal of the Gandhian[2] Indian in the West and exalted by the Indian nationalists involved in the independence project. This vivid kind of representation requires the on-lookers' attention and engagement, and may even demand participation.

These forms are non-classical/non-Brahmanic expressive forms as a result of the long arms of video technology, the availability of audiocas-settes, and other electronic and digital musical media, the distribution of films, the facility of international travel, the shifts of migration patterns. These technologies provide culture that travels light and relatively cheap, whereas classical arts require musicians, costumes, an imported guru, a hefty income—accoutrements that are tied tightly to the geographical India, as well as to her elite classes. These structures can be mimicked here, but they are only mimicries, that is, if India is perceived as the site of the original, authentic Indianness. To validate one's expertise in classi-cal dance for example, an aspirant must go to India for a few months or years to learn the dance in a prestigious school there. To perform a true classical dance, one must have live musicians; taped music is a begrudg-ing substitute. The burden to represent India this way is heavy, whereas the technolocal arts are light. This bearable lightness of being Indian out-side India is a new form of Indianness, portable and democratic. You or I, Indian-born or American born, Indian or not can perform it after school or work, on the weekends, with very minimal interruption of the week, or lifestyle of mainstream America, yet vivifying mainstream American life with spice and color, at will. At our will.

Forms that are not perceived to be indigenously Indian, or even available to other non-elite classes are made vernacular through spoof-ing, owning, appropriating, Indianizing, doing it the Desi way. The world of European and American haute couture, Hollywood popular cinema, mainstream television and popular music, are used to express the senti-ments of American youth of South Asian heritage. At a community per-formance in Forest Hills, Queens, March of 1996, a group of young dancers who named themselves after a Indian sweet dish, *Jelebi Babies* performed modern jazz to a mix of hip-hop Hindi filmi songs while their admirers, family and extended kin, and friends squeal in delight at their voluptuousness. The dance is an invitation to party, enjoy each other. So come, let's party!

The Party

And so off I go
to a Barney party
to become one

with my people!
Let me be fair
My friends will be there
and they will be perplexed to see
that I am yet unmarried
have done so much university
and be kind nevertheless,
because my name sounds
familiar, familial, filial,
and has a hint of royalty.

So we will commiserate
about our heavy hips
despite diets and aerobics
and how to groom out our body hair
over the Chinese buffet
at a restaurant in Queens
interrupting our conversation
with exclamations
that the delectable morsels
though sumptuous, do need
a little more spice.

The purple dinosaur will romp
with children whose complexions
are various hues of masala chai[3]
They ache to touch his body,
take His darshan[4]
be blessed by his magnanimity.
And in unison, we all will sing, devotedly
about I loving you, you loving me,
we loving everybody, A bhajan[5]
about being one big happy family!

The mimicries illustrate the doubleness of same and different. We are, but not quite. A true hybridity of being not wholly Indian, not wholly Western, not wholly other. We are all, and are not, because identity is a compelling but spurious myth.

Almost the same but not quite, almost the same but not white . . . The discourse of mimicry is constructed around an ambivalence [continually] producing its slippage, its excess, its difference . . . Mimicry is, thus, the sign of the inappropriate. . . . Black skin splits under the racist gaze, displaced into signs of bestiality, genitalia, grotesquerie, which reveal the phobic myth of the undifferentiated whole white body. (Bhabha, 1984:126. 130, 132-133)

Though Bhabha specifically speaks about the supremacist yearning for the purity of whiteness over the grotesquerie of blackness, I use his notions of mimicry producing what marga aficionados, i.e., Indian elites and proponents of official Indianness would consider as inappropriate or excessive. So to dance film dance in a hip-hop beat, and sing a bhajan to Barney reveals the tenuousness and fallibility of the undifferentiated authentic and pure Indianness. Thus, to turn a polemic phrase, I yearn for another much preferred pre-lapsarian impulse. The narrative of the intercultural:

Learn to be intercultural? More like: unlearn what is blocking us from returning to the intercultural. For as far back as we can look in human history peoples have been deeply, continuously, unashamedly intercultural. Borrowing is natural to our species . . . What is borrowed is swiftly transformed into native material—at the very same time as the borrowing remakes native culture . . . Syncretism and the making of new cultural stuff is the norm of human activity. (Schechner, 1991:313)

The story of interculturalism rebuffs the myth of an undifferentiated, authentic, pure, original identity, be it Whiteness, or Indianness. Though, Indians outside India may search and invent an authentic Indianness, its elusive and slippery characteristics, necessitate continuous mimicry and performance.

These are the kinds of Indiannessess in the diaspora (at least covered in this book): The **authenticated**, the **parochial**, the **hyphenated**, and the **Desi hybrid.**

An **authenticated**, essentialist, nationalist Indianness is depicted by the Indian elites in New York during festivals and parades in Manhattan, utilizing bourgeois notions of all that is true, good and beautiful about India, and its most folkloric, exotic and colorful aspects. The truth of the matter is that India is all that, too. But due to the nasty habit of ex-nomination, these elites are unable to admit follies, foibles and problems, and certain kinds of difference that are believed to taint and mark all that is true, good and beautiful about being Indian. Or these are shamefacedly veiled in a heavy purdah of exclusion, rejection, even denial. Or, at least, not be displayed publicly, especially to non-Indians. The ex-nominated, undifferentiated 'We' must continue to be a model minority, showing that despite our minority status we can excel because of our traditional family values, the resilient spirituality of our ancient civilization, the profound efflorescence of our aesthetics. We market these aspects of our culture, and are convinced of it ourselves to a large extent, so as to be recognized as part of the human species as human and humane beings by those (imperialistic mercantile colonialists) who historically have regarded us as barbaric, excessive, bestial, grotesque.

But 'we human and humane beings' are minority, nevertheless, and must be considered for affirmative action so we can get that job, fill that space, have access to abundance, to excel! Hence the category of 'Asian Indian' in the U.S. Census. We, Asian Indians, are different from you European Americans, because we are your racial and cultural other, but we, Asian Indians are the same as you European Americans because by virtue of immigrating, living, and working, and being born here are entitled to all the privileges of U.S. citizenship.

Indianness has multiple definitions. Official Indianness is encouraged by the National Endowment of the Humanities, the Ford Foundation, and others. These forms are not of the people, being the class arts of Indian heritage. They are also not of the white people, and in fact, show how different Indian culture is to that of Western. Classical traditions, folk arts and crafts, are some of the representations of official Indianness. These forms need official governmental support whereas popular, commercial entertainments, i.e., vernacular forms have the support of community businesses and the avid participation of the community members already. Though these vernacular forms are conservative at one level, they, are subversive of class/caste structure and ideologies at another. The spurious dichotomy of official Indianness as the soil and soul of Indian culture and vernacular expressions as its body and goods ignore the fact that the body is present and reconfigured in both. What aspect of the body is emphasized depends on class and caste biases: pelvic thrusts, broad movements, flamboyant costuming are used in popular forms while graceful, delicate movements of the upper body are used for official forms. These broad movements are regarded as earth-bound, calling attention to the erogenous parts of the human body, miming the sex act and its potentiality at times. The latter movements are regarded on the "higher plane" of spirituality, away from the body. The duality is a Platonic intrusion—a vestige of Anglican Victorian education—a gift from colonial imperialism.

Because the authenticated Indianness is a nationalist one, this identity is directed towards an allegiance to the nation-state of India. There is an underlying resistance to being inclusive of other South Asians, an assertion of an exalted *Indian* and *Hindu* culture. This kind of Indianness is an argument against invisibility, an assertion of presence and clout.

Here is an example of the acknowledgment of **parochial** Indianness along sectarian or regional lines:

> Upon approaching the desi-looking ticket taker at New Jersey turnpike, a desi truck driver asked: Should I say 'Namaste', 'Salaam', 'Sat Sri Akaal' or 'Hi! How ya doin?' To which she replied amusedly— 'Namaste'! This response indicated that she was not Muslim (Salaam), Sikh (Sat Sri Akaal), or Christian—Westernized—American Born (Hi! How ya doin?), but an Indian Hindu.

There's a pick-up line to beat all pick-up lines!! From being a generic Desi, the kind of Desi the ticket taker was cleverly extracted. Asian Indians also associate with others who speak the same language, eat the same kind of food, and would prefer for themselves and their offspring to marry endogamously. The ideal is to build family, and reinforce community with someone from the same class, caste, religion, and linguistic group propagating sameness within an environment of difference. There are specific variations and their enactments depending on family background and individual preference. Coming to the United States, specifically New York City, where there are not only many non-Indians to contend with, there are other kinds of Indians (South Asians) to associate with, befriend, desire, and even procreate with. Asian Indians here, during the work week may allow for associations with other Indians as well as non-Indians but on the weekends, they associate with like-minded family members, relatives and friends. To smell aromas, taste flavors, undulate to rhythms, guffaw at jokes that are familiar and that are shared are comforting amidst the hostilities and aloofness of the competitive and unemotional work environment. These "vernacular" Indians are members or participate both in their specific linguistic associations, as well as in Pan-Indian organizations. In their lived lives, too, they can watch a Tamil film on video at home, but also watch a Hindi film on screen in one of the cinema houses, or eat Gujarati food at home and have Mughlai Indian cuisine in an Indian restaurant, or go to the Sindhi

Hindu temple in Woodside every Sunday, but attend a wedding in the (South Indian) Hindu Temple of North America in Flushing, or dance the Dandya during Navratri in Jersey City, and dance disco *Bhangra* on a float blaring the latest Hindi film songs during Independence day down Madison Avenue. The binaries of what is Indian other and not-other are not rigid, or fixed. The boundaries of what is official Indianness and vernacular are malleable, always shifting, depending on the situation.

The vernacular Indianness takes into account the specific religious, regional, and caste affiliations that may have been diluted in a Pan-Indian configuration. The assertion of self is for the pleasure of familiarity amongst co-ethnics. The parochial identity is an argument against being made invisible by larger forces within the Indian community by declaring an allegiance to a particular culture within the Indian panorama.

These excerpts from an NYU freshman student paper on identity illustrate the consciousness of an emergent **hyphenated** Indianness[6] among American-born Indian young adults:

Ethnicity is enjoyed and celebrated through a performance genre of the Gujarati folk dance Garba and through the comfort of the Hindu religion:

> I would consistently participate in Garba and would enjoy learning the intricate steps and rhythms involved. The Hindu culture also provided me with a spiritual outlook...that making money and having material pleasures are not the only things in life...it is important to be a hardworking individual who is also sensitive to other's need. The religious aspect has . . . given me . . . mental peace.

Religion, cultural origin, linguistic/regional affiliations conflate to form ethnic distinctiveness. Being Hindu is too simplistically conflated with being Indian, a glaring indication that a bulk of the definition of Indianness depends on the characteristics, idiom and iconography of Hinduism. Indianness is defined by what non-Indianness is negatively perceived to be. A clear boundary is set up between 'us' and 'them'.

> [My parents] believed that Americans in general were immoral untrustworthy people who have no stability and directions in their lives . . . they would always point out things like how high the divorce rate and how it would damage family values . . . They felt that only immoral American people who have promiscuous sex habits had AIDS.

It is not surprising how similar the vocabularies are between the rhetorics of American Moral Right and the claims to the superiority of a non-American ethnicity. An obedient child from a protective home begins to experience a more diverse life in school:

> I began to learn about sports and other things that Hindu culture did not have. I learned it was okay to have friends who are girls, which is usually frowned upon in the Hindu culture. Other positive things that I learned about this culture was it was okay to question authority as long as you can substantiate your opinions. When I was younger, I accepted everything my parents said as law and I would never question them.

The young man learns to have more control of his body and his mind, enjoys the rush of his hormones. His Americanization and individuation from his parents' value system is facilitated by western-style U.S. education. In severing the umbilical cord, crisis is palpable.

> Probably the most absurd manner in which I try to convince myself that I was not Indian involved my skin color. Being lighter skin than most Hindus, I thought I could blend in with the American kids. I would get great satisfaction in hearing from others, especially Americans, that I didn't look Hindu.

The young man has taken advantage of a racism that allows him to gain acceptance, and assimilate to white American culture because he can pass as white. But nevertheless he is still a brown (albeit a light shade of) Hindu, and not white. He is neither here nor there, both here and there— "in between".

> This conflict came more to the forefront when I went to a [picnic] in a park in upstate New York. . . . As people were mingling amongst themselves, I felt very lonely. I didn't know anyone because I had cut off ties from the Hindu culture for almost seven years. The cultural games and speeches no longer had any significance to me. I felt so hurt and ashamed at not knowing what was going on.
>
> The Americans who were picnicking near our group were picnicking in their own way. They had their barbecues and games, something I was not familiar with. So I stood there between these two groups, feeling very clearly that I was 'in between' the two cultures.

Confronting again the heritage of his childhood from which he had cut himself off from, and realizing that the host country's culture was distinct from what he was used to, the young man sees himself as neither wholly Indian (Gujarati/Hindu) nor wholly American (White) That bleeding wound of the hyphen is sutured with the salve of redefinition.

> I then realized that I had been living according to the expectations of others and not considering what I wanted. I didn't have to label myself "American" or "Hindu". No one was holding a gun to my head and telling me to choose. I learned I could be both and incorporate the positive aspects of both in my life.
>
> I could still enjoy the Indian Garba and at the same time appreciate the liberal thinking that I learned in school. So why not be both and be an "American Hindu".

A graduation from parochiality and essentialisms, to a hyphenated identity; from obedient boy to a self-possessed young man, wearing the stigma of his fracture hopefully. He has invented a new identity for himself. It is a new amalgam, a third psychic space where he can live and play that is neither wholly Hindu or wholly American. As Trinh T. Minha asserts:

> The challenge of the hyphenated reality lies in the hyphen itself: The becoming Asian-American [or American Hindu]; the realm in-between, where predetermined rules cannot fully apply [the laws of mom and dad; of passing as white] . . . becoming Asian American affirms itself at once as a transient and constant state: one is born over and over again as hyphen rather than as fixed entity, thereby refusing to settle down in one world or another. (1991:157)

Though the young man scuttled between the essentialisms of Hinduness/Indianness and Americanness, indeed, no one held a gun to his head to choose either. His world expands to include many others. In expanding, he breaks off from his infantile space of parochialism, resists melting into the pot of oblivion, but instead, creates a 'third space' of hyphenation (where he may dance disco Garba!) much like the South Asian American youth in the Shruti show.

The complex, exciting, new, emerging **Desi Hybrid** identity is shared by those of South Asian origin who feel committed in the hereland they find themselves in and acknowledge the similarities in the colonial histories, in the multicultural politics of their present, and the pleasures they derive from the melange of American, African, and South Asian expressive forms that they share with others like them. Caste, Region, Religion, National origins hold no bar in coming together to advocate for an issue, to party, to represent, to coalesce. This Desi Hybridity is shared amongst ourselves whereas we may call ourselves *South Asian* when we speak to other non-South Asians, or speak officially about our coalition.

Following are excerpts of a recipe of Lasagna Keema—a hybrid blend of an Italian-American dish with some typically Desi ingredients. The pleasure of this dish, besides it's hearty taste, is also in performing a hybrid Desiness in its preparation- going to the Desi stores in Jackson Heights to purchase the spices and meat, blending the spices, and eating this in company. Besides its nutritive value, a new punchy taste is added to a standard American dish, satisfying to both mainstream Americans and to Desis. An apt metaphor for adding spice to an otherwise mundane, workaday, bland, impersonal existence that highly industrialized and mechanized city life is believed to provide for most of its residents.

Though New York city can boast of having the most varied and at times delicious array of ethnic foods, preparing and eating an ethnic food is an important form of performing and participating in Desiness, and reassuring Desis in America that despite being here, they have maintained their 'taste' for their homelands by preferring and yearning for Desi spice. And also that in their sojourn here, Desis are 'American' enough to enjoy food that is not 'native' to them. The recipe is also an act of appropriation—taking a foreign artifact and making it one's own, adjusting it to the Desi palate, and in doing so, overpowering its distance and otherness. Thus, here are excerpts of this amalgam, an attempt to create a transnational cuisine:

Ingesting Hybridity
while being Hospitably Desi:
Recipe for Lasagna Keema
(excerpts)

This is an arduous dish because it takes time to prepare. It is not a diet dish either. It calls for a special occasion, or for the weekend, or when the spirit moves you. Your friends and family will enjoy it and their compliments are worth the effort. Do not fall into the trap of "Indian womans means cooking"[7]. Such nonsense! I insist you include your partner, your family, your friends in the preparation of this dish, in shopping for the ingredients, in assembling the dish, in eating it—making it a communal, egalitarian affair. Hey! A party!

Much of the recipe can be followed by reading the directions off the box of lasagna. I present here only the variations, especially the secrets in the sauce.

This dish is good for six people of medium appetite, for four of hefty appetite. It can be served with fresh salad greens, garlic bread, ice-cold draft, red wine, or whatever you want.

A. For the Sauce

1. 2 pounds of goat meat ground and cleaned by any of the Muslim halal butchers in Elmhurst, or Jackson Heights. Divine intervention of this ilk, a must. I am not Muslim, but I feel that halal meat is lean, clean, fresh and tasty. The butcher cleans and cuts the meat for you which reduces your preparation time in half—a welcome relief, indeed. You can substitute with halal chicken, turkey, or beef. For the vegetarians, minced gluten will have to do or you could leave the 'meat' out altogether and add four cups of vegetables.

(steps 2 to 4 omitted)

. . .

4. One big red onion. It's pungency makes the meat fragrant.

5. 1 tablespoon each of garlic powder, ginger powder, cumin powder, coriander powder, chili powder, garam masala, mango powder. I prefer that you purchase these spices from any Desi grocery store rather than from general supermarkets. Though they may be ground and processed in New Jersey, these spices are authenticated because they are used by Desis in the NYC tri-state area, so they must be good. (All other ingredients you can purchase in any supermarket). You may increase the amount of spices to more than one tablespoon but that might be too hot. The sauce must tingle your tongue not burn it, but then again it's your tongue.

So that the spices are more pungent, you can purchase them in seed form and grind them yourself using a coffee bean grinder. To perform the ultimate in folksiness, you may want to pound these spices with a pestle and mortar, instead—but we all work, and there is much to do, so who has the time!!

(steps 6 & 7 omitted)

. . .

8. Corn oil for sautéing will do but you can up the notch of 'authentic' Desiness by using ghee—clarified butter. Most Desis in the U.S.A. use corn oil. It is healthier and easily available.

B. For the Cheeses .

3. 1 tablespoon each of cumin seeds, dried red peppers, ground black pepper added to the 1.5 pound of ricotta, and 1.5 pounds of mozzarella.

Procedure: Most of the procedure can be followed from the lasagna box however, goat meat may take longer to cook so add 10 minutes if you are not convinced of its done-ness. The sauce must be fragrant and not smell of the meat.

Then with gusto serve, eat and relish this hybrid dish which will win the hearts of both your Desi buddies, American colleagues, multi-culti chums, and all those in between.

And while preparing this dish, how about listening to this song by Taj in which the grand qualities of the Desi girl are extolled:

> I was walking in Jackson Heights
> My favorite part of Queens
> In the window of an Indian Store
> I saw her face on a magazine
> Babababbabbabaaaaby!!!
> Namaste!
> I think I'm in love
> A red lenga boom banga!
> C'mon give me your handa!
> Be the one I'm dreaming off
> I don't know how to get to you
> But there is nothing I wouldn't do
> For the love of a Desi Girl
> You are making me crazy
>
> I have been living in the Bronx so long
> Thought my life would slip away
> Never knew that the girl I'd love
> Would be somewhere from Bombay!

> Babababbbbabby!!
> Asalaam-Alaikum!
> I think I'm in love
> If its Hindi or a Sindhi
> Put on a little Mehndi
> Be the one I'm dreaming off!

MULTI-CULTURALISM AND COALITION

> From World Music to exotic holidays in Third-World locations, ethnic
> TV dinners to Peruvian knitted hats, cultural difference *sells.* This is
> the 'difference' of commodity relations, the particular experience of
> time and space produced by transnational capital. In the commodifica-
> tion of language and culture, objects and images are torn free of their
> original references and their meanings become a spectacle open to al-
> most infinite translation . . . Otherness is sought after for its exchange
> value, its exoticisms and the pleasures, thrills and adventures it can
> offer. The power relation is closer to tourism than imperialism, an ex-
> propriation of meaning rather than materials. (Rutherford, 1990:11)

The South Street Seaport Deepavali Festival is an example of this
barter of essentialisms, of otherness sought for its pleasures, thrills and
adventures. The myth of authentic, different and exotic Indianness is exchanged for U.S. American privilege. Exotic others provide bland, enter-
tainment-hungry U.S. American life with color, variety and spice besides
the talent, hard work, productivity of their labor. Besides being an em-
ployee, professional, laborer, exotic others, by virtue of their difference
provide amusement. Though ethically contentious, exoticness becomes a
commodity that is exploited in order to be endowed U.S. citizenship and
the U.S. dollars it can bring. The artificiality of Indianness is underscored in it's flamboyant celebration. It is a put-on, an invention, a conceit.

> I come to these shows
> dressed in kitsch gold and cherryred
> a dot winking suggestively
> in the middle of my forehead
> a tourist in my own culture
> to be reassured that
> those other Indians

> though unlike me
> can like me
> because I am passing
> as one of them.
> Because I like to see,
> I dance, and inflect my speech
> with the proper intonation
> choice words of dialect
> Mimicking Indianness
> And because I can cook with spice
> and eat everything Indian nice.
> Now I am ripening
> readying myself
> to contribute to community
> without being a part
> through the authority
> of my dubious ethnicity
> and that elusive NYU Ph.D.

Multi-culturalism began as a response in academic and educational circles against the oppressive Eurocentrism of texts, values, and aesthetics. At its worse, the term seems to emphasize difference leading to divisiveness between cultures rather than a coalition against Eurocentric hegemony. Many ethnic minorities organize on grounds of ethnicity defined and authorized by cultural elites, not on grounds of issues that we are commonly grappling with. In the subcontinental community in the US, the first step of coalition is toward a construction of South Asianness, rather than merely an Indianness. Commendable are the efforts of the left-off center groups like *SAKHI—for South Asian Women*, and *SALGA*—South Asian Lesbian and Gay Alliance who coalesce on the issues of domestic violence and alternative sexualities. Multiple valences of gender and sexuality, ethnicity, and empowerment strengthen the groups' clout, and further their influence and effectivity. The historically and politically split up subcontinent is reunified in the Diaspora as South Asia especially in organizations such as South Asian Youth Action, South Asian Women's Creative Collective, to name a few.

Growing up in white communities, South Asian gay men and lesbians often depend on the support they can get from their families, who share, at least, a commonality in heritage that becomes of immediate

importance in the face of white racism. The bonding in communities
becomes an act of protection. (Rasiah, 1993:271)

Grouping ourselves as South Asians increases our numbers as a category
to contend with.

The next step of coalescing is then toward Asianness or Asian-
Americanness with the history of exclusion and discrimination as valences of bonding. We could coalesce on the basis of issues: poverty or
economic disenfranchisement, emaciated education and health care, discrimination, domestic violence, sexuality, immigration, and even the oppressive US foreign policy. It is strategic since there is strength in
numbers.

> The grouping "Asian American" is not a natural or static category; it is
> a socially constructed unity, a situationally specific position that we as-
> sume for political reasons . . . It is possible to utilize specific signifiers
> of ethnic identity, such as Asian American, for the purpose of contest-
> ing and disrupting the discourses that exclude Asian Americans while
> simultaneously revealing the internal contradictions and slippages of
> Asian American so as to insure that such essentialisms will not be re-
> produced and proliferated by the very apparatuses we seek to disem-
> power . . . in the 1990's we can afford to rethink the notion of ethnic
> identity in terms of cultural, class, and gender differences, rather than
> presuming similarities and making the erasure of particularity the basis
> of unity. (Lowe, 1991:48)

Ritin Chakraborty, an ex-officer of the NYU South Asian Student
group Shruti quit to join an Asian organization on campus because there
he felt he could be recognized as Indian rather than as a "North" Indian
who spoke Bengali. He felt that the larger and more generic identity of
'Indian' allowed him to participate in Indianness more fully, using his
talent as variety show producer without having to defend his authenticity
as an Indian to other fellow Indians (as was discussed in the Chapter 5).
In 1995, as an undergraduate instructor in a private college in New Jersey, he asserts that the controversies of difference and divisiveness that
he had to confront in both Shruti and the Asian organization have helped
him educate his multicultural students to live harmoniously, and to de-
nounce discrimination, to think beyond racial difference. Thus to co-
exist in *shruti* or harmony.

Another example of a coalition based on a shared Asian-American political issue rather than a particular ethnicity is the *Committee on Anti-Asian Violence*. The Committee was founded on the basis of a shared history of criminal acts of discrimination against Asians in the United States, and seeks to intervene, and prevent further violence and discrimination. Other examples of organizations that share a common political agenda are the Asian Americans for Equality who strive for equality in housing opportunities for low-income Asian Americans, The Asian American Legal Defense and Education Fund who help provide legal services especially in discrimination cases, Asian/Pacific Islander Coalition on HIV and AIDS for the increased awareness, research and funding for AIDS. There are many others.

Another important group to coalesce is with the African American community. The African American community is not a community of immigrants, but is a diasporic one. It continues to suffer the tyrannies of racism, and experience similar problems of disenfranchisement. Having a historically longer foothold in the United States, strength in numbers, as well as highly politicized civic life, the community is a formidable ally to have against the Anglo-centrist hegemony. It is predicted by the National Immigration Forum that by the year 2040, 40% of the U.S. population will consist of people of color—immigrant and native-born Latinos, Asians and Blacks (1994).

It is unfortunate that even within Asian communities there is racial discrimination against the African American community, (there is discrimination in the Indian community against dark-colored skin in general as described in Chapter 3). Amongst Asian Indians, African Americans are also condemned as a criminal underclass to be feared. Unlearning stereotypes and rethinking racist predilections only benefit the Asian communities. After all we do not want to be discriminated against by both white and black!!

Indeed in the areas of performance, and in the presentation of self, Asian Indian youth adopt the popular art forms, the dress sense, and speech—the aesthetic and style of the hybrid African American youth culture. Understandably these forms are construed not necessarily as 'black' but as 'American' or even 'youthful', and 'modern' which they also are. Its visibility and difference sets the youth apart from the staidness of the older generation. Their inherent physical exuberance, expressive sexuality, and petulance against the sobrieties of out-dated values individuates and enlivens the Desi youth who participate in this type of hybrid aesthetics. The motivation to adopt the hybrid African American style slips between defying the conservatism of an older generation, and identifying with a racial other. But even moreso, these mixing of hip-hop with *Bhangra* and with Hindi film musics, opens up lines of communication and expressivity which are inclusive rather than divisive, participatory rather than passive. It reflects a new community being formed or that needs to be formed in the hereland of not-not Desis who are Americans, and who are also diasporic. These are the seedlings of a coalitional identity. Dick Hebdige's observations in the "cut n' mix" multiple versions of hybrid Caribbean musics as expressions of anti-Eurocentric belongingness seem to apply to the beginnings of a new community forming amongst hybrid Desis:

> Nobody can own a sound. Nobody can pin it down or put a copyright on it....As the pressure in the cities has mounted, the old national culture and national identity have started cracking at the seams...There is an army of in-betweens and neither-nors out there who feel they belong to no given community. They realize that any community they might belong to in the future will have to be *made by them* or it won't get made at all...Perhaps there is another nation being formed for the future beyond the boundaries of race. If that nation can't yet be visualized, then it can perhaps be heard in the rhythms of the airwaves, in the beat that binds together histories, cultures, new identities. The future is as blurred and as uncertain as the roots. It is as shapeless and as colorless as music itself (Hebdige, 1988:158).

Hebdige's speculation concurs with the utopian lyrics of pop singer Janet Jackson, "We are a part of the Rhythm nation". Music, dance, rhythm are the valences of coalition amongst youth of different American ethnicities.

And finally, as I have discussed earlier,

> Coalitions must be formed *around issues*, rather than racial groups. Poverty, injustice, poor education, and inadequate health care affect citizens and immigrants, blacks and whites [and all those in between, if I may add] . . . Unfortunately, enemies of social progress are always pleased to see groups who ought to be allies fighting each other over turf or status. (Bernard Watson, 1994)

Celebrating difference is all very well and good in making ourselves visible, inscribing our humanity in this society, and imprinting our presence in the imaginative space of US life, but concurrent with this agenda is the predilection to use these differences to shun others who have the same agenda of visibility, history of exclusion and disenfranchisement. We divide ourselves up, much to our detriment. These coalitions are political strategies or counterarguments against Western/white/Eurocentric hegemony. It would be imprudent of me to suggest that people in their daily lives, in their personal lives, in all aspects of their lives form alliances. Being with those who share some "sameness" of heritage, taste, and culture can be powerfully comforting but we do need to learn to live with each other, to live with difference, and work together for our greater good. A utopian ideal worth aspiring towards rather than constantly deconstructing and being cynical about it.

Flushing Meadows Park

I love picnicking families
They reek of forgiveness
Laughing at each other's silly jokes
Lolling about on the dog poo grass
Swaying their hips to salsa
Barbecuing slabs of meat
And even if it's pumped up with chemicals
or the marinade's really not that great
Everyone's really hungry
and say it's yummy.

I love picnicking families
Children romp about
while the breeze balloons out
their kurta pajamas[8]
Convinced that the mutant ninja
turtle sludging through
that murky lake does love it
will live long,
will win that race
It doesn't.

I love picnicking families
Couples lay facing one another
their coffee thighs entwined,
exchanging sighs and glances

forgetting at least for now that
last night she faked her orgasm
and he's been laid off again
because of his bad English.

I love picnicking on families
The sun numbs them
into lethargic bliss
at least for these few hours
they reek of forgiveness.

LIVING THE METROPOLITAN LIFE

The common material languages of money and commodities provide a
universal basis within market capitalism for linking everyone into an
identical system of market valuation and so procuring the reproduction
of social life through an objectively grounded system of social bonding.
Yet within these broad constraints, we are 'free' . . . to develop our own
personalities and relationships in our own way, our own 'otherness',
even to forge group language games, provided, of course, that we have
enough money to live on satisfactorily . . . As a social power that can be
held by individual persons it forms the basis for a wide-ranging individual liberty, a liberty that can be deployed to develop ourselves as free-
thinking individuals without reference to others. *Money unifies precisely
through its capacity to accommodate individualism, otherness, and extraordinary social fragmentation.* (Harvey, 1990:102-103. Italics mine)

The logic of money rather than ethnicity is the source of power in
the city. War, communal and racial hostilities, and other excessive forms
of divisiveness are bad for business. Ah yes, there is strength in demo-
graphic numbers, too. Throngs of people populate prime areas of the
city, especially during festivals and other public celebrations and displays. Some areas in the city are designated as "Indian" or Little Indias
such as 23rd St to 30th St. on Lexington Ave., and East 6th St. between
First and Second avenues, and, of course, 75th St. and Roosevelt Ave in
Jackson Heights, Queens with the proliferation of Indian businesses
there. We indeed must have enough economic clout to be able to use the
Empire State Building during Independence Day, finance the use of
South Street Seaport and its environs and the extravagant production of
the Deepavali festival, yes, to buy art in Sotheby's art auction. A paint-

ing of the superstar Madhuri Dixit of *Choli Ke Peeche* fame by contemporary Bombay-based master artist M.F. Hussain sold for $50,000.00 to an Indian investment banker based in New York at a recent Sotheby's auction. In this example we have the convergence of popular culture, Indian elite culture, New York commercial but elite art circle, and Indian Non-Resident immigrant wealth purchasing an artifact from the homeland for a Manhattan/Long Island/Connecticut home. An Indo-Persian painting was bought by an Asian Indian living in Connecticut for 1.3 million dollars! (Melwani, May/96:10). During the 50th year anniversary of India's independence, there were enough funds from the Indian community to produce a large number and variety of performance events to celebrate.

There is enough wealth to purchase artifacts of Indianness, to indulge in the consumption and participation of Pan-Indianness as well as participate in mainstream American life. The median Indian family income is $48,320.00, (mean family income of $64, 243) nearly 60% higher than the national average. The per capita income of Indians is $25, 275.00 compared to the $15, 000.00 national average. The annual receipts of Indian American firms reached $19.3 billion in 1990. Indians have the third largest number of businesses among Asian groups with New York City having the largest number of 5,744 (Little India Business Directory, 1996—1997). We have money, we can organize, we can represent, we can purchase visibility!! With visibility there is a presence to contend with, there is audibility, expressiveness, politicking, clout! This is how the educated and professional elites of the AIA were able to advocate for the category of Asian Indian in the US census, enabling the Asian American of Indian descent to take advantage of the affirmative action minority quota. (Despite the apparent wealth of the Indians in America, one out every 12 Indians live in poverty. Twenty per cent of all Indians who arrive in the U.S. between 1987—1990 live in poverty!! Of course this allows for expressions of philanthropy amongst the civic, parochial, and community organizations. Philanthropic acts becomes another manifestation of Indianness through "sheva" or community service.)

Where to represent Indianness is a conscious choice of self-assertion. Parades, variety shows and festivals are used to mark territory. An event held in Manhattan indicates the clout and power of a particular ethnic group; thus, tourist spots like the South Street Seaport, and Madison Avenue are prime locations, because they are visible, and they are commercial nerve centers of the city. There is a formidable Indian community living in New York. In fact, New York City has the largest Indian population in the country (106,270; 1.24% of the New York Metropolitan area's population)—enough to warrant this public display of ethnicity, enough to become part of the consciousness of New York life.

> In the hierarchy of New York City ethnic parades, Fifth Avenue, the most coveted venue, is reserved by provisions of the City Charter for older and now more powerful ethnic groups: the Irish, Jews, Italians, Germans, Poles, Greeks, Hispanics. Latecomers such as the Koreans, Pakistanis, Sikhs, Indians, Dominicans, Cubans, and Muslims are relegated to Lexington, Sixth Avenue, Broadway, or, lowest on the urban grid, Battery Park, the southern tip of Manhattan. (Slymovics, 1995:161).

Madison Avenue, where the India Day parade perambulates is one block away from the much coveted Fifth Avenue, but the FIA did manage to keep the Empire State Building ablaze with the three colors of the Indian flag for the Independence Day weekend in 1994[9]. These are potent symbols of visibility politics, and diplomatic savvy on the part of the FIA.

Besides being introduced to the diversity within South Asian cultures, the cosmopolitanness of the city provides the opportunity to create the aspects, accoutrements, and aesthetics of Pan-Indianness. As I mentioned earlier, variety entertainments which include the Masala film and its systemics, the salwar khameez, a certain type of North Indian Mughlai cooking, the colorful and varied Indian dances, and other hybrid forms become the symbols of Pan-Indianness. As do the events of the South Street Seaport Deepavali Festival, India Day Parade, and university shows, among others, become symbols of Pan-Indianness. Pan-Indianness is displayed also for fellow Indians to understand their belonging to a larger community, as well presented to non-Indians to indicate presence and the existence of a community.

CLASS AND CASTE

> Certainly the question, "Where are you from?" is never an innocent one. To pose a question of origin is subtly to pose a question of return, to challenge not only temporarily, but geographically, one's place in the present. For someone who is neither fully Indian nor wholly American, it is a question which provokes a sudden failure of confidence, the fear of never replying adequately. (Visweswaran, 1993:301)

The community is divided due to immigration patterns, economic classes, and expansion of professions. There are thus, different types of Indianness. There is a carry over of casteist claims, a tribalism when we are bombarded with questions by other Desis such as: Where are you from? What part of India are you from? What do you do? Are you married? Do you have children? Do you have a green card? Besides wanting to know what kind of Indian you are, a new class distinction emerges between documented and undocumented aliens, one's length of stay in the US, where you live in the city, or out in the boroughs, in a hi-rise, or a home, with roommates or alone, what kind of roommates you have, what kind of food you cook at home, how often you eat at home, how often you eat out. The array of possibilities are made facile by these distinct categories. So you are a more assimilated to America if your roommates are not all Desi, if you cook a variety of foods rather than just Desi. You have, of course done well economically if you are working in an American company, have stayed here for more than five years, have a home, and are a documented alien. Plus you are Punjabi Hindu, and your family's from Delhi, your last name will decide your historic casteist link.

Classism juts its vicious head in the performances that I have discussed in this dissertation. The moneyed, well-established Indian elites 'run' the cultural organizations that dictate the texture of Indianness to be represented. However, despite their dominance, the participants and audience belong to a variety of classes. These vernacular forms bubble forth even within these elite-managed performance event, an assertion of their resistance against elite hegemony and an indelible fracture to a homogeneous Indianness. In an effort to be inclusive, expand their audience and encourage participation, and to present the Indian community as united, these elites have to include these new vernacular forms in the repertoire of their programs. It also helps that non-Indians are beginning to enjoy and appreciate these new vernacular forms, affording it a validity, and a new market.

MIGRATION & DIASPORA

The migrant sensibility for those of Indian origin is a great romance with India concocted in the hereland. The India they fantasize through the rose-tinted glasses of nostalgia is that of their carefree childhood while in contrast to their adult life in the American present is pockmarked with bills, mortgage, competition, immigration hassles and racism. For some, the dreamy American promise of opportunity is hollow. To recapture, recreate, and maintain that ideal Indianness, the ultimate fantasy is a wedding with other Indian hyphenates—a not too desi parochial, and a not too Americanized mate who understands the experience of displacement, of having South Asian heritage while being well-adjusted to the United States. And to have American-born children who despite their "American" accents love them and "Desi values". A young British-Indian divorcee medical doctor visiting New York told me that she indeed would like to remarry but would not want to marry either an Anglo, or a man from India, but one who was of mixed heritage (not necessarily of "mixed blood"), another British Indian (who most likely would himself prefer an Anglo woman)—someone who would understand her hyphen. My British Indian cousin-in-law does not want her sons to go to boarding school in England because she fears she would loose them to English wives. Better that they have an Indian home to come to after school (in London, of course! The new India!) so they don't forget her and India. Wives of Indian descent, so the hope is, may understand this bond and attachment to Indianness and may not require their spouses to sever ties with mother and land—unlike Western women, I suppose.

MADE IN INDIA[10]

Dekhi yeh sari duniya
I 've seen the whole world
Japan se leke Russia
From Japan to Russia
Australia se leke America
From Australia to America
Dekhi hai pyar ka sapna
I 've even seen love's dream
Dil chahi koi apna
My heart wants someone
Mil jai ek sathiya, ek desiya
From home, from there
Made In India
Ek dil chahi yeh
My heart desires one from there.
Made in India
Ek pyara soniya
A precious love from there.
Tan ho gora ya aur kala

> *Dark or fair, I don't care*
> Par ho sacha dilwala
> *So long as his heart is true*
>
> Chandi nahin, sona nahin
> *I've no use for gold or silver*
> koi hira
> *not diamonds, too.*
> Dil Jiska Hindustani
> *That whose heart is Indian*
> Nai koyi Inglistani
> *No please, not an Englishman!*
> Raat aur din , Mujhe piyar
> *Someone who could love me*
> ko hi karnewala
> *Night and day.*
> *I desire one*
> *Made in India* (Alisha/Biddu, 1995)

Despite this bad Indian girl going everywhere[11], she does prefer, ultimately to come home to a desi mate. On a literal level, this song is more of an Indian man's fantasy since many Indian men in the United States, even after living here for more than 20 years, travel back to India to find their 'made in India' wives. Many Indian women, on the other hand are not too enamored of this process of a "meat market" arranged marriage in India because they experience greater freedom of choice in this "open" society of the US, whereas Indian men lose their foothold and stronghold having lived in such an open and sexually egalitarian society. For men, maintaining a semblance of this power occurs in an arranged marriage with that sweet, innocent, subservient female phantasm from back home.

On a metaphoric level, the fantasy of loving the true Indian despite experiencing other objects and subjects of desire bespeaks of the stubborn love for the imagined India. Besides being a great piece of music to dance to, this song expresses the underlying anxiety of exogamous bonds, not out of a free-floating fear but based on the experience of confronting non-Indian difference, and being one's self stigmatized for being Indian-different. Moreover, the tenuousness of courtship and ephemerality of romantic love become ever-more repugnant when compared to the security and community bonding that an arranged marriage is argued to provide. Consorting with a like-minded and like-hearted hyphenate is a happy compromise between the culturally prescribed arranged marriage and yearnings for romance. The life partner can have his or her parts 'made in India' but these parts can be assembled or re-assembled locally.

The song "Made in India" is a derivative of an older film song:

> Mera joota hai Japani
> Ye patloon Inglistani
> Sar pe lal topi Rusi
> Phir bhi dil hai Hindustani
>
> O, my shoes are Japanese
> These trousers, English, if you please
> On my head, red Russian hat
> My heart's Indian for all that.
> (Rushdie, 1991:11)

Indian popular culture acknowledges hybridity and the presence of foreign influences in the Indian identity. These impurities are subsumed into Indianness, though.

Amitav Ghosh aptly described the diasporic relationship to the homeland as an epic one. It is imaginative, it is larger than life, melodramatic, mythopoetic. The genres of the cinema—film, song and dance—the Ramayana epic of exile, and amongst the educated elites—Indo-Anglian literature such as those of Rushdie and Naipaul are the expressive texts. I must include music and dance as sensuous manipulations of time, space, and rhythms as part of this epic spectacle, the media with which stories are told about that relationship to India. Because stories are re-tellable, so is "the symbolic spatial structure of India infinitely reproducible" (Ghosh, 1989:76) here, there, everywhere, and elsewhere. And since stories have multiple versions, Indianness, too, has multiple versions here, there, everywhere, and elsewhere. Much like folklore, Indianness continuously innovates, invents, imputes meaning, and meaningfulness in life experience. What remains constant is the process and structure of the story-telling. The details may change.

> In a story told about Aristotle in Europe, and about an Indian philosopher in India, the philosopher meets a village carpenter who has a beautiful old knife and asks him, "How long have you had this knife?" The carpenter answers, "Oh the knife has been in our family for gener-

ations. We have changed the handle a few times and the blade a few times, but it is the same knife" (Ramanujan, 1991:xx)

"Thus, India exported with her population, not a language, as other civilizations have done, but a linguistic process—the process of adaptation to heteroglossia" (Ghosh, 1989:75). The heteroglossia is not limited to multi-linguistic cognizance but to multiple ways of being. These multiple ways of being is described nevertheless as "Indian".

As an active participant in the production of Indianness in my lived life and in my intellectual/artistic pursuits, I have come to understand the artificiality and arbitrariness of and the ambivalence towards Indianness. Not being Indian born, but of Indian descent, my engagement with Indianness has acquired multiple refractions and a double distance. Being Indian is not "natural", it has to be put on, it cannot be taken for granted, it is a phenomenon. But even before that it has to be constructed, learned, authenticated, looked for, discovered, and then performed. In the spirit of a performance event, though very unlike the celebration of difference and assertion of visibility that the South Street Seaport Deepavali festival, the India Day Parade and cultural program, and the University variety programs that NYU young adults produce, I have composed a performance piece to express my ambivalence and, therefore, critique of some kinds of Indianness that I have come to understand in the production of this study. The performance entitled *It's a Drag Being an Indian Woman* is parodic, and is done in 'drag'. The drag underscores the distance between the 'essence' of the actor and the performance of Indianness. Judith Butler's discussion of the meaning of the ironic imitation of the cultural construct of woman via the genre of drag is the impetus to understand, though in hyperbolic terms, the put-on-ness of Indianness:

> The performance of drag plays upon the distinction between the anatomy of the performer [looking and sounding Indian] and the gender [Indianness] that is being performed. But we are actually in the presence of three contingent dimensions of significant corporeality: anatomical sex [looking and sounding Indian, i.e., being 'racially' Indian, having Indian parents], gender identity [Indianness], and gender performance [performing Indianness] …[In this gender parody] we see sex [looking and sounding Indian] and gender [Indianness] denaturalized by means of performance which avows their distinctness and dramatizes the cultural mechanism of their fabricated unity . . . so gender parody [this particular Indian drag] reveals that the original identity

after which gender [Indianness] fashions itself is an imitation without
an origin . . . a production that postures as an imitation. (1990:137-
138)

Consequently, in this performance that I have composed, I reveal the
tenuousness of Indianness and that "the various ways in which a body
shows or produces its cultural signification are performative. [There] is
no pre-existing identity with which an act or attribute might be measured; there would be no true or false, real or distorted acts of [Indian-
ness], and the postulation of true [Indianness] would be revealed as a
regulatory fiction." (Butler, 1990:141). This fiction of true Indianness is
used by elites to exclude, approve, limit participation. This fiction is nevertheless constantly deconstructed, even exploded by counterarguments
performed by other groups who feel that they have claims to other kinds
of Indianness.

IT'S A DRAG BEING AN INDIAN WOMAN:
AN EMPOWERED RESPONSE TO INDIANNESS

The multi-media interactive performance is largely autobiographical
based on my experience of an ambivalent Indianness while completing
my Ph.D. in Performance Studies, while researching this study, as I continue to grapple with Indianness. It offers an ironic and powerful solution
to the handling of this slippery identity from the point of view of a left-
off center intellectual/artistic woman of a bourgeois background (that's
me!). The performance consists of five parts. The lights are set low. On
the wall are slides of my family, my friends in Manila, Bombay, San
Francisco, and New York, interspersed with slides of Indian miniature
paintings and photographs of classical dance poses and erotic postures-
Marga—brahmanic as well as courtly sources of official Indianness combined with a personal life of one dispersed Indian. Two video monitors
run simultaneously, blaring loudly. On one is a continuous loop of gar-
ish, and very popular Hindi film song and dance sequences. On the other
monitor are clips from VH1 and MTV. These are the popular media representations and images which are resources for the construction of Indianness in the diaspora. In the middle of the room on the floor is the site of
learning- a shrine, so to speak, to scholarship marked off with an Indian
chaddar or bedspread. This valorized reading space consists of certain
significant objects such as earthen lamps, Hindu idols, framed and gar-
landed portraits of Indian nationalist leaders, tourist objects depicting the

arts and crafts of India, bottled spices, various salwar khameezes and sarees. With these objects are brochures, programs, fliers that I have collected from the performance events that I attended and observed for this
study. In these reading materials, tied with twine are the direct quotes
and poems I have collected and have discussed in this concluding chapter. These new 'books' of learning are arranged in a semi- circle. In the
middle of this semi-circle is a golden box. I sit behind the box towards
the end of the ceremony. The audience come into the space and can take
any number of the books, undo the ribbons and read what is inside. They
must redo the ribbons so that the next person can read the books. As they
are reading the books, I sit with my back towards the audience, transforming into an Indian woman: donning on my flamboyant costume,
putting on my long braid, my kohl-liner and red red lipstick, my kitsch
jewelry. The audience must try to remain silent throughout this part of
the performance. The slides, the videos, my 'dressing up', and the indi-
vidualized reading occur simultaneously.

The second part of the performance is the "performance of Indianness". In gaudy costume, long plait, reddest lipstick, the biggest dot on
my forehead, and exaggerated kohl-lined eyes, i.e., in Indian drag, I perform my reinterpretation of a Hindi Film dance. The original dance from
the film will be seen on one monitor, on the other, the dance as reinterpreted by a child in one of the local community performances, i.e., Preeti
in the Indian Independence Day cultural show. The text of the dance is
about romantic love with very strong sexual suggestions—"Choli Ke
Peeche Kya Hai"—"(Guess) What is underneath my veil? Underneath
my blouse? Underneath my veil is my heart, underneath my blouse is my
heart. This I will give to my lover" and so on which I have discussed at
length in Chapter 4. As the dance continues, it becomes through the sheer
mimicry of the film's choreography, a grotesque, exaggerated alterity of
Indian classical dance steps, a parody of Indianness created by the
media, bourgeois history (personal and academic) and nationalism. As
the music climaxes, I discombobulate, reacting against and exorcising
the demons of heterosexual oppressions and bourgeois chauvinisms,
communal violence and discriminations—Much like what the members
of SAKHI for South Asian Women and SALGA, the disenfranchised immigrants, and even the agonies young adults have to deal with within
their community, and from the dominant community.

The third portion consists of my disheveled, breathless, bespecta-
cled self sitting behind the box for a formal and dramatic reading of the
books. On both monitors is a montage of selected and telling video

footage from the events that I have observed such as scenes of protest during the Independence Day parade juxtaposed with Preeti's dance, the stiff BJP float contrasted with the flamboyant film float, the whirl of folk dances from South Street Seaport, excerpts from the fashion show, and other group dances. I read out loud portions of the quotes, poems that are included in this concluding chapter, and relevant parts of the dissertation. This intertextuality brings out the attractiveness to and ambivalence for this colorful though contentious Indianness. After the readings, I remove from the box an object wrapped in a shimmering veil. I unwrap the cloth to reveal a rust-encrusted kitchen cleaver. I read what has been pencilled on the wooden handle—"I am going to have a hysterectomy". I pretend to gouge out my uterus—that ultimate mimetic apparatus, "the mimetic organ par excellence" of Indianness (Taussig, 1993:35) from under my skirt. What emerges is a little doll of myself/my probable daughter/ the archetypical little dancing girl in a blood-red shimmering costume/the infantile citizen of Indianness which I affectionately fondle, coddle and place tenderly into the box saying firmly but not without affection, "I place you here, sweet thing, for now. Later, we can play!". I quickly sit on the box as if afraid it might escape or be stolen, and laugh unabashedly, fearlessly for I have excised my reified Indianness only to be used at my will when necessary and discarded her when I want to just be! That is when I am not playing at being Indian, for after all, being an Indian woman is not all that I am! I am also just and primarily, Sunita.

For the fourth part, as I undergo my last transformation, the following verse is heard as muted video footage of the three performance events that I analyzed in this study are projected:

> *Naach meri jaan, phata phat!*
> *(Quick! dance, my sweet)*
> *Boys want to kiss me, ya ya ya*
> *Girls want to hug me, ya ya ya*
> *I am wanted, wanted everywhere!*[12]

> Dance, little girl, dance!
> Imprint your presence
> World the city with heritage
> That lives here and there
> and elsewhere
> Your infant body

bumps and grinds
ululating in fragile unity
with diasporic gyrations

Though you mouth
words of desire
in a hip-hop beat
and sway your tiny hips
to the yearnings
of a love-ravaged heroine
You must stay home and
not love-make with boys
in real flesh and time.

On stage, in costume
Bedecked and beautiful
How dazzling and glamorous
You must feel!
At least, up there
no mess of fluid exchanges
and torn hymens
and loving the wrong sorts
which later, mother and India
may need to clean up
with your bridal shawl.

I transform into the emancipated and hopeful Shrimati Liberty, the Indian hybrid of that lady on the Hudson, in a saree of five stripes—red, white, blue, saffron and green—the colors of the US and Indian flags, with a star-shaped bindi, and Ashoka wheels for earrings in this parody of the accoutrements of Indianness and Americanness. On one raised hand I carry an earthen lamp—a diya used in the Deepavali celebrations, on the other at my side, this book (my academic representation of Indianness), and the doll (portable Indianness). The audience shout out "Zindabad Shrimati Liberty[13] !" three times.

Shrimati Liberty in a fit of hospitality, serves portions of her delicious lasagna keema to one and all to ingest Desiness. To encourage participation in the celebration of being emancipated from the regulatory fiction of true Indianness as well as realizing that playing at being Indian can be delightful, too, choice cuts of Disco Bhangra, and Hindi film songs blast in the background. If the spirit moves us, yes, we can boogie the rest of the night away as one undulating vibrating Desi body!

RECAPITULATIONS AND RECOMMENDATIONS: THE SENSIBLE MIGRANT PERFORMS INDIANNESS

This project has vividly described how the slippery, tenuous Indian identity is defined, authenticated, and performed for the consumption of both those who think of themselves as Indian and for those who are not. Because the identity is not fixed, because it is comprised of multiple histories, memories, origins, religious affiliation, and inchoate notions of taste and aesthetics, and cultural practices, there is a constant need to reiterate it, reproduce it, perform it because an individual can never be wholly it. Indianness is performed within a community of like-minded individuals who have agreed on certain notions of Indianness at least for a certain time in a particular place. This Indianness may also be performed for individuals who are identified as not belonging to the Indian community but who expect to witness aspects of Indianness that are recognizable as Indian. Indeed, though a certain official type of Indianness may be touted by certain elite groups, this type of Indianness is simultaneously being deconstructed and subverted by other kinds of Indians and other kinds of South Asians who assert their own, sometimes opposing views of what it means to be Indian. The performance events that I have analyzed in these pages are problematic but prime examples of this dialogic.

The Association of Indians in America's (AIA) Deepavali Festival at the South Street Seaport is a public performance event in which on the occasion of a Hindu festival, Indian ethnicity in the U.S.A is displayed and celebrated. What is considered as part of Indianness has expanded through the ten years that I witnessed it, and will continue to in accordance to the changing demographics, needs and tastes of the ever-growing and ever-diversifying Asian Indian and South Asian community in the tri-state area. Originally, the members of the AIA board were earnest to present only the most traditional and folkloric aspects of the Indian expressive arts based on the colonialist criteria of Marga/Desi aesthetics. Now they have succumbed to include Hindi film dances, bhangra, rock and hip-hop dance parties, western and Indian dance amalgamated innovations, Indo-Caribbean and Asian dances and musics. This is an acknowledgement that Indianness is produced not only from the South Asian subcontinent but also from the diaspora. The shift of identification is from "Indian" to "Persons of South Asian descent", i.e. Desi. It would be valuable to continue the study, record and analyze the changes in the South Street Seaport Deepavali festival as an indicator of the shifting demographics as well as the shift in aesthetic and cultural values of the community.

Part of the agenda of the AIA Deepavali festival is to assert that the Asian Indian is an active citizen of America, and part of what we can offer to this new hereland is the spice, color, variety of our expansive Indian difference. In exchange for that orientalist, touristic difference, we claim our rights to US American privilege—the rights to happiness, property, employment, political and legal representation. I predict that with the inclusion of more hybrid forms from the other sites of the Indian diaspora such as the Indo-Caribbean, the British Indian and even in Asia, being Indian will take on a more deterritorialized and transnational flavor. Cohesiveness will emerge on the basis of shared issues of displacement and adjustments to the herelands.

In the private sphere of our parochial communities, as was seen with the Sindhis of Rego Park, the pleasure of displaying our particular regional/religious identity instead of our Pan-Indian one already dismantles the notions of a nationalist, ostensibly secular and diverse Indianness. Amidst the sameness of individuals who speak the same mother tongues, practice the same folk religions, and socialize with familiar as well as familial others, a particular cultural citizenship which reduces the confrontations with difference is performed. In this case, Sindhiness is performed amidst sameness to validate a belonging to a particular community rather than expressing allegiances to either the Indian or US nation-states. Cultural identity incurs more refractions, involves multiple splits. These kinds of refractions can occur in a society that prizes multiculturalism. One can live as one pleases in one's private sphere as long as certain universal civic duties are performed in public.

In the Federation of Indian Associations' India [independence] day parade and cultural program the melodramatic contest and protestations of multiple kinds of Indianness are performed. The libidinal and lively citizenship is practiced via the sexually suggestive dances reinterpreted live from Hindi film song and dance sequences by young Indian women and girls. Through these dances, the Indian audience is reassured of a link with the phantasmagoria of Indian life as depicted in popular Hindi film. The fantasy of being participant in Indianness is kept alive in the ability of the young performers mimicking expertly but not pat, the gestures, idioms, sentiments of that particular fictive life. Despite, being

away, and even here in America, Indianness is reproducible in the bodies
of these performers.

Amidst these reassuring, delightful, though conservative dances,
other perceived to be contentious service oriented groups by the FIA
such as SAKHI for South Asian Women, and SALGA—South Asian
Lesbian and Gay Alliance are excluded from participating in these celebrations. These groups assert their presence and visibility in the performance of their protests, in incurring broad media attention, in anarchic
disavowals of the rules and regulations of the FIA using the rhetoric of
Indian tolerance, inclusion, and hospitality. After all, these groups are
also servicing Indians as well as other South Asians who, though they are
not mainstream, claim certain aspects of their selves as Desi. They de-
serve to participate in any public display of Indianness. These left-off
center groups can also be the subject of further research especially in
their configurations what it means to be Desi, and how these notions af-
fect the effectivity of their organizations. Moreover, it is well-worth exploring how despite the rigid geopolitical boundaries set up by the South
Asian countries, here in the diaspora, on the level of civil society, those
of South Asian descent come together on the basis and acknowledgement
of a shared heritage, creating solutions to similar problems, and even on
the level of social interaction. Amongst South Asians there seems to be
much fluidity

Though dangerous and life-threatening, the nationalist machismo
performed during one of the India day celebrations brings to the fore the
potency of communalist politics even when away from the subcontinent.
Much of what it means to be identified as Indian is dependent on the borders—psychic, symbolic and territorial that one sets up to resist being
infected or subdued by the "enemy". With the rise to power of Hindu
fundamentalism in India, and even in the diaspora, capitalizing on the
paranoia and hatred against Muslims in India and against Pakistan, Indianness has become conflated with Hinduness. Though this kind of ahistoric and propagandistic Indianness is not succumbed to wholesale, in
recent years it has, quite dismally, gained popularity in leaps and bounds
in the mainstream of Indian life in India as well as here in the U.S. More
specific and quantitative information on how these fundamentalist
groups wield their influence here and in India would indeed be helpful in
seeing the relationship with Indians in the diaspora and the rise and triumph of Indian communal politics.

The New York University South Asian Organization Shruti practice
their brand of youthful Indianness by unabashedly coopting, spoofing,

borrowing, and adapting expressive genres from both Indian diasporic and American diasporic popular entertainments. Within the Shruti show, these young second generation Indian Americans, create, not a revivalist space to perform Indian heritage nor a space depicting only non-Indian American life but an entirely different third space in which to negotiate their somewhat hostile and disturbing encounters with conflicted inter-generational and intercultural value systems. Dating and sexuality seem to be areas of concern since their parents through their economic and emotional clout can thwart romance, influence partner choice, and se-verely restrict dating with non-Indians, or even with other 'undesirable' Indians. On stage, in Indian costume, as they dance like a love-ravaged pair, these young Indian Americans can represent their notions of cou-pling and familiarize their parents who are in the audience to see them with partners of their choice who happen to be Desi. During rehearsals, Shruti outings and meetings, of course, actual coupling can and does occur.

The concerns of (heterosexual) dating and sexuality may not be con-sidered as radical or vital for left-off center groups dealing with more po-litical and broad-ranging issues. But within the conservative strictures of the bourgeoisie middle class Indian family system where marriages arranged by parents are still the preferred norm even here in the United States, asserting one's own partner choice is fraught with tension and careful consideration. Family ties bind and are binding. More detailed substantive research can be conducted on the sexuality of Indian Ameri-can youth and how this bears upon the intergenerational conflicts over sexual politics, partner choice, and family-building.

My involvement in this project is also another kind of performance of Indianness. As I watched the shows, talked to people, wrote this dis-sertation, I am constantly aware of the tenuousness and at times spuri-ousness of an essential Indianness. Like my compatriots, I seem to yearn for an authentic, true, and inclusive Indianness in the vast number and types of expressive behaviors that are available to me. The yearning stems from wanting to belong to a group, to be recognized as part of the family as such, to claim a cultural landscape as familiar and as one's own and a personal, sensual, habituated preference for the dynamic aesthetic of Indianness. For the time that I am performing this Indianness in the form of gyrating to a bhangra tune, in the form of watching a dance, in eating Indian food, in being in the presence of other Indians, in wearing an Indian dress, in creating performance pieces which resonate with other like-minded contemporaries of Indian descent—I can feel the thrill of recognition, the delight of being Indian with other Indians, of being part of a Desi community. But it only lasts for the time of the performance process because it slips away, is ephemeral and needs to be performed or attended to again and again in the near future. To be convinced of (my) Indianness, these celebrations and other expressive behaviors repeat year after year, even day after day. One needs an Indian fix once in a while and for others more often than not. Indianness has to be perpetually performed.

Performing Indianness is singularly dissatisfying, too, because being Indian is only a part of one's (my) being. People are also their gender, their age, their profession, their ideas, their individuality, their selves. Culture, though, important, is merely only one aspect of the human gestalt. Many of one's activities, beliefs, choices are not only motivated by being true to one's culture. Moreover, to be solely identified as Indian restricts one's being recognized for the whole self, for one's individual difference, for one's transnational, transcontinental and even transcendental humanity. Coalitions based on shared issues (for e.g. ecology, AIDS awareness, economic stability), shared professional and vocational interests allow for the dismantling of ethnic divisiveness, racism, and spurious nationalism.

It is for this reason that Indianness is constantly being argued about, defined and redefined, regulated and deregulated, and deconstructed. Individuals bring to it the uniqueness of their life experiences, splintering that monolith constantly. In every public display of Indianness, there is within it an exclusion of another equally valid aspect of Indianness bubbling forth. There is a perpetual oscillation between the yearning of the stasis of an unchanging culture and the reality of the dynamism of flux, choice, and adaptation. Both aspects of this perpetual oscillation are practiced by at times disparate groups of individuals, even within one performance event.

To invoke that exiled and much misunderstood man, Salman Rushdie, what then does it mean to be Indian outside India? How do we live that aspect of ourselves that we recognize as Indian in the world that is not Indian?

Indeed, through the process of performance, by donning the conceit of Indianness as a strategic bartering and visibility device we cross frontiers, break open boundaries, shift borders, and disperse. We may even have to dance unabashedly on the wounds of our hyphens in quint-colored drag, knowing full well that it is only an act to persuade ourselves of our impure, unstable Indianness.

NOTES

[1]The nationalists of India's independence movement against the British Raj, too, redefined the diverse cultures and religions of the subcontinent as Indian. It seemed expedient then, to cohere as a united Indian front against British tyranny. Currently, the subcontinent is being torn apart by the polemical assertions of the religio-political fundamentalists in their invented definitions of what is true, pure, authentic Indianness. Now in India, the communal card is being played against another kind of difference, that of religion. True Indianness is being defined as Hinduness against Muslim "others"—not a Hinduness of diversity but of a certain Rama-centered North Indian kind at that.

[2] Though I cannot say that M.K. Gandhi was self-effacing or passive. It is the reinterpretation of Indian pacifism in the midst of dissent or hardship that I am recoiling from.

[3]Sweet, milky tea brewed with spices.

[4]be blessed by the sheer act of "exchanging glances" with a deity.

[5]a song of religious devotion.

[6]I thank Raewyn Whyte, my colleague at the Expository Writing Program and Performance Studies Department for giving me her student's paper.

[7] an edict that an aunt hurled at me constantly when I resisted kitchen work. Today, I am grateful for the culinary prowess of Indian women and now even men.

[8]A South Asian attire consisting of a loose shirt and loose trousers.

[9]Prabhir Roy of FIA was able to negotiate the use of the much coveted 5th Avenue for 1997's India Day parade. In the arena of visibility politics of New York City, this is an indication that the Indian-American community has finally arrived, though in subsequent years, the parade is back on Madison.

[10]There is another version of this song with the refrain "made in Pakistan" sung more appropriately by a man. Both versions, though, acknowledge the themes of loss and nostalgia as a result of dispersal.

[11]this phrase is based on the joke: Good girls go to heaven, bad girls go everywhere!

[12]lyrics from a Hindi film song.

[13]long live Lady Liberty!

Bibliography

"An American Hindu", 1992. Unpublished, anonymous paper.

"Choli Ke Peeche Kya Hai?". 1993. in *Khalnayak*. Music by Laxmikant Pyare-lal. Lyrics by Anand Bakshi. Sung by Alka Yagnik and Ila Arun. Performed by Madhuri Dixit.

"Court Battle over Shooting" in *India Abroad*, August 20, 1993, p. 40

"Fireworks Ramayana". 1993. Deepavali: Festival of Lights brochure. Association of Indians in America–NY Chapter.

"Indian Independence Day" in *India Abroad*, August, 19, 1995, p. 42

"Pakistani Shoots at India Day Parade" in *News India*, Aug. 20, 1993, p.1

"Parade and Other Events Around U.S." in *India Abroad*, August 26, 1994, p. 42.

"Parade Victim in Critical Condition" in *India Abroad*, August 27, 1993, p. 34.

"Song Ruled not Obscene" in *India Abroad*, August 26, 1993, p. 31.

"South Asian Gay and Lesbian Group Marches for India" in the *New York Times*, Aug.22, 1994, p. B2.

"What are we to Believe About Communal Relations in India?". 1993. Pamphlet by *Concerned South Asian*.

Abrahams, Roger. 1987. *Time Out of Time: Essays on the Festival*. Ed. by Alessandro Falassi. University of New Mexico Press.

Agarwal, Priya. 1991. *Passage from India: Post-1965 Indian Immigrants and their Children—Conflicts, Concerns and Solutions*. California: Yuvati Publications.

Agnihotri, Ramakant. 1987. *Crisis of Identity: The Sikhs in England*. New Delhi: Bahri Publications.

Aguiar, Arun. 1994. Statement in the Deepavali: Festival of Lights Brochure. Association of Indians in America-NY Chapter.

Aguiar, Arun. Interview and conversations from 1991 to 1995.

Alisha/Biddu. 1995. "Made in India". audiocassette.

Allen, James Paul. 1988. *We the People: An Atlas of America's Ethnic Diversity*. New York: Macmillan.

Amin-Patel, Smita. 1995. "Authentic Chutney or Masala Mayonnaise: An American Compromise of Indian Folk Art". Paper presented in the first National Conference on Indian-American Identity Conference: Little India & Montclair State University.

Amladi, Parag. Sept., 1995. "Comforting Illusions" in *Little India*.

Anderson, Benedict. 1991. *Imagined Communities: Reflections on the Origin and Spread of Nationalism*. New York: Verso.

Anwar, M. 1979. *The Myth of Return: Pakistanis in Britain*. London: Heineman.

Appadurai, Arjun, Frank J. Korom & Margaret A. Mills, eds. 1991. *Gender, Genre and Power in South Asian Expressive Traditions*. Philadelphia: University of Pennsylvania Press.

Appadurai, Arjun. 1981. "The Past as a Scarce Resource" in *Man: Journal of the Royal Anthropological Institute*,16/2: 201-219.

Appadurai, Arjun. 1986. *The Social Life of Things: Commodities in Cultural Perspective*. Cambridge: University Press.

Appadurai, Arjun. 1988. "How to Make a National Cuisine: Cookbooks in Contemporary India" in *Comparative Studies in Society and History*. vol. 30 #1: 3–24.

Appadurai, Arjun. 1988. "Putting Hierarchy in its Place" in *Cultural Anthropology*, 3:1, Feb., 1988. pp. 36 to 49.

Appadurai, Arjun. 1990. "Disjuncture and Difference in the Global Cultural Economy" in *Public Culture*, vol. 2, no. 2, Spring. pp. 1 to 24.

Appadurai, Arjun. 1991. "Global Ethnoscapes: Notes and Queries for a Transnational Anthropology" in *Recapturing Anthropology*, ed. by Richard Fox. Santa Fe: School of American Research Press.

Appadurai, Arjun. 1993. "Patriotism and its Futures" in *Public Culture*, 1993, 5: 411 to 429.

Asad, Talal. 1990. "Multiculturalism and British Identity in the Wake of the Rushdie Affair" in *Politics and Society* 18, #4, December 1990. pp. 455 to 80.

Ashley, Wayne. 1993. *Recodings: Ritual, Theatre, and Political Display in Kerala State, South India*. Dissertation, Performance Studies Dept., New York University.

Awasthi, Suresh. 1989. "Theater of Roots: Encounter with Tradition" in *The Drama Review* 33, 1989.

Bahadur, Gaiutra. 1998 (Nov). "Indian Looking" in Little India, vol. 8. #11. pp. 20 to 21.

Banerjee, Sumanta. 1991. " 'Hindutva'—Ideology and Social Psychology" in *Economic and Political Weekly*, Jan. 19, 1991. pp. 97 to 101.

Barnouw, Erik & S. Krishnaswamy. 1980. *Indian Film*. New York: Oxford University Press.

Barth, Frederik. 1969. *Ethnic Groups and Boundaries: The Social Organization of Cultural Difference*. Oslo: Norwegian University Press.

Barthes, Roland. 1990. *Mythologies*. New York: Noonday Press.

Bateson, Gregory. 1972. "Culture Contact and Schismogenesis" in *Steps to An Ecology of Mind*. New York: Bantam.

Baudrillard, Jean. 1983. *Simulations*. New York: Semiotext(e) Inc., Columbia University.

Bauman, Richard, ed. 1992a. *Folklore, Cultural Performances and Popular Entertainments: A Communications-Centered Handbook*. New York : Oxford Press.

Bauman, Richard, Inta Carpentar, et al. 1992b. *Reflections on the Folklife Festival: An Ethnography of Participant Experience*. Bloomington, Indiana: Indiana University Press.

Baumann, Gerd. 1990. "The Reinvention of Bhangra" in *World of Music*, v. 32, #2.

Bausinger, Herman. 1990. *Folk Culture in a World of Technology*. trans. by Elke Pettner. Bloomington: Indiana University Press.

Benjamin, Walter. 1969. "The Works of Art in the Age of Mechanical Reproduction" in *Illuminations*. New York: Schocken Books.

Benjamin, Walter. 1979 (1933). "Doctrine of the Similar" in *New German Critique*, #7, 1979. pp. 61 to 69.

Benjamin, Walter. 1986 . "On the Mimetic Faculty" in *Reflections: Essays, Aphorisms, Autobiographical Writing.* trans. Edmund Jephcott.

Berlant, Laurie. Spring, 1993. "The Theory of Infantile Citizenship" in *Public Culture*, vol. 5, #3.

Berrol, Selma Cantor. 1980. "Strangers in the City: Migration and Ethnicity in New York" in *The New Ethnics*, ed. by Parmatma Saran & Edwin Eames. New York: Praeger Press. pp. 86 to 105.

Bhabha, Homi. . 1984b. "Representation and the Colonial Text: A Critical Exploration of Some Forms of Mimeticism" in *The Theory of Reading*. Gloversmith, Frank, ed. New Jersey: Barnes & Noble.

Bhabha, Homi. 1984 "Of Mimicry and Man: The Ambivalence of Colonial Discourse" in *October* #28, 1984.

Bhabha, Homi. 1986. "The Other-Question: Difference, Discrimination and the Discourse of Colonialism" in *Literature, Politics and Theory*.

Bhabha, Homi. 1990. "The Third Space" in *Identity, Community & Difference* ed. by Jonathan Rutherford. London: Lawrence & Wishart.

Bhabha, Homi. 1992. "Race and the Humanities: The 'Ends' of Modernity?" in *Public Culture*, Vol. 4, No.2, Spring, 1992. pp. 81 to 85.

Bhabha, Homi. "Signs Taken for Wonders: Questions of Ambivalence & Authority Under a Tree Outside Delhi, May 1817" in *Critical Inquiry*, Autumn, 1985.

Bhachu, Parminder. 1985. *Twice Migrants: East African Sikh Settlers in Britain.*

Bhachu, Parminder. 1995. "New Cultural Forms and Transnational South Asian Women: Culture, Class, and Consumption among British Asian Women in the Diaspora" in *Nation and Migration: The Politics of Space in the South Asian Diaspora*. Philadelphia: University of Pennsylvania.

Bharata Muni. *Natyasastra*. 1956. Trans by Manmohan Ghosh.

Bharucha, Rustom. 1990. *Theater and the World: Essays on Performance and Politics of Culture*. Columbia, Missouri: South Asia Publications.

Bharucha, Rustom. 1992. "Anatomy of Official Cultural Discourse: A Non-Government Perspective" in *Economic and Political Weekly*, August 1 to 8, 1992. pp. 1667 to 1676.

Bhatacharjee, Annanya. 1992. "The Habit of Ex-Nomination: Nation, Woman, and the Indian Immigrant Bourgeoisie" in *Public Culture*, vol. 5, #1, Fall, 1992.

Birbalsingh, Frank. ed. 1989. *Indenture and Exile: The Indo-Caribbean Experience*. Toronto: TSAR, Ontario Association for Studies in Indo-Caribbean Culture.

Blatti, Jo. 1987. *Past Meets Present*. Washington, D.C.: Smithsonian Institute Press.

Bloch, Maurice. 1974. "Symbols, Song, Dance and Features of Articulation: Is Religion an Extreme Form of Traditional Authority?" in *European Journal of Sociology* 15: 55 to 81.

Bourdieu, Piere. 1984. *Distinction: Social Critique of the Judgement of Taste*. Cambridge: Harvard University Press.

Brennis, Donald. 1991. " Aesthetics, Performance, and the Enactment of Tradition in a Fiji Indian Community" in *Gender, Genre and Power in South Asian Expressive Traditions*. ed. by Appadurai, Arjun, Frank J. Korom & Margaret A. Mills Philadelphia: University of Pennsylvania Press.

Brereton, Bridget & R. Dookeran. 1982. *East Indians in the Caribbean: Colonialism and the Struggle for Identity*. New York: Kraus.

Burchfield, Robert. 1980. "Dictionaries and Ethnic Sensibilities" in *The State of the Language*. Ed. by Leonard Michaels & Christopher Ricks. Berkeley: University of California Press.

Burek, Deborah M., ed. 1992. "National Federation of Indian American Associations" in *Encyclopedia of Associations in the United States*, 26th ed., vol. 1, Part 2, Section 10. Detroit: Gale Research.

Burghart, Richard. 1987. *Hinduism in Great Britain*. London: Tavistock

Butler, Judith. 1990. *Gender Trouble: Feminism and the Subversion of Identity*. New York: Routledge.

Byron, Reginald. 1992. "Ethnography and Biography: On the Understanding of Culture" in *Ethnos*, vol. 57: III–IV. pp. 170 to 181.

Castle, S.H. & T. Wallace. 1984. *Here for Good: Western Europe's Ethnic Minorities*. London: Pluto Press.

Chada, Gurinder. 1989. "I'm British But…"presented in Sakhi for South Asian Women's Fourth Annual Film Festival Women Directors from South Asia, 1995.

Chakrabarty, Dipesh. 1992. " The Death of History? Historical Consciousness and the Culture of Late Capitalism" in *Public Culture*, vol. 4, No. 2: Spring 1992. pp. 47 to 65.

Chakrabarty, Dipesh. 1992. "Postcoloniality and the Artifice of History: Who speaks for the 'Indian' Pasts?" in *Representations* 37: 1 to 26.

Chakraborty Ritin, 1995. Executive Producer of *Harmony, Pride and Heritage: Reflections of Our Artistic Heritage* (1992). Produced by Shruti, South Asian Student Association of New York University. Interview.

Chakravarty, Sumita. 1993. *National Identity in Indian Popular Cinema*. Austin: University of Texas Press.

Chatterjee, Partha. 1989. "Colonialism, Nationalism, and Colonized Women: The Contest in India" in *American Ethnologist*, vol. 16, #4. Nov. 1989. pp. 622 to 633.

Chatterjee, Partha. 1993. *The Nation and its Fragments: Colonial and Post-Colonial Histories*. New Jersey: Princeton University Press.

Chaudhuri, Una. 1991. "The Future of the Hyphen: Interculturalism, Textuality and the Difference Within" in *Interculturalism and Performance: Writings from PAJ*. ed. by. Bonnie Maranca & Gautam Dasgupta. New York: PAJ Publications.

Chin, Daryl. 1991. "From Popular to Pop: The Arts in/of Commerce" in *Performing Arts Journal* # 37, January, 1991.

Chin, Daryl. 1992. "Multiculturalism and its Mark: The Art of Identity Politics" in *Performing Arts Journal* 40. January, 1992, p. 1-15.

Chin, Daryl. "Interculturalism, Postmodernism, Pluralism" in *Performing Arts Journal* 11 3-12 1: 163-75.

Clarke, Colin, Ceri Peach & Steven Vertovec, eds. 1990. *South Asians Overseas: Migrations and Ethnicity*. Cambridge: Cambridge University Press.

Clifford, James. 1988. "Histories of the Tribal and the Modern"; "On Collecting Art and Culture", "On Ethnographic Authority" & "On Ethnographic Surrealism" in *Predicament of Culture: Twentieth Century Ethnography, Literature & Art.*. Cambridge, Mass: Harvard University Press.

Committee on South Asian Women Bulletin (COSAW), 1993. Vol. 8 (Nos. 1-2).

Connerton, Paul. 1989. *How Societies Remember*. Cambridge University Press.

Cowsik, Shyamala. 1995. Remarks of Indian Ambassador to Washington D.C. National Advisory Committee on South Asian Affairs Workshop, Washington, D.C.

Dabydeen, David & Brinsley Samaroo, eds. 1987. *India in the Caribbean*. London: Hansib.

Das Dasgupta, Shamita. 1998. A Patchwork Shawl: Chronicles of South Asian Women in America. New Jersey: Rutgers University Press.

Das Gupta, Chidananda. 1991. *The Painted Face: Studies in Popular Cinema*. Delhi: Roli Books.

Davis, Fred. 1979. *Yearning for Yesterday*. New York: Free Press.

Davison, Robert. 1966. *Black British: Immigrants to England*. London: Oxford.

Devji, Faisal Fatehali. 1992. "Hindu/Muslim/Indian" in *Public Culture*, vol. 5, No. 1, Fall 1992.

Dirks, Nicholas, ed. 1992. *Colonialism and Culture*. Ann Arbor: University of Michigan.

Dominguez, Virginia. 1986. " The Marketing of Heritage" in *American Ethnologist* 13,3|: 546-555.

Dorfles, Gillo. 1970. *Kitsch: The World of Bad Taste*. New York: Universe Books.

Drewal, John. 1988. "Performing the Other: Mami Wata Worship in Africa" in *The Drama Review* 34 (2) 1988.

Dundes, Alan. 1985. Nationalistic Inferiority Complexes and the Fabrication of Fakelore" in *Journal of the Folklore Institute*.

During, Simon. 1987. "Postmodernism or Postcolonialism?" in *Landfall*, vol. 3 # 39.

Dusenbery, Verne. 1995. "A Sikh Diaspora? Contested Identities and Constructed Realities" in *Nation and Migration: The Politics of Space in the South Asian Diaspora*. ed. by Peter Van der Veer Philadelphia: University of Pennsylvania. pp. 17 to 42.

Eck, Diana. 1985. *Darsan: Seeing the Divine Image in India*. Pennsylvania: Anima books.

Eco, Umberto. 1983. *Travels in Hyperreality*. New York: HBJ

Erdman, Joan L. 1983. "Who Should Speak for the Performing Arts: The Case of the Delhi Dancers" in *Pacific Affairs* 56 (20): 247-69.

Eriksen, T. Hylland. 1991. "Ethnicity Versus Nationalism" in *Journal of Peace Research*, 26 (3). pp. 263 to 278.

Eriksen, T. Hylland. 1992. "Multiple Traditions and the Question of Cultural Integration" in *Ethnos*, vol. 57: I–II. pp. 6 to 30.

Falassi, Alessandro, ed. 1987. *Time Out of Time: Essays on the Festival*. University of New Mexico Press.

Fanon, Frantz. 1966. *The Wretched of the Earth*. trans. by Constance Farrington. New York: Grove Press.

Feng, Peter X. 1994. "Discussion of S. Mukhi's Indian-Americans Perform their Hybrid Identity". *Rethinking the South Asian Diaspora* Workshop. unpublished ms.

Film Utsav. 1985. *Indian Cinema 1980-1985*. ed. by Rani Burra. New Delhi: Directorate of Film Festivals.

Fine, Elizabeth & Jean Haskell Speer, eds. 1992. *Performance, Culture, and Identity*. Connecticut: Praeger.

Fine, Elizabeth. 1991. *Performance as Cultural Storage*, ms. Virginia Polytechnic Institute and State University.

Fisher, Maxine P. 1980. *The Indians of New York City: A Study of Ethnic Identity*. Columbia, Missouri: South Asia Books.

Fisher, Maxine P. 1980b. "The Indian Ethnic Identity: The Role of Associations in the New York Indian Population" in *The New Ethnics: Asian Indians in the United States*. Saran, Parmatma & Edwin Eames, eds. New York: Praeger Publishers.

Flynn, John J. 1991. "Postcards From the Rim" in *Performing Arts Journal* # 37, January, 1991.

Foucault, Michel. 1980. *Power/Knowledge: Selected Interviews and Other Writings, 1972-1977*. ed. and trans. by Colin Gordon. Brighton: Harvest.

Ganti, Tejaswini. 1995. "Gimme Something to Dance To" presented in Sakhi for South Asian Women's Fourth Annual Film Festival Women Directors from South Asia, 1995.

Gardner, Katy. 1993. "Desh-Bidesh: Sylheti Images of Home and Away" in *Man: Journal of the Royal Anthropological Institute*, March 1993, vol. 28, no.1.pp. 1 to 16.

Gargi, Balwant. 1962. *Theatre in India*. New York: Theatre Art Books

Gargi, B.D. 1996. *So Many Cinemas: The Motion Picture in India*. India: Eminence Design Ovte. Ltd.

Garnham, Nicholas. 1993. "The Mass Media, Cultural Identity, and the Public Sphere in the Modern World" in *Public Culture*, vol. 5 #2, Winter 1993.

Geertz, Clifford. 1973. "Deep Play: Notes on the Balinese Cockfight" & "Ethos, Worldview & the Analysis of Sacred Symbols" in *The Interpretation of Culture*. New York: Basic Books.

Geertz, Clifford. 1983. "Blurred Genres: The Refiguration of Social Thought" & "Art as a Cultural System" in *Local Knowledge*. New York: Basic Books.

Ghai, Subhash. 1993. *Khalnayak*. (feature film) Bombay: India.

Ghei, Kiren. 1988a. "Hindi Popular Cinema and the Indian American Teenage Dance Experience". Unpublished ms.

Ghei, Kiren. 1988b. "Accessible Choreographies: Hindi Cinema on Videotape in Los Angeles" in *UCLA Journal of Dance Ethnology*, vol., 12, 1988.

Ghosh, Amitav. 1990. "Diaspora in Indian Culture" in *Public Culture*, Spring, 1990.

Giddens, Anthony. 1991. *Modernity and Self-Identity: Self and Society in the Late Modern Age*. Cambridge: Polity Press.

Gilroy, Paul. 1991. 'There Ain't No Black in the Union Jack'. Chicago: University of Chicago Press.

Gilroy, Paul. 1993. *Small Acts: Thoughts on the Politics of Black Culture*. London: Serpent's Tail.

Goffman, Erving. 1973. *The Presentation of Self in Everyday Life*. New York: Overlook Press.

Golub, Leon, Guillermo Gomez-Peña, et al. 1991. "On Nationality: 13 Artists" in *Art in America*, September, 1991. pp. 124 to 131.

Gomez-Peña, Guillermo. 1988. "Documented/Undocumented" in *Multi-Cultural Literacy*. ed by Rick Simonson and Scott Walker. Saint Paul: Graywolf Press.

Gomez-Peña, Guillermo. 1989. "The Multicultural Paradigm: An Open Letter to the National Arts Community" in *High Performance*, Fall 1988.

Gopinath, Gayatri. 1994. "Bombay, U.K., Yuba City: Bhangra Music and the (En)gendering of Diaspora", *Rethinking the South Asian Diaspora* Workshop, University of Iowa. unpublished ms.

Goswamy, B.N. 1986. *Essence of Indian Art*. San Francisco: Asian Art Museum.

Goswamy, B.N. 1991. "Another Past, Another Context: Exhibiting Indian Art Abroad" in *Exhibiting Cultures: The Poetics and Politics of Museum Display*, ed. by Ivan Karp & Steven Lavine. Washington, D.C.: Smithsonian Press. pp. 68 to 78.

Graburn, Nelson. 1976. "Arts of the Fourth World" in *Ethnic and Tourist Arts: Cultural Expression From the Fourth World*. Berkeley: University of California Press.

Grant, Catherine S. 1980. *Six Immigrant Groups in Queens: A Pilot Study*. Flushing, New York: City University, Queens College.

Gunawardana, A.J. " From Ritual to Rationality" in *The Drama Review* vol. 15 #3 T50, Spring 1971.

Guthikonda, Ravindranath, et al., ed. 1979. *Indian Community Reference Guide and Directory of Indian Associations in North America*. New York: Federation of Indian Associations.

Hall, Stuart. 1981. "Notes on Deconstructing 'The Popular' " in *People's History and Socialist Theory*, ed. Raphael Samuel. London: Routledge and Kegan Paul. pp. 227 to 232.

Hall, Stuart. 1987. "Minimal Selves" in *Identity: The Real Me*. ed by Rutherford, Jonathan . London: ICA.

Hall, Stuart. 1988. "New Ethnicities" in *Black Film, British Cinema*, ed. by Kobena Mercer, et al. London: Institute of Contemporary Arts

Hall, Stuart. 1990. "Cultural Identity and Diaspora" in *Identity, Community & Difference* ed. by Jonathan Rutherford. London: Lawrence & Wishart.

Handler, Richard and Joycelyn Linnekin. 1984. "Tradition, Genuine and Spurious" in *Journal of American Folklore* 97/385. pp. 273 to 290.

Handler, Richard. 1986. "Authenticity" in *Anthropology Today*. 2/1: 2 to 4.

Hansen, Kathryn. 1995. "From Bharat Natyam to Bhangra: The Cultural Politics of South Asian Dance in the U.S., U.K. and Canada". paper presented in "Diaspora South Asians: Identities, Politics and Performance" panel at the Association for Asian Studies Conference. Washington, D.C.

Harvey, David. 1994. *The Condition of Postmodernity*. Cambridge, Mass.: Blackwell.

Hasan, Ihab. 1987. *The Post-Modern Turn: Essays in Postmodern Theory and Culture.*

Hebdige, Dick. 1987. *Cut N' Mix: Culture, Identity and Caribbean Music*. New York: Methuen & Co.

Hegeman, Susan. 1991. "Shopping for Identities: 'A Nation of Nations' and the Weak Ethnicity of Objects" in *Public Culture*. Vol. 3 #2, Spring, 1991.

Helweg, Usha. 1990. *Immigrant Success Stories: East Indians in America.* Philadelphia: University of Pennsylvania Press.

Hing, Bill Ong. 1993. *Making and Remaking Asian America Through Immigration Policy, 1850–1990*. California: Stanford University Press.

Hollan, Douglas. 1992. "Cross-Cultural Differences in the Self" in *Journal of Anthropological Research*, vol. 48, #4, Winter, 1992. pp. 283 to 300.

hooks, bell. 1990. *Yearning: Race, Gender, and Cultural Politics*. Boston: South End Press.

Huyssen, Andreas. 1986. *After the Great Divide: Modernism, Mass Culture, Postmodernism*. Bloomington: Indiana University Press.

Intercultural Performance Issue, *The Drama Review* T94, Summer 1982.

Interviews with Preeti & Rakhee, Oct. 1994.

Isar, Yudhishthir Raj. 1986. *The Challenge to Our Cultural Heritage: Why Preserve the Past?* Washington, D.C.: Smithsonian Press.

Islam, Naheed. 1993. "In the Belly of the Multicultural Beast, I am Named South Asian" in *Our Feet Walk the Sky: Women of the South Asian Diaspora,* ed. by Women of South Asian Descent Collective. San Francisco: Aunt Lute Books. pp. 242 to 245.

Iyer, Pico. 1989. *Video Nights in Kathmandu and Other Reports from the Not-So-Far East*. New York: Vintage.

Iyer, V.R. Krishna. 1992. "India, Islam and the Pall of Postmodernism" in *Economic and Political Weekly*, November 7, 1992. pp. 2417–19.

Jameson, Frederic. 1983. "Postmodernism and Consumer Society" in *The Anti-Aesthetic: Essays on Postmodern Culture*. Ed. by Hal Foster. Washington: Bay Press.

Jameson, Frederic. 1984. "Post-Modernism, or the Cultural Logic of Late Capitalism" in the *New Left Review*, 61.

Jameson, Frederic. 1989. "Nostalgia for the Present" in *South Atlantic Quarterly*, 88 #2.

Jameson, Frederic. *The Political Unconscious: Narrative as a Socially Symbolic Act*. Ithaca: Cornell University Press.

Jameson, Frederick. 1986. "Third World Literature in the Era of Multinational Capitalism" in *Social Text* 15 (Fall, 1986), 65-88.

Jarvie, I.C. 1986. *Movies and Society*. New York: Garland Publishing, Inc.

Jensen, Joan. 1989. *Passage From India: Asian Indian Immigrants in North America*. New Haven: Yale University Press.

Juhasz, Alex, Indu Krishnan, et al. 1992. "Shifting Communities/Forming Alliances: A Cross-Circuit Videologue" in *Felix*, Spring 1991.

Kadaba. Lini & Tanya Barrientos. "Balancing Two Worlds" in *Little India*, July 1993, vol. 3, #7.

Karamcheti, Indira. 1992. "The Shrinking Himalayas" in *Diaspora* 2:2.

Karp, Ivan & Steven Lavine, eds. 1991. *Exhibiting Cultures: The Poetics and Politics of Museum Display*. Washington, D.C.: Smithsonian Press.

Katrak, Ketu. 1989. "Decolonizing Culture: Toward a Theory for Postcolonial Women's Text" in *Modern Future Studies*, vol. 35, #1, Spring 1989.

Khandelwal, Madhulika. 1992. *Patterns of Growth and Diversification: Indians in New York City 1965-1990*. Phd. Dissertation, ms. History Dept: Carnegie-Melon University.

Kirshenblatt-Gimblett, Barbara. 1983. "The Future of Folklore Studies in America: The Urban Frontier" in *Folklore Forum* 16, 2. pp. 176 to 233.

Kirshenblatt-Gimblett, Barbara. 1988. "Authenticity and Authority in the Representation of Culture: The Poetics and Politics of Tourist Productions" in *Kulturkontakt/Kulturkonflict*, band 28, October 1988. pp. 59 to 69.

Kirshenblatt-Gimblett, Barbara. 1988. "Mistaken Dichotomies" in *Journal of American Folklore*, vol. 101, no. 400. pp. 140 to 155.

Kirshenblatt-Gimblett, Barbara. 1989. "Objects of Memory as Life Review" in *Folk Groups and Folklore Genres*. Oring, Elliot, ed Utah: Utah State University Press.

Kirshenblatt-Gimblett, Barbara. 1990. "On Producing Ellis Island" in *Artforum*, December, 1990. pp., 17 to 19.

Kirshenblatt-Gimblett, Barbara. 1991. "Objects of Ethnography" in *Exhibiting Cultures: The Poetics and Politics of Museum Display*, ed. by Ivan Karp & Steven Lavine. Washington, D.C.: Smithsonian Press. pp.387 to 442.

Kirshenblatt-Gimblett. 1990. "Confusing Pleasures" in *By Means of Performance: Intercultural Studies of Theatre & Ritual.* Schechner, Richard, ed New York: Cambridge University Press.

Klass, Morton. 1991. *Singing with Sai Baba: The Politics of Revitalization in Trinidad.* Colorado; Westview Press.

Kondo, Dorinne K. 1990. "M. Butterfly: Orientalism, Gender and a Critique of Essentialist Identity" in *Cultural Critique*, Fall, 1990, pp. 5-29.

Korom, Frank. 1994a. "Community Processes and the Performance of Muharram Observances in Trinidad" in *The Drama Review* 38, 2 (T142), Summer, 1994. pp. 150 to 175.

Korom, Frank. 1994b. "The Transformation of Language to Rhythm: The Hosay Drum of Trinidad" in *The World of Music*, 36(3). pp. 68 to 85.

Korom, Frank. 1995. Discussion Paper for "Diaspora South Asians: Identities, Politics and Performance" at the Association for Asian Studies Conference. Washington, D.C.

Kupiers, Joel. 1990. *Power in Performance.* Philadelphia: University of Philadelphia Press.

Kurin, Richard. 1985. "Mela! An Indian Affair" in *Festival of American Folklife Program Book.* Washington, D.C.: Smithsonian Institution.

Kurin, Richard. 1991. "Cultural Conservation through Representation: Festival of India Folklife Exhibition at the Smithsonian Institution" in *Exhibiting Cultures: The Poetics and Politics of Museum Display*, ed. by Ivan Karp & Steven Lavine. Washington, D.C.: Smithsonian Press. pp. 315 to 343.

La Guerre, John Gaffar, ed. 1974. *Calcutta to Caroni: The East Indians of Trinidad and Jamaica*: Longman Caribbean.

Lannoy, Richard. 1971. *The Speaking Tree: A Study of Indian Culture and Society.* New York: Oxford University Press.

Larson, Gerald. 1995. *India's Agony Over Religion.* Albany: State University of New York.

Lent, John, ed. 1995. *Asian Popular Culture.* San Francisco: Westview Press.

Lent, John. 1990. *The Asian Film Industry.* Austin: University of Texas Press.

Lewis, George H. 1981. "Commercial and Colonial Stimuli: Cross-Cultural Creation of Popular Culture" in *Journal of Popular Culture* 14,2: 142-156.

LiPuma, Edward & Sarah Keene Meltzoff. Fall, 1990. "Ceremonies of Independence and Public Culture in the Solomon Islands" in *Public Culture*, vol. 3 #1, pp. 77 to 92.

Little India Business Directory, August 1996–July 1997.

Little India Business Directory, 1998 -1999

Lobel, Meriam. 1996. "From Rice Fields and Temples to High School Auditoriums and American Legion Halls: Rituals of Asian Indian Dance in a New

Country". *New Routes: Traditional Music and Dance in America,* Summer/Fall 1996.

Lowe, Lisa. 1991. "Heterogeneity, Hybridity, Multiplicity: Marking Asian American Differences" in *Diaspora,* Spring 1991.

Lutgendorf, Philip. 1990. "Ramayan: The Video". in *The Drama Review,* summer 1990.

Lynch, Caitrin. 1994. "Nation, Woman, and the Immigrant Bourgeoisie: An Alternative Formulation" in *Public Culture,* 1994 6: 425-437.

Lyotard, Jean-Francois. 1984. *The Post-Modern Condition: A Report on Knowledge.* Minneapolis: University of Minnesota.

Macaloon , John, ed. 1984. *Rite, Drama, Festival, Spectacle: Rehearsals towards a Theory of Cultural Performance.* Philadelphia: University Press

Manning, Frank, E., ed. 1983. *The Celebration of Society: Perspectives on Contemporary Cultural Performance.* Philadelphia: University Press.

Manuel, Peter. 1991. "The Popularization and Transformation of the Light-Classical Urdu Ghazal Song" in *Gender, Genre and Power in South Asian Expressive Traditions.* ed by Appadurai, Arjun, Frank J. Korom & Margaret A. Mills Philadelphia: University of Pennsylvania Press.

Manuel, Peter. 1993. *Cassette Culture: Popular Music and Technology in North India.* University of Chicago Press.

Marranca, Bonnie & Gautam Dasgupta, eds. 1991. *Interculturalism and Performance: Writings from PAJ.* New York: PAJ Publications.

Mayo, Katherine. 1927. *Mother India.* New York: Harcourt Brace.

McNamara, Brooks, ed. 1983 "Defining Popular Entertainments" in *American Popular Entertainments: Jokes, Monologues, Bits and Sketches.* New York: PAJ Publications

Meduri, Avanthi. 1988. "Bharat Natyam: What Are You?" in *Asian Theatre Journal 5, 1:1-22*

Melendy, Howard Brett. 1977. *Asians in America.* New York: G.K. Hall & Co.

Melwani, Lavina. 1996. "The Great Indian Art Bazaar" in *Little India,* May.

Melwani, Lavina. Nov. 1995. "Trick or Treat" in *Little India.* vol. 5 #11. 10–19.

Melwani, Lavina. Sept. 1995. "Bollywood Live in New York" in *Little India.*

Melwani, Lavina. Nov. 1998. "Strangers in Our Midst" in Little India, vol.8 #11 . pp. 28 to 36.

Melwani, Lavina. Dec., 1998. "The Knotty Knot" in Little India, Vol. 8.#12.pp.28 to 39.

Memmi, Albert. 1991. *The Colonizer and the Colonized.* Boston: Beacon Press

Miller, Jane. 1980. "How Do You Spell Gujarati, Sir?" in *The State of the Language.* Ed. by Leonard Michaels & Christopher Ricks. Berkeley: University of California Press.

Mishra, Vijay. 1985. "Towards a Theoretical Critique of Bombay Cinema" in *Screen*, vol. 26, # 3-4, May–Aug., 1985. pp. 133 to 146.

Mitchell, Timothy. 1992. "Orientalism and the Exhibitionary Order" in *Colonialism and Culture*. Ann Arbor: University of Michigan. ed by Dirks, Nicholas.

Motwani, Jagat. "Arranged Marriage and Dating: A Source of Intergenerational Conflict". Paper presented at *Conference on Family*, Washington DC, May 26 to 27, 1984.

Mukhi, Sunita Sunder. 1989. *The Imagined Audience*. Master's Thesis. San Francisco State University.

Nag, Dulali. 1991. "Fashion, Gender and the Bengali Middle Class" in *Public Culture*, vol. 3, no. 2, Spring 1991. pp. 93 to 112.

Naipaul, V.S. 1990. *India: A Million Mutinies Now*. New York: Viking

Narayan, Kirin. 1993. "How Native is a "Native" Anthropologist?" in American Anthropologist , 95, pp. 671 to 686.

National Immigration Forum: A Guide to Immigration Facts and Issues, 1994.

Nehru, Jawarhalal. 1946. *The Discovery of India*. New York: John Day

O'Brien, Conor Cruise, Edward Said & John Lucacs. "Response to 'Intellectual in the Post-Colonial World' " in *Salmagundi* # 10/71, 1986.

Olalquiaga, Celeste. 1992. *Megalopolis: Contemporary Cultural Sensibilities*. Minneapolis: University of Minnesota Press.

Oring, Elliot, ed. 1989. *Folk Groups and Folklore Genres*. Utah: Utah State University Press.

Pandey, Gyan. 1992. "In Defense of the Fragment: Writing About Hindu-Muslim Riots in India Today" in *Representations* 37: 27 to 54.

Parekh, Bhikhu. 1993. *Some Reflections on the Indian Diaspora*. London: Lady Services Ltd.

Partha Chatterjee. 1993. *The Nation and Its Fragments: Colonial and Post-colonial Histories*. New Jersey: Princeton Universtiy.

Patel, Manhar. Chairperson, Cultural Committee of India Day, 1994, Federation Of Indian Associations, NYC Chapter Nov., 1994. Interview.

Pendakur, Manjunath. 1990. "India—Introduction and Notes on the Film Industry" in *The Asian Film Industry* ed. by John Lent. Austin: University of Texas Press.

Pfeiderer, Beatrix & Lothat Lutger. 1985. *The Hindi Film: Agent and Re-Agent of Cultural Change*. Delhi: Manohar Books.

Pillai, A.K.B.. "Asian Indian Family: Psychological and Cultural Adaptation". Paper presented at *Conference on Family*, Washington DC, May 26 to 27, 1984.

Postman, Neil. 1985. *Amusing Ourselves to Death*. New York: Penguin Books.

Prakash, Gyan. 1992. "Writing Post-Orientalist Histories of the Third World: Indian Historiography is Good to Think" in *Colonialism and Culture*. Ann Arbor: University of Michigan. ed by Dirks, Nicholas.

Radhakrishnan, R. 1987. "Ethnic Identity and Post-Structuralist Differance" in *Cultural Critique*, No. 6, Spring 1987.

Rajadhyaksha, Ashish and Paul Willemen. 1994. *Encyclopedia of Indian Cinema*. New Delhi: Oxford University Press.

Ramanujan, A.K. 1991. *Folktales From India*. USA: Random House.

Ramaswamy, Srikant. 1995. "Union of Families" in *Little India*, July, 1995.

Rasiah, Dharini. 1993. "Mississippi Masala and Khush: Redefining Community" in *Our Feet Walk the Sky: Women of the South Asian Diaspora*. San Francisco: Aunt Lute Books.

Ratti, Rakesh, ed. 1993. *A Lotus of Another Color: An Unfolding of the South Asian Gay and Lesbian Experience*. Boston: Alyson Productions.

Redfield, Robert. 1955. *The Little Community: Viewpoints for the Study of the Human Whole*. Chicago: University of Chicago Press.

Ricoer, Paul. 1965. "Universal Civilizations and National Cultures" in *History and Truth*. Evanston, Illinois: Northwestern University Press.

Roy, Probhir. President, Federation of Indian Associations, NYC Chapter, 1994. Oct., 1994. Interview.

Rushdie, Salman. 1992. "Imaginary Homelands" in *Imaginary Homelands: Essays and Criticisms 1981-91*. London: Granta Books.

Rushdie, Salman. 1992. "The Location of Brazil" in *Imaginary Homelands: Essays and Criticisms 1981-91*. London: Granta Books.

Rutherford, Jonathan, ed. 1987. *Identity: The Real Me*. London: ICA

Rutherford, Jonathan. 1990. "A Place Called Home: Identity and the Cultural Politics of Difference" in *Identity: Community, Culture, Difference*, ed. by Jonathan Rutherford. London: Lawrence & Wishart.

Said, Edward. 1979. *Orientalism*. New York: Vintage

Said, Edward. 1986. "Intellectuals in the Post-Colonial World" in *Salmagundi* #70/71, pp. 45–81.

Said, Edward. 1986. "Orientalism Reconsidered" in Cultural Critique, vol. 1, #1.

Sapir, E. 1924. "Culture, Genuine and Spurious" in *The American Journal of Sociology*, vol. 29 #4, Jan. 1924. pp. 401 to 429.

Saran, Parmatma & Edwin Eames, eds.. 1980. *The New Ethnics: Asian Indians in the United States*. New York: Praeger Publishers.

Saran, Parmatma. 1985. *The Asian Indian Experience in the United States*. Massachusetts: Schenerman Pub., Co., Inc.

Schechner, Richard, ed. 1990. *By Means of Performance: Intercultural Studies of Theatre & Ritual*. New York: Cambridge University Press.

Schechner, Richard. 1985. *Between Theater and Anthropology.* Philadelphia: University of Pennsylvania Press.

Schechner, Richard. 1985. "Performer Training Interculturally" and "Restoration of Behavior"in *Between Theater and Anthropology.* Philadelphia: University of Pennsylvania Press.

Schechner, Richard. 1985. "Performer Training Interculturally" and "Restoration of Behavior"in *Between Theater and Anthropology.* Philadelphia: University of Pennsylvania Press.

Schechner, Richard. 1991. "Intercultural Themes" in *Interculturalism and Performance: Writings from PAJ.* ed by. Bonnie Maranca & Gautam Dasgupta. New York: PAJ Publications.

Scheffauer, Herman. Jan. 1993. "Invasion of the Heathens" in *Little India.* vol. 3, #1: 22–25.

Schieffelin, Edward L. 1981. "Performance and the Cultural Construction of Reality" in *American Ethnologist,* 12: 707-724.

Schjeldal, Peter, Edward Said, et al. 1991. "Art and National Identity: Critics' Symposium" in *Art in America,* September, 1991. pp. 80 to 83.

Scott, Joan. "Multiculturalism and the Politics of Identity" in *October*/61. pp. 12 to 19.

Sharma, Rashmi. 1995. "Crossing the Dark Waters" in *Living in America: Poetry and Fiction by South Asian American Writers,* ed. by Roshni Rustomji-Kerns.

Sengupta, Somini. 1998 (October 7). "United Ethnically, and by an Assault" in *New York Times http://saxakali.com/Rishi1.htm.*

Shils, Edward. 1981. *Tradition.* Chicago: University of Chicago Press.

Shruti Handbook, 1992 to 1993. New York University.

Sikand, Nandini. 1994. "Bhangra Wrap" presented in Sakhi for South Asian Women's Fourth Annual Film Festival Women Directors from South Asia. 1995.

Singer, Milton. 1980. *When a Great Tradition Modernizes: An Anthropological Approach to Indian Civilization.* Chicago: University of Chicago Press.

Slemon, Stephen. 1988. "Post-Colonial Allegory & the Transformation of History" in *Journal of Commonwealth Literature,* vol. 23 #1.

Slymovics, Susan. 1995. "New York City's Muslim World Day Parade" in *Nation and Migration: Politics of Space in the South Asian Diaspora.* ed by Peter Van der Veer. Philadelphia: University of Pennsylvania Press.

Sollors, Werner, ed. 1988. *The Invention of Ethnicity.* England: Oxford.

Spivak-Chakravorty, Gayatri. 1987. "Explanation and Culture: Marginalia" *In Other Worlds: Essays in Cultural Politics.* New York: Methuen.

Spivak-Chakravorty, Gayatri. 1987. *In Other Worlds.* London: Routledge.

Spivak-Chakravorty, Gayatri. 1988. "Can the Subaltern Speak" in *Marxism and the Interpretation of Culture*. Cary Nelson and Larry Nelson, eds. Urbana: University of Illinois Press.

Spivak-Chakravorty, Gayatri. 1990. *The Post-Colonial Critic: Interviews, Strategies, Dialogues*. New York: Routeledge.

Spratt, P. 1966. *Hindu Culture and Personality*. Bombay: Manaktalas.

Srivatsan, R. 1991. "Looking at Film Hoardings: Labor, Gender, Subjectivity and Everyday Life in India" in *Public Culture*, vol. 4, No. 1: Fall 1991. pp. 1 to 21.

Steinberg, Stephen. 1981. *The Ethnic Myth: Race, Ethnicity and Class in America*. Boston: Beacon Press.

Stewart, Kathleen. 1988. "Nostalgia—A Polemic" in *Cultural Anthropology*, Vol. 3 #3, August, 1988. pp. 227 to 241.

Stewart, Susan. 1984. *On Longing: Narratives of the Miniature, the Gigantic, the Souvenir and the Collection*. Missouri: Johns Hopkins Press.

Stewart, Susan. Winter, 1991. "Notes on Distressed Genres" in *Journal of American Folklore*, vol. 104, # 411.

Takaki, Ronald. 1989. *Strangers from a Different Shore: A History of Asian Americans*. Boston: Little Brown.

Tallapragadha, Sridhar. July, 1994. "Out in the Trenches" in *Little India*. vol. 4, #7: 31–35.

Taussig, Michael. 1993. *Mimesis and Alterity: A Particular History of the Senses*. New York: Routledge

Taylor, Diana. 1991. "Transculturating TRANSCULTURATION" in *Performing Arts Journal*.38, vol. 8, #2, May 1991. pp. 90 to 104.

Thomas, Rosie. 1985. "Indian Cinema: Pleasures and Popularity" in *Screen*, vol. 26, # 3-4, May–Aug., 1985. pp. 116 to 131.

Tiffin, Helen. "Post-Colonialism, Post-Modernism and the Rehabilitation of Post-Colonial History" in *Journal of Commonwealth Literature*, pp.169–181.

Tillman, Lynne. 1991. "Report from Ellis Island: The Museum of Hyphenated Americans" in *Art in America*, September, 1991. pp. 55 to 61.

Toelken, Barre. 1979. "A Matter of Taste: Folk Aesthetics" in *The Dynamics of Folklore*. Boston: Houghton Mifflin.

Trinh T. Minh-ha. 1991. *When the Moon Waxes Red*. New York: Routeledge.

Trinh, Minh Ha. 1989. *Woman, Native, Other*. Indiana: Indiana University Press.

Turner, Victor. 1986. *Anthropology of Performance*. New York: PAJ

Ury, John. 1987. *Cultural Change and Contemporary Holiday-Making*.

Van der Veer, Peter, ed. 1995. *Nation and Migration: The Politics of Space in the South Asian Diaspora*. Philadelphia: University of Pennsylvania.

Van der Veer, Peter. 1988. *Gods on Earth*. London: Atheone Press.

Vasudeva, Aruna & Philippe Lenglet. 1983. *Indian Cinema Super Bazaar.* New Delhi: Vikas.

Vasudeva, Aruna & Philippe Lenglet. 1983. *Indian Cinema Super Bazaar.* New Delhi: Vikas.

Vasudevan, Ravi. 1993. "Shifting Codes, Dissolving Identities: The Hindi Social Film of the 1950's as Popular Culture" in *Journal of Arts and Ideas*, nos. 23 to 24, Jan. 1993. pp. 51 to 79.

Visweswaran, Kamala. "Predicaments of the Hyphen" in *Our Feet Walk the Sky: Women of the South Asian Diaspora*. San Francisco: Aunt Lute Books.

Wade, Peter. 1993. " 'Race', Nature and Culture" in *Man: Journal of the Royal Anthropological Institute*, March 1993, vol. 28, no.1. pp. 17 to 34.

Wagner, Roy. 1975. *The Invention of Culture*. New Jersey: Prentice-Hall.

Wallis, Brian. 1991. "Selling Nations" in *Art in America*, September, 1991. pp. 85 to 91.

Walzer, Michael, Jean Bethke Elshtain, et al. "Nationalism and Ethnic Particularism: Roundtable Discussion" in *Tikkun*, vol. 7, no. 6. pp. 49 to 56.

Watson, Bernard. 1994. Quote in *National Immigration Forum: A Guide to Immigration Facts and Issues*.

Watson, J. L., ed. 1977. *In Between Two Cultures: Migrants and Minorities in Britain*. Oxford: Basil Blackwell.

Webster's Encyclopedic Unabridged Dictionary of the English Language. 1989.

Williams, Raymond Brady. 1988. *Religions of Immigrants from India and Pakistan*. New York: Cambridge University Press.

Williams, Raymond. 1958. "Culture is Ordinary" in *Conviction*, ed. by Norman Mackenzie, et al. London: MacGibbon & Kee.

Williams, Raymond. 1982. "Identifications" in *The Sociology of Culture*. New York: Schocken Books.

Zuberi, Nabeel. 1995 (summer). "Paki Tunes" in *SAMAR: South Asian Magazine for Art & Reflection*. #5, p. 35 to 39.

Dance Data Guide
by Joann Kealiinohomoku, 1966

Introduction:

1. This guide is designed to focus the attention of anthropologists who are confronted with an opportunity to view dance; it is also a research reminder for dance ethnologists.

2. It is hoped that information compiled from this guide will be made available to archives and dance ethnologists

3. The guide-user should not feel confined to the guide, but should amplify and adjust any item which pertains to the particular dance or set of dances being viewed.

4. This guide may be used for a total dance culture, or for a particular performance.

A. Identification
    1. Name and type of dance
    2. Locality and environment
    3. Time and length
    4. Occasion
    5. Participants

B. Dance Background
    1. Function and Purpose

2. Meaning or story of dance
3. Classification of dance as art, ritual, and/or recreation. Its relationship with comparable forms of art, ritual and/or recreation
4. Comparisons of dance with other dances of area.
5. Owner of dance and procedure of transmission
6. Composer of dance
7. Methods of learning and rehearsing dance
8. Nomenclature used for dance and dancers
9. Ethnoevaluation of dance and performance, especially what constitutes a good dance and a successful performance

C. Participants' Background
1. Organizational arrangements for both dancers and audiences (e.g. age grade and secret societies)
2. Number, ages and sex of performers
3. Body types and special physical characteristics of performers
4. Status of performers
5. Rewards to performers (e.g., economic gain, prestige)
6. Training of performers
7. Ethnoevaluations of what constitutes a good dancer
8. Special roles of leaders, teachers, soloists, proxies
9. Role of audience

D. Elicitation (from informants)
1. What is the meaning and purpose of the dance?
2. When are dances performed? For how long?
3. How are dances composed? Invented? Borrowed?
4. Who owns the dance?
5. Who are the dancers?
6. How are the dances learned? Special training? Imitation? Rehearsed? Improvised?
7. What qualifies a person as a dancer? Belonging to some society? Special talents?
8. What are the most important criteria (in the culture involved) for judging a good dancer? Grace? Strength? Endurance? Ability to improvise? Good memory?
9. How does one dance type of the area significantly differ from another dance type of the area?
10. How do these dances compare with dances of other ethnic groups in the same culture area?

E. Other Considerations
1. Texts
2. Posture and body alignment—What characterizes ordinary posture? How does posture change for dance?
3. Source of movement within body or its parts
4. Use of energy and qualities of movement (texture; e.g., precise, smooth, jerky)
5. Degree of predetermination (e.g., improvised on basic patterns, or set patterns performed in unison, etc.)
6. Communication and Projection of performers—what and how much
7. Dance gesture codes—esoteric, exoteric, correlation of gesture with texts
8. Dynamics and changes during performance, especially in tempi, rhythms, meters, styles, spatial levels
9. Accompanying performers, singers, instrumentalists

Brief Chronology of Indian Diaspora—Focus U.S.A.[1]

1790	Federal Immigration Law passes, reserving US citizenship for whites only.
1834	Indentured labor recruited from India to serve the varied and globally dispersed colonies of the British Empire in Asia, West Indies, Africa, and UK. Other colonial empires will proceed to require Indian labor, also.
1851	Six Indians march in the Fourth of July parade in Salem, Massachusetts.
1865	Hawaiian Board of Immigration recruits Indian laborers.
1868	W. Whitman writes "Passage to India"
1893	Swami Vivekananda lectures at the World Parliament of Religions in Chicago.
1900's	Surging 'Tide of Turbans' in the West Coast.
1907	Anti-Asian riots in Bellingham, Washington State.
1908	Tarakanath Das starts publishing *Free Hindustan*.
1913	Gadar movement in San Francisco agitates for a free India.
1917	U.S. government under pressure from British government, prosecutes, imprisons and deports Gadar movement members.
1923	U.S. Supreme Court rules that 'white' in Immigration Laws refers only to the European continent or landmass attached to Asia. Therefore, Indians of Aryan stock cannot be US citizens, and all citizenships granted on previous rulings are null and void.
1946	U.S. citizenship granted to those of Asiatic descent.
1947	Partition of the Indian subcontinent into the nation states of India and Pakistan. Massive displacements, and migrations of people within the subcontinent, and emigration globally.
1957	U.S.S.R. launches Sputnik. Increased funding for aeronautic, space,

and other Science research in the U.S. Many foreign scientists and researchers recruited.

1965   European bias in U.S. immigration laws removed. Medicare and Medicaid instituted. Increased demand for medical personnel and health professionals in the U.S. Many foreign medical personnel recruited. Family reunification category allowed for the emigration of relatives of foreign born U.S. citizens. Many Indians are granted investor visas for the ownership and management of small businesses.

1967   Association of Indians In America formed. Members belonged to the elite, affluent and professional classes.

1971   Federation of Indians in America formed as an umbrella organization for the coordination of the ever-increasing number of parochial organizations.

1976   Severe cutbacks in the granting of immigration status to Foreign medical personnel in the Health Professionals Education Assistance Act.

1980   "Asian Indian" designation included under the Asian/Pacific Islander category of the U.S. Census with the persistent efforts of the AIA.

1987   Amnesty granted to illegal laborers in farmlands.

1987   Anti-Asian violences by the Dotbusters of New Jersey resulting in the
to 89   murder of Navraz Mody. Attack on Indian Muslims in Woodside, Queens.

1989   First Global Convention of Overseas Indians held in NYC.

1990   Rally against the increase of Indian businesses in Jackson Heights, Queens by the Jackson Heights Beautification Group.

1992   Protest against Jackson Heights, Queens being renamed *Little India*.

1994   Lottery opened for underrepresented countries for immigration to the U.S. Pakistan and Bangladesh are included but not India.

1998   Rishi Maharaj, an Indo-Caribbean was battered by three young Whites in South Ozone Park, Queens. This assault unifies the South Asian as well as Indo-Caribbean communities to protest.

NOTES:

[1] Rustomji-Kerns, 1995; Khandelwal, 1991; Hing, 1993;

U.S. Population of Indian Descent[1]

Year	Number of Immigrants[2]
1820	1
1830	8
1840	39
1850	36
1860	43
1870	69
1880	163
1890	269
1900	68
1910	4,713
1920	2,082
1930	1,886

Year	Number of Immigrants	Foreign Born	Native	Illegal
1940	496			
1950	1,761			
1960	1,973			
1965	2,602			
1970	27,859			
1980	164,134			
1990	815,447	797,304	218, 031	28,000
1995	1,000,000[3]			
2000	1,332,691			

NOTES

[1] Until 1947 'India included the areas that are now Pakistan and Bangladesh.

[2] Sources: Rustomji-Kerns, 1995, p. 18; Khandelwal, 1991, p. 219; Hing, 1993, p. 70; Immigration and Naturalization Service, Statistical Yearbook, 1993, Little India Business Directory, 1996-1997.

[3] Estimate by Youth Against Racism, 1994.

Index